"A heartwarming love story set against the backdrop of communist rule and oppression in post-war Hungary— an engaging read that puts you in the middle of inter- national intrigue and conflicting family loyalties as a young girl comes of age and discovers her own values and boundaries."

—Teresa Carlson
VP, Global Public Sector, Amazon

A Single Yellow Rose

A Single Yellow Rose

| a memoir |

Anna Koczak

TATE PUBLISHING
AND ENTERPRISES, LLC

Published by Tate Publishing & Enterprises, LLC
127 E. Trade Center Terrace | Mustang, Oklahoma 73064 USA
1.888.361.9473 | www.tatepublishing.com

Tate Publishing is committed to excellence in the publishing industry. The company reflects the philosophy established by the founders, based on Psalm 68:11,
"The Lord gave the word and great was the company of those who published it."

Book design copyright © 2012 by Tate Publishing, LLC. All rights reserved.
Cover design by Shawn Collins
Interior design by Chelsea Womble

Published in the United States of America

ISBN: 978-1-61862-906-7
1. Biography & Autobiography / Personal Memoirs
2. History / Europe / Austria & Hungary
12.04.24

Dedication

To my husband, Stephen Andrew, with love forever; and to Robin Steussy, a true friend; to my parents, brothers, sister, and their compatriots who were willing to die and suffer for what was good and right; and to every brave soul who is willing to extend a helping hand to those in need, in danger, or suffering from injustice.

Acknowledgments

I would like to thank my three daughters and their families for their wonderful help and support and for their enthusiastic encouragement without which I might have given up completing this manuscript long ago: Andrea and her husband, Dendy, and their children, Michelle, Kaelan, Alex, and Brendan; Christina and her children, Athena, Roya, Maya, and Robert Mustafa; Gabriela and her husband, Michael, and their children, Austin, Ryan, Skyler, Quincy, and Maguire. You are Stephen's and my pride and joy. I wrote this book with all my love so that you may have a way to remember and tell your children and the world our story.

To my editor, Herta B. Feely, I owe special thanks for her sensibility and ability to transform my often Hungarian way of thinking into flowing English without altering what I intended to say. I appreciate her thoroughness and patience, sorting out six hundred pages to 340. She did a superb job.

I want to thank her two assistants, Amanda Vacharat and Emily Jones. I am also indebted to all my pre-publication readers Jannette Baja Jones, Emily Jones, Lawrence Russel, Laura S. Grillo, Kay Glendale, Beatrice Santorini, and Debra Robertson. They gave generously of their time and effort to both read my manuscript and to share their thoughtful comments, suggestions, and encouragement. I want to thank Nancy Bouton for retouching my photographs for the book.

Finally, I thank my husband Stephen for his wisdom, honor, and courage. I thank God for His infinite grace in guiding Stephen safely at my side during his lifetime of dedication to helping others who would have suffered or perished without his help.

Author's Brief Historical Note to the Reader:

It is fair to say that 85 percent of Hungarians did not support Hitler's politics. But they were faced with a double edged sword: join the Axis or be overrun by Hitler. Hungary was geographically situated between Hitler's and Stalin's domain. At the time, Hitler seemed to present the lesser of two evils, so Hungary joined the Axis. In addition, the Hungarian government hoped, based on Hitler's promise, to regain the territories Hungary had lost at the Treaty of Trianon in 1920 after WWI. History, of course, has its own answers.

At the point that my story begins, in mid-1947, the struggle for political power dominated Hungary. WWII had ended only two years earlier, a few months after the violent one hundred day siege of Budapest. The war had inflicted substantial devastation on my country, with approximately three hundred thousand Hungarian soldiers and eighty thousand civilians killed, hundreds of businesses and buildings—including beloved historical structures—destroyed, and bridges spanning the Danube bombed.

After the war, the allied powers—the United States, Great Britain, France, and the Soviet Union—had taken charge of war-torn Europe, drawing an imaginary line through the middle of the continent, north to south. The former German-occupied countries to the west came under the rule of the United States, Great Britain, and France, and those territories that lay east were under the power of the Soviet Union. The latter included the eastern part of Germany, part of Austria, Poland, Czechoslovakia, Romania, Bulgaria, and Hungary.

This temporary arrangement was aimed at restoring order and rebuilding the devastated countries. An agreement was signed by the four nations, stating that all but a minimal force of occupying troops would be withdrawn by February 1947. However, the Soviet Union, with its eye on controlling the Eastern Bloc countries, had little intention of leaving. Perhaps in retaliation for its own heavy losses, on arrival in Hungary, the Russian occupiers raped thousands of women and girls, seized assets and resources, and sought to gain control of the government through whatever means necessary.

In the first round of elections after the war, in 1945, the Hungarian Communist Party received only 17 percent of the vote, while the Small Landholders Party gained 57 percent, resulting in a coalition government with the Presidency going to Zoltan Tildy (a Smallholder, as party members were also known).

The Russians were quite unhappy with this poor showing. Stalin backed Hungarian Communist Mátyás Rakosi and helped him maneuver into a position of power. Though he was only the Deputy Premier, Rakosi, not Zoltan Tildy, was the real head of the country and would prove to be a ruthless dictator. Stalin expected the Communist Party to do better in the next set of elections, scheduled for late summer, 1947, and Rakosi was determined to succeed.

Key to Communist control was the secret police, known as the AVO, part of the Ministry of Interior, housed at 60 Andrássy Street, in an attractive part of Budapest, which formerly had been the headquarters of the Hungarian Nazi Arrow Cross movement during the country's German occupation. The AVO's task was to suppress all political opposition to communist rule through intimidation, false accusations, coerced confessions, imprisonment, torture, exile to Siberia, and even execution. Approximately 350 thousand Hungarian officials, intellectuals, and assorted other citizens viewed as threats and enemies of the state were purged between 1946 and 1956.

But the number one enemy of the state, as early as 1945, was the Prince Primate of Hungary, Cardinal József Mindszenty, the spiritual and moral leader of a large majority of the Hungarian populace, including many non-Catholics. (Approximately 70 percent of Hungarians were Catholic, which included my family and me.) Because of his popularity, getting rid of Cardinal Mindszenty would be far trickier than eliminating most other political opponents. However, those in power would go to extraordinary lengths to achieve their goal.

This memoir takes place over the course of twenty months, from mid-1947 to January 1949. This is a personal account about the life I experienced in Hungary during this time.

Prologue

July 20, 2000, Washington, DC

László Harsányi stood at my door clutching a cane. Though his curly hair was now white and his face creased with the passage

Anna in July, 1947.

of time, I could still see the handsome young man who had wooed me some fifty years earlier, and who, despite declarations of love, had planned to betray me. At the time, László was an agent of Hungary's feared and hated secret police, the AVO.

I last glimpsed him on the night of my escape in 1949, when my country was in the throes of turmoil and our freedom steadily eroded by our Russian occupiers. Now, after half a century, László stood before me again. Events of so long ago sped through my mind, the backward motion dizzying.

Briefly, I wondered what he was thinking as he gazed upon me. Back then, he'd endlessly praised my looks. And now, like a supplicant before a priest, he asked to come inside.

May-June 1947

It was a balmy spring day just two weeks before final exams at the public high school I attended in Nagykőrős, a farming town about fifty miles southeast of Budapest. The classroom windows were open, allowing the scent of spring to enter the high-ceilinged room painted the color of daffodils. I sat, head in hand, staring outside and pretending to listen to the history professor, though I couldn't wait for class to end.

The church bell tolled three times, interrupting my reverie. It wasn't time for the bells. Maybe a funeral service, I thought. What a shame to be buried on a lovely day like this.

"Miss Tóth!" our silver-haired professor shouted. "Tell us when Constantinople was renamed, and what is its new name?"

Luckily for me he'd asked an easy question. "In 1930 the name was changed to Istanbul."

"Right," he said, shaking his head at me. "You were lucky to—"

A knock at the door stopped him mid-sentence. An unfamiliar man entered the room. As was etiquette, we twenty-six students sprang up to greet this guest who wore no necktie and whose shoes needed a good shine. Before we could wonder who he was, our professor introduced him as "Comrade." Then he told us to sit down and to give the man our attention. "Come and see me before you go home," our professor commanded, then he left to wait for us in his office.

"Young comrades," the sloppily dressed man said. "I am here on a mission from the government." He handed a sheaf of papers to one of the students in the front row and asked her to pass them out. "Please read this letter carefully and then sign it. Use your good judgment, and we will reward your cooperation."

As he spoke, I quickly scanned the letter. While I can't remember the exact language, essentially, the letter declared that Cardinal Mindszenty, the highest church official in Hungary, was a traitor and a friend of capitalist America, and it accused him of attempting to overthrow the government. At the bottom there was a place for a signature.

As my fellow students read the letter, the air grew thick and still, so still that it seemed I could hear the silence breathing. We were all in shock.

If we refused to denounce the Cardinal, the document stated we would not be allowed to take final exams, which were mandatory for continuing on to the University. As a devout Catholic and a great admirer of the Cardinal, I could not believe what was being asked of us. The accusations were lies. The truth was that the Russians believed Cardinal Mindszenty to be a threat to communism and to their plans. It was to him that at least 70 percent of Hungarians looked for moral and political guidance, not to the Russian-backed Hungarian communist leaders.

The tolling bells broke the silence. I think it's safe to say that few, if any, of us wanted to sign the letter. Someone declared, "These bells are ringing for us." Yes, it seemed they were mourning the terrible decision we faced. By unwillingly signing the document, we were betraying the Cardinal, not to mention ourselves. And not signing it meant we were choosing to limit our futures.

I knew almost immediately that I would do what my parents would do. With little hesitation, I gathered my books, passed by the man on my way out, and entered the professor's office. He sat there, his face filled with undisguised grief and sadness.

I handed him the letter.

"You're not signing it?" he asked.

"No."

"Are you certain, Anna?" He studied my face. "You know what this means."

"Yes," I said. "How could I live with my conscience otherwise?"

"I'm sorry to have to say this, because you are an excellent student with a future," he whispered. "But today is your last day of school. In a week or two, you will receive an official letter from Budapest."

My two-mile walk between school and our twenty-acre farm took me through orchards, cornfields, and a meadow—one full of assorted wildflowers. I can still remember inhaling the wonderful scent of spring and at the same time wanting to cry but being unable to. I felt angry at this man and the government officials and sad for the Cardinal, but for some reason, I also felt relieved. Perhaps it was the fact that I'd stood up for what I believed in. The consequences of my action, however, hadn't fully sunk in. I had always received excellent grades, and it was assumed I would go on to study at the University.

At a roadside crucifix I stopped to pray—for myself, for our country, and for Cardinal Mindszenty. I had no idea what good or bad fortune lay ahead. But if things had been disastrous before the war ended, in due time I would learn that the future would become even bleaker—for me, my family, the Cardinal, and the entire country.

Family picture—top left to right: Mihaly, Margit, Károly, Gyula, Lászlo
—bottom left to right: István, Father, Mother, and Anna

On returning home, my parents couldn't believe what had taken place. They were proud of my stance, but feared for me. Not long after, one night around the dinner table with my parents and four siblings, our conversation grew rowdy and contentious. All but my two older brothers felt I'd done the honorable thing not signing the letter. They'd capitulated, because "they had families to provide for and needed the money." They insisted that my stubbornness would be my ruin. How could I throw away my future? I knew they were approaching the issue from a practical standpoint, and I didn't want to think they were right.

When they mentioned that I should do what was in *my* best interest, my mother attacked them vehemently. "You may have signed that document, but don't tell your sister to do so. And I don't want to hear that you've borne false witness against anyone! Do you understand?" Generally soft-spoken, her passionate response astounded all of us.

The two things everyone agreed on were that, first, I'd be more likely to find work in Budapest than in Nagykörös, and second, that as long as Cardinal Mindszenty maintained his position and power, we had hope for the future. Little did we realize how tenuous his situation was.

On the seventh of June, my family sat together waiting for my sister to join us. As soon as she arrived, Pista told us in a hushed voice that the police had confiscated his radio for listening to foreign broadcast.

"Tell us at least what you heard," we urged him.

"Deputy Rakosi was bragging about the Communist Coup he accomplished without America's knowledge." Pista explained.

"So, what was America's answer?" my father wanted to know.

"President Truman said that the whole thing is outrageous."

A long silence ensued.

"I am sorry about your radio, son. I am glad I don't have one," my father said. "Being well informed has its' price."

July-August 1947

On July 28, 1947, the day I left, only Pista, my youngest brother, accompanied me to the train station. We decided it would become too much of an emotional scene if everyone came, and I didn't want that. Pista, with whom I had always been closest, treated me like a mother hen: Are you sure you have enough money? Will you be all right alone? As for me, I put on a brave front reassuring him that I had plenty of money, and if anything happened, I could turn around and come home. "It's not as though I'm traveling to the other side of the world, Pista."

The train arrived early, announcing itself with shrill whistles and screeching brakes. Our conversation cut short, we only had time for a hug. Pista helped me lift my bags onto the train where I found an empty seat by a window so I could wave to him, which I did, until losing sight of my beloved brother. My eyes then clung to our town's two church towers until they too faded into the distance.

My emotions were mixed. I was a rural girl going to the big city, something I'd often dreamed of, but under different circumstances. Now, I was leaving my family and striking out on my own. It made the trip both exhilarating and intimidating.

The countryside raced by, and as the train clattered over the tracks, I tried to imagine what Budapest would be like and what sort of work I'd be able to find without a Communist Party membership card.

The train track unspooled across the flat countryside, tall poplars framing wheat fields, orchards, and vineyards. Here and there we passed small villages of red-shingled, whitewashed houses with vegetable gardens. Children ran alongside the train and waved.

I grew sad, wondering what I was leaving behind and what life would have held had I agreed to sign the cursed letter. Undoubtedly, I would have traveled a different path. So often, decisions we cannot fully appreciate at the time determine our future. If I had known of the treacherous times that lay ahead, would I have left home?

Sunday, July 28, marked my arrival in my new home—two months after my last day of school and eight days after my nineteenth birthday. I'd been in glamorous pre-war Budapest once and then only briefly. Now that formerly elegant city on the Danube, while functioning, was populated by poorly dressed, underfed people whose eyes often registered fear and avoided one's gaze. I only had a vague sense of why this was true, though soon I'd come to better understand.

Exactly three weeks after my arrival, on August 18, 1947, twenty-nine-year-old Stephen Koczak was enjoying his flight from Berlin to Budapest, where he looked forward to working with Minister Selden Chapin, the head of the American Legation in Hungary, and his friend and colleague, Vice Consul Robin Steussy, two years his junior. Joining them, in his position as American Legation attaché, was the true beginning of his career, a career which had been delayed by mandatory service in the military during the war.

Stephen, born in 1917, grew up in the Hungarian community in Trenton, New Jersey, where he became fluent in English and Hungarian, the language of his family and many neighbors. Both parents were of Hungarian descent, though only his mother had been born there. Like millions of Americans, he and his family struggled through the depression, but with the assistance of a full scholarship, Stephen fulfilled his dream of graduating from Harvard University in 1942. "Cum laude," his father had said, beaming with pride as he toasted Stephen at a family celebration.

Though he received a fellowship from Harvard to continue his studies, he also received a letter from Uncle Sam, enlisting him in the army. He was sent to officer training school, then overseas to France and England. This detour placed his future plans on hold.

After his return to civilian life, he took the Foreign Service exam with Robin. Both passed with flying colors. Stephen, with his fluent Hungarian, requested a posting in Budapest, and Robin chose Berlin. When the assignments were handed out, their destinations were reversed. "How completely illogical," Stephen protested, "a waste of our talents."

Now, finally, through the intervention of Minister Chapin, he would be exactly where he wanted to be. He looked out the window. The plane was circling, preparing to land. The slanting afternoon sun lit up the large city of Budapest sprawling beneath him. The half called Buda was situated in the hills, and the other half—Pest—in the plains. The two were divided by the Danube, a winding silver ribbon that originated in Germany's Black Forest and flowed southeast through Austria, Hungary, Yugoslavia, Bulgaria, and Romania, finally emptying into the Black Sea.

As he peered down, he saw the devastation wreaked on the city by the war. During the three-month siege from 1944 to 1945, what British bombs hadn't destroyed, Russia's did. Buildings lay in ruin, bridges had crumbled into the water, and the airport consisted of a few temporary buildings and a potholed landing strip.

Like me, Stephen could not predict the future, even from the aerial heights of the plane. He could not foresee the political turbulence that lay ahead—the oppressive Soviet-imposed regime, the stifled democracy, the hundreds and thousands of Hungarians desperate to get out—and the risk-filled role he would play. He would meet several women with designs on him, and he would meet me.

Budapest in August, 1947.

His friend and colleague, Robin Steussy, picked him up and drove through town, pointing out various landmarks and briefing him on current events. In particular, he explained to Stephen that two days earlier, the State Department had allowed Ferenc Nagy, the exiled former Premier, to broadcast an appeal over the *Voice of America* urging his fellow Hungarians to boycott the coming election. The entire issue was a hot one and this was stirring up more trouble for the Legation. "That and the dicey situation with the Cardinal are posing major challenges for us, Koczak," Robin said.

He pulled up in front of a large house bearing the sign Society of Sisters of Social Service. "Welcome to your new home. Don't worry. The Sisters will take good care of you. You can come and go as you please, as long as you don't bring a lady friend to your room." He grinned. This would be Stephen's home in Budapest for the next five months.

The woman who greeted him was Sister Margit Slachta, not only the foundress and head of this secular order, but also a member of Parliament. During the war the Sisters of Social

Services had sheltered scores of Jewish women. Sister Slachta was a well-educated nun of middle age with a no-nonsense attitude. Stephen would learn that she was unafraid to speak her mind, even to the Russians. To them she would prove to be an especially prickly thorn.

The following day, with the August sun pouring its golden rays over the city, a limousine picked Stephen up to drive him to his first day of work. Despite the devastation of war along the route, Stephen saw that Budapest was still majestic, alive, and beautiful. Around the Legation, in the fashionable part of town, there was little evidence of war. When Stephen stepped out of the limo, he could smell the scent of roses that bloomed in the square just across the street.

At the elevator, Stephen encountered a clear-eyed, balding man in his midfifties, wearing a priest's frock. When the doors to the elevator opened, Stephen waved the priest inside and then followed him. Extending his hand, he introduced himself in Hungarian. "Stephen Koczak. I'm a new political attaché."

The priest smiled. "Cardinal József Mindszenty. Glad to meet you." His eyes were magnetic, his bearing elegant but relaxed. So this was the man around whom swirled a political storm. Before Stephen could say anything else, the elevator came to a halt, and the doors opened.

Minister Chapin awaited the Cardinal in the hallway. "Your Eminence," he said, bowing slightly. "So good of you to come." When Chapin noticed Stephen, he welcomed him and asked if he would join them. "We can benefit from your knowledge of Hungarian."

The Cardinal was paying his respects to the minister, having arrived that morning to prepare for the following day's Mass honoring St. Stephen, the first king of Hungary. Before leaving, he thanked Stephen for the "easy conversation" and invited him to the celebration. "It will be an experience for you."

When the door closed behind him, Chapin said to Stephen, "*Ecce homo*, here is the man that the entire Communist government hates and fears. They do not know what to do with him. They think if he would leave or could be done away with, all will be right. But they are wrong." He paused for a moment, thinking. "Something, isn't it, that you should meet him like this?"

"He's quite impressive," Stephen answered, having no idea that his path and the Cardinal's would be so intertwined in the months to come.

"Let me explain, Mr. Koczak," Sister Slachta said. "St. Stephen established Hungary as a Christian country one thousand years ago and became its first king. That is why August twentieth is one of our most important holidays of the year."

They were on their way to the St. István Basilika, a cathedral bombed during the war and still undergoing repair. "When the Cardinal comes to Budapest, he insists on staying in the badly damaged palace next to the Basilika, which, by tradition, has been the Cardinal's residence. He says that it is fitting for the Primate of a devastated country to stay in a devastated house, and he cannot accept better accommodations."

Worshippers filled the huge cathedral and spilled outside, overflowing the plaza. "This is what irks the Communists," Sister Slachta said. "This devotion of the people to Cardinal Mindszenty."

At one point during the Mass, gunshots and screams could briefly be heard outside. Stephen turned to the nun, who said, "You will have to get used to it. We are in for some cruel times. One war just ended on our soil, and another has already begun."

Though he had just arrived, Stephen knew she was right. What he couldn't know was the intensity of the future violence, nor could he imagine his own significant role.

Stephen was stirred by the Cardinal's sermon, and afterward, at a reception, he had the chance to tell him so personally. There he also met the Cardinal's secretaries, Father András Zakár and Father Sándor Csertö.

By the time he and the nun left the reception, the church and the square outside had nearly emptied of worshippers. "The Cardinal is very popular," Stephen said to Sister Slachta.

"Yes," she said. "Thanks to the Cardinal, the church is held in high esteem, and we look to him as our moral, spiritual, and political leader." She offered some history on the man. "He grew up poor and has never forgotten it. He is a man of the people, Mr. Koczak. First he became a country priest, then a monsignor, and then bishop. During the war, he confronted the Nazis, and for that he was thrown into prison. And now, at risk to himself, he continues to challenge and draw people's attention to injustices. He pushes our political leaders to stand up to the Russians and the Communists, not to capitulate or compromise. He reminds them of their moral obligation to the people they represent."

The air grew unusually still. The sister cast her gaze at the army of dark clouds gathering on the horizon. "A storm coming from the east is always destructive," she said. "Take note of this uneasy, suffocating air, Mr. Koczak. It describes perfectly the political situation in our country—ready to explode, like this rainstorm."

My friend Julia and I reached a small coffee shop just around the corner from the cathedral as the storm began. I had been staying with her at her parents' home for two weeks. They'd offered to put me up until early August when a small apartment my family owned would become available. Safely inside the café, we sipped hot coffee and watched tiny pieces of hail ping against the window and bounce on the street.

"What did you think of the Cardinal's sermon?" Julia said, her gaze fixed outside.

"My father would say he is an oak tree standing straight," I said.

"Occasionally oak trees get cut down when they are in the way," Julia answered. Then turning to me and wearing a quirky smile, she said, "I haven't told you, but I got the job at the botanical gardens."

Her announcement took me aback. It had been a job I'd interviewed for and had hoped to get. Julia knew that. Not wanting her to see my hurt, I shifted my eyes outside. Not even an apology. Jobs were hard to come by, and I knew all along that I stood little chance of snagging the position, but how could a friend do such a thing? Then I realized what must have happened. "So, you signed the party membership card?"

"Yes, I did," she said defensively. "I'm not about to take a job as a maid in some rich family's home. Forget that. Anyway, what difference does it make if I sign the thing or not?"

"How can you say that, Julia?" I felt the heat rise up my neck.

She laughed. "Oh, don't get all upset. You can always get married. That's really what I want—a husband who loves me and takes care of me and a couple of kids."

I looked at her silently, though I wanted to say, "Then why didn't you let me have the job?"

The Cardinal leaned against the wall beside the large crucifix. He was tired. Father Csertö could see that. Just then, his face and that of the suffering Christ bore a startling resemblance, he thought.

A small number of dignitaries were still there, needling him or flattering him, depending on what they sought to accomplish. Father József Jánosi, a Jesuit priest, made no secret of his feelings of superiority to the Cardinal when it came to understanding political matters. In stark contrast to the Primate, he leaned toward compromise in dealing with the Russians. István

Barankovics, the leader of the Democratic Peoples' Party, gave the Cardinal his party's whole-hearted support. He chatted with him, complimenting him on the sermon. There were others, reporters, some of whom had great respect for him and were willing to tell him so.

Fathers Csertö and Zakár were about to usher Cardinal Mindszenty out of the church when they became aware that everyone seemed to be staring at him. The storm had stopped, and sunshine poured in through the window, illuminating the statue of Christ and casting a shadow of his crown of thorns onto the Cardinal's head.

There was a brief spell of silence. Then the doors opened and the two priests led the Cardinal out into the square, sprinkled with a myriad of tiny pebbles of ice glistening like diamonds in the sun.

———•———

The national elections were to take place in a few days, on August 31, 1947. Most people believed the Hungarian Communist Party was planning to cheat at the polls and foreign news reports said as much. There was much at stake. Stalin had demanded that Deputy Premier Mátyás Rakosi bring home a victory, and it was clear from events that he would use what he called "salami tactics" to slice away the other parties' power, bit by bit.

September-October 1947

Protests citing election fraud erupted after news announcements that the Communists had received the most votes, just over a million, of any party. The fairly new opposition party, the Democratic People's Party, came in second, having garnered just over eight hundred thousand votes. The DPP's success was attributed to support provided by the Roman Catholic clergy, despite claims the church was neutral. The Smallholders and Social Democrats gained over seven hundred thousand votes each, as did the Independents despite the brutal attack on Zoltan Pfeiffer and several others at a party rally a few days earlier.

However, on September 6, in Millennium Square, Rakosi made it clear he was not finished threatening the Independents' leader and his party. In a menacing statement at a Communist rally, the Deputy Premier said that "there is absolutely no reason for Pfeiffer's existence," and added, "His party slanders Hungarian democracy to Hungary's enemies abroad and enjoys the support of foreign reactionaries. We shall continue an unrelenting fight against this party. We shall teach Pfeiffer a lesson that this is 1947 and not 1945. With the help of the workers we shall break up any attempt at a Rightist putsch."

At this same meeting, Rakosi announced that Hungarians would be limited to an income of no more than three thousand forints, or about $273 per month, and that the state would begin to "store flour, potatoes, sugar, lard, and other food staples to bring down the high prices and that all necessaries of life must have two prices, one for the poor and the other for the rich."

Stephen could hardly keep up with the daily problems that this situation had created at the Legation. People fearing for their lives came to the Legation begging for help to escape from the country. Because Stephen spoke Hungarian, many of these people were sent to him.

After another grueling day, he returned home exhausted only to be summoned by Sister Slachta moments later. She introduced him to a man he had recently seen at the Legation but could not recall in what capacity he had been there.

"Mr. Koczak," she said, "I want you to help Mr. Sági out of the country. If they find him, he will be killed or imprisoned. The AVO has mistaken him for his brother who is a member of parliament."

"But Sister," Stephen protested, "I don't even know the way to the border, let alone how to smuggle people out." *And what if we get caught*, he thought to himself. *What then?*

The short-statured nun drew herself very erect. "Mr. Koczak, if you are as decent a man as I think you are, you will find a way to help." She pierced him with her steely eyes. "During the war, German soldiers raided this convent every night, and yet we never lost a single fugitive to the police. We planned everything to the smallest detail. Mr. Sági has to leave in two days; we cannot shelter him beyond that." With that pronouncement she left the dumbfounded Stephen alone, taking Mr. Sági with her.

In the short time he had spent in Budapest, Stephen had already heard numerous stories about the Legation agreeing to assist people's escape and then reneging on their promise. In two instances, this negligence had resulted in death. Nevertheless, Stephen resented being put in this position.

That night, his sleep was fitful; he was unable to shake the words *if you are as decent as I think you are* from his mind.

Two days later, Stephen and Robin started for the Austrian border with Mr. Sági in Robin's Chevrolet. Heeding Sister Slachta's advice, they planned everything out to the smallest detail. Though Stephen counseled against it, Robin insisted on taking a gun.

As long as they were risking their careers and even their lives to smuggle this man out of the country, Stephen thought Sági at least owed them an explanation of what had happened that forced him to this drastic measure.

He was willing to oblige. "Just a few days before St. Stephen's Day, I was jumped by two strong fellows. They twisted my arms and pushed me into a car. The next thing I knew, we were at AVO Headquarters. As we entered a long corridor, one of them gave me a powerful kick in my buttocks. It was unexpected, as you can imagine," he said, taking a moment to pause. "I flew against the wall, face first. Blood dripped from my nose onto my shirt. My vision was blurry, and I could hardly see where I was stepping.

"Finally, we arrived in a room with a narrow table and four chairs in the middle. On the wall, hanging with artistic precision, were the instruments of torture. One man sat on a chair and gave the orders. 'Boys, tenderize him a little.' They beat me senseless. I fainted, and when they revived me with a bucket of water, the interrogation began. 'You are Ákos S, member of parliament?'"

"'No,' I said, and they struck me again. I realized they had confused me with my twin brother, who, just a day before, had attempted to escape with his wife to Austria. I wasn't sure that they'd succeeded, and so thought it better to pretend that I was him.

"'Are you Ákos?' he said again and shoved me against the chair. 'Give him a strong cup of coffee. He'll need it,' the man ordered. With the coffee came a white sheet of paper with no writing on it. 'Sign it!' he commanded.

"'I am not signing a blank sheet of paper,' I said. The next thing I knew, I was pulled up from the chair, and one of the men kicked me in the groin, and I passed out. When I came to, I felt a warm pungent liquid streaming onto my face. Then I saw a man standing over me zipping up his pants. I threw up.

"'Finish your coffee,' the interrogator ordered.

"I reached for the coffee, the taste of which mingled with the blood in my mouth. 'Be a good boy now and sign.' He paused. 'If you don't, you'll get the full treatment.' And he pushed the paper at me.

"'What am I signing?' I asked.

"'In time, you will know.' He motioned to his boys, who both held rubber truncheons in their hands. I took the pen and signed my name, Péter Sági, forgetting that he thought I was Ákos. 'What's this,' he said.

"I realized my mistake, and quickly added Ákos' name. 'I sometimes go by my middle name.'

"Apparently satisfied, the AVO man said, 'I am a good man so I'll let you go.' He squinted at me. 'Tell me, what kind of man am I?'

"'You're the kind of man who would rape his mother,' I said. Then thinking better of it, I added, 'You're a good man.'

"'That's more like it,' he said and extinguished his cigarette on my forehead. I was allowed to go to the washroom to clean up as best as I could. Then they let me go. The next morning, I heard that my brother Ákos and his wife were safe. I don't know why they wanted him, though. If I get out, I'll be sure to ask him and tell him how I suffered on his behalf."

Not long after he'd told them his story, about half an hour from the Hungarian-Austrian border, Robin pulled the car off the road and told Péter Sági to get in the trunk. "No matter what," Stephen instructed, "don't say a word."

Ten hours later, they were taking the same 250 or so mile route back to Budapest, relieved that they'd accomplished their mission.

———◆———

I was clearing teacups from the table while my Uncle Ferenc relaxed on the sofa, appearing content, an almost happy look on his face. Since the death of his wife during the waning days of the war, it was a rare sight. He lived about ten blocks from my family's apartment on Benzcur ut in a fashionable neighborhood. I'd moved there a few weeks earlier, and now, since he was so nearby, I visited him regularly.

Uncle Ferenc wasn't actually my uncle; he was my father's cousin, but because he came to live with my father's family as a child after his parents' untimely deaths, my sister and brothers and I always referred to him that way. I'm not sure when he became a Communist, but I do know that he fought in the Spanish Civil War in 1937 alongside men like Tito and László Rajk and then became a member of the Hungarian Communist Party. Because of this, he was offered a job in the Interior Ministry with the AVO. In any case, a rift occurred between him and my father in 1946 over this.

Despite this, I continued to care about him and knew that, deep down, he was a decent man. Too, I knew I was his favorite niece. Probably because he and his wife had remained childless, I was the daughter he would have liked to have had.

He had just turned fifty, and with only a touch of silver in his dark hair, he was still handsome and youthful despite the demands of his work and a life that had been filled with hardship.

A knock at the door startled us both. Uncle Ferenc jumped up from the sofa and hurried to the door. He opened it only a foot or so, exchanged a few words with a man, pulled a file from his hands, and then closed the door. He went to his desk and sat down to study the documents it contained. He seemed to have forgotten about me, so intent was he on the pages before him. At one point, he simply dropped the papers on his desk and left for another room to make a call.

Curious about what had so captivated him, I went to the desk to have a look, knowing it was none of my business and would have angered my uncle had he known. I could hear my uncle's voice on the other side of the wall as I leafed through the pages. A photo of a man caught my attention. I thought his face a bit on the plump side, but attractive, with an open expression and friendly eyes. A wave of light brown hair capped his head. Though he had a slightly receding hairline, he didn't look older than thirty, if that. He wore a mustache, typical for the time, which I thought looked quite distinguished. The name beneath the photo said: Stephen Andrew Koczak, American.

Stephen—as I saw him in the file in 1947.

I heard my uncle's footsteps, so I quickly shuffled the papers back into the folder. Then I heard his agitated voice and realized he was still on the telephone and probably pacing back and forth.

"I know what the file says. But explain to me how this SOB is crossing the border twice in the same night and slipping between your agents' fingers?"

There was silence as he listened to whoever was on the other end of the line.

"It's obvious," Uncle went on, "the man's taking people across the border. Or do you think he goes to Vienna to make love for a few hours?" Another pause. Then, "Just send László over. I want to talk to him."

When he returned to the room, my presence seemed to startle him, perhaps realizing I might have overheard his conversation. He regarded me, and for a moment I thought he would ask me what I'd heard, or maybe even confide in me.

Instead he said, "You should get married, Anna." Smiling, he joked, "You know a girl's looks don't last forever."

Playing along, I said, "Uncle, I'm hardly nineteen. Hopefully my looks will keep for a few more years. Anyway, I'm not ready to get married. I want to experience life."

As if his thoughts had already traveled back to his work, he gazed off distractedly. "Could you mail these letters on your way home?" he asked and handed them to me.

"Of course." A few minutes later, I kissed him on the cheek and departed.

Just as I was reaching the bottom of the stairs, a youngish looking man entered the building. For a moment we were face to face, then he passed me. Tall and lean, with dark curly hair and equally dark eyes, he was almost as handsome as the American in the photo I'd just seen. *Two good-looking men in one afternoon*, I thought.

The September sun was warm, and a light breeze blew the fragrant aroma of autumn flowers into the air. My uncle's suggestion that I get married coiled through my mind. I gave it some more thought then laughed at myself, because I knew that wasn't what I wanted. Not yet. Besides, after several weeks of unsuccessful job hunting, I'd finally found one I liked. The job was in a flower nursery where the owner, who hadn't requested a Communist Party card, said I would be working on developing new varieties of hybrid flowers. I would be starting after I returned to Nagykörös to help my family harvest our potato and corn crops, which I'd done every year since I was eight.

Just a block from my uncle's apartment, a huge gray building blotted out the sun. When I looked, I saw that I'd been cast into the shadow of the infamous headquarters of the AVO at 60 Andrássy Street. Located in the bowels of the building were solitary cells and rooms where torture was routinely administered. I couldn't help shuddering whenever I passed by the place.

Knowing that my uncle's office was in there somewhere, despite his kindness to me, I always wondered how he could serve such an unjust regime, a government that not only was taking away our freedoms bit by bit, but also was responsible for imprisoning and torturing innocent people, executing them or exiling them to Siberia by the thousands. It made no sense.

I was going home to help with fall harvest. It had been five weeks since I'd left my family, and I brimmed with excitement at the prospect of seeing them. I'd succeeded in making a home for myself in the capital city despite all that was happening and couldn't wait to tell them about it. I'd acquired a job (which I would rub my brothers' noses in!) and had become quite adept at navigating Budapest. I'd added my own flair to my family's small apartment on the top floor of the ornate French style, four-story building. It featured tall, white-framed, bay windows, elegant, wrought iron balconies, and an arched, twelve-foot-high entry-way. The tall spiked fence with locked gate kept residents safe and my parents less worried. In fact, I hoped they might come for a visit.

Of course I was greeted as though I'd been gone for a decade, but their affection was welcome. Other than my uncle and Julia, I had yet to create a circle of friends in Budapest.

The work in the fields was physically demanding, and at the end of the day, we were all exhausted. Sitting with my father outside in the slanting late afternoon sun, I extended my hands toward him and flipped my palms up. "These are the last blisters I'm going to have on my hands from a hoe!"

I expected my father to laugh. Instead, his expression turned from a smile into a worried frown. "That might well be," he said, then pointed at the lane leading to our gate. I followed the aim of his finger.

Four rangers on horseback—police with jurisdiction outside our city limits—and two civilians approached the house. One of the men dressed in street clothes was a man my father knew well, Feri Korsos, a self-appointed authority in our town and a hard-nosed Communist.

None of my family liked him, nor did most of the town's citizens—and for good reason. Under his command and with his guidance, the expropriation of land, euphemistically referred to as "nationalization," was progressing at a rapid pace. Anyone owning more than twenty acres of land was at the mercy of Feri Korsos. Half the landowners of Nagykörös had already lost all but five acres of their property. Not nearly enough to make a living. Hardly enough for a garden of vegetables to feed themselves. Those who protested often landed in jail. Others had committed suicide.

Bodri, our dog, barked incessantly, defending his territory against intruders. With confident strides, the six men entered the gate into our courtyard as my mother came out to investigate the source of the noise.

My father ordered Bodri to be quiet. With a cursory greeting, Korsos opened a document and handed it to Father. "It's your turn, Gyula," Korsos said flatly. The paper bore the stamp of the government. Like those before him, my father was being asked to sign away his land. It was bad enough that this man treated others in the town with contempt, but that he could be so cold-hearted to someone who was part of his extended family shocked me.

"And if I don't?" my father asked.

Waving his hand at the policemen, he said, "You will."

"Sign it, Gyula," my mother said, a catch in her throat. "The land is not worth the price we'll pay if you don't."

At age sixty-two, with the flourish of a pen, my father lost most of his land, his horses, his vineyards, his fields, his fruit trees, everything he'd worked for over a lifetime. My mother too lost what she loved. And so did all of us.

Father dropped the document on the ground. "It's all yours, Feri." Then in a calm voice and looking him in the eye, he added, "Men like you disgust me."

Tears tugged at my eyes. I was furious and already imagined strangers cultivating and harvesting our land and the land of our neighbors. How could this man so casually destroy people's lives? Father was right. He was disgusting.

Abruptly, my father rose and went inside. That night, dinner was a quiet affair. The food and wine tasted bitter in our mouths. My departure the following day was the exact opposite of my arrival. No enthusiasm, excitement, or semblance of happiness. In that defeated spirit, my father accompanied me to the train station.

For a time, we chatted, ignoring events of the day before. Then, quite seriously, he said, "The next time you see your uncle, tell him that I've retired. No more worrying about the grain harvest or the quality of the grapes. With my five acres, I can smoke my pipe to my heart's content."

I knew what he was really saying—that he hoped Ferenc was happy with the Communists' methods. And I felt the same. How could Uncle be one of them? It was difficult to depart, seeing a robust, still youthful man look so beaten. At the station, I embraced him. "Leave it up to me what I tell him, Father."

The entire way back to Budapest, I stared outside, trying to make sense of the world. The train traveled through the countryside where most crops had been harvested, and all that remained were mounds of straw, secured with rope to withstand the wind, and dried cornstalks tied in bunches and leaning against each other like tepees. Flocks of birds rippled over the fields like waves on the sea, hunting for scattered seeds.

The next morning, back in Budapest, I dressed for my first day on the job. I felt simultaneously excited and guilty for experiencing such emotions after my family's misfortune. I arrived promptly at the gate of the nursery, where several other employees were gathered and waiting. I wondered why they hadn't gone inside. Then I noticed a sign that read: "Keep Out—Government Property."

Inside the gate, a man none of us knew approached and shooed us away like pigeons. "Go home. You're all fired!"

I took the bus home in a state of disbelief. Between that day and the day before, everything that had seemed so promising and solid had crumbled. What now? Without money, I couldn't stay in Budapest, and things could hardly improve in Nagykörös. Jobs there were even harder to find. And if I went home, I would just be another mouth to feed.

Perhaps Julia's outrageous suggestion a month ago was my only option. Be a maid to a wealthy family. Was I too proud for that? Yes, but what choice did I have? What other work could I get without a Communist party card?

In the tiny efficiency apartment, sitting beside one of the tall windows overlooking the courtyard, I began reading newspaper ads listed under the heading "Domestic Help." Each one seemed more demeaning than the previous. Could I really take care of strangers' houses—change their sheets, clean their toilets, wash their dishes, and possibly be yelled at in the process? The thought was humiliating. I felt sorry for myself and several times was tempted to burn the papers in the stove.

About to give up, an ad caught my eye. "Seeking intelligent young woman for three or four months." It said nothing about cleaning. Why would they want an "intelligent" girl? Then I noticed the most peculiar thing. The location of the work, 41 Benczur Street, was my address, the apartment on the floor below mine. Could that be? Having lived there only a short time, I knew few tenants.

I dressed hastily and rang the doorbell. A heavyset woman with an attractive face answered the door. "Yes?" she said.

The way she stared at me made me realize that I'd been impulsive and hadn't taken the time to think this through. "I wanted to inquire about your ad in the paper."

"You should have called." Her tone was formal.

"I apologize, but you see, I live in this building and I thought—"

After eyeing me shrewdly, she released an exasperated sigh. "Well, as long as you're here, you might as well come inside." I followed her through several large, elegantly furnished rooms to a library with hundreds of books neatly lining mahogany shelves. A man sat in a leather chair reading.

He rose and extended his hand. "I am Dr. Ernő Doroghy, and this is my wife." In turn, I introduced myself, taking great care to be polite. Dr. Doroghy went on to explain the position. Light housework—no cooking since they already had a cook—and taking care of telephone calls. The job would become even simpler after they left for Switzerland for a two- to three-month visit to see their son. The salary was excellent.

The job sounded ideal until Dr. Doroghy added, "After we return from Switzerland, your job will be terminated." If he hired me, I would have work for about three or four months. He inquired about my education and what had brought me to Budapest. When I told him where I was from, he looked a little surprised.

"Any relation to Gyula Tóth?" he asked.

"Why yes."

He and his wife exchanged a look but said nothing further about it, and I didn't feel it was my place to ask. A few minutes later he offered me the position. I would start in early October, and a week later they would leave.

<hr />

During the war, Uncle Ferenc became involved in hiding Jews from the Germans after meeting Raoul Wallenberg through his wife's work at the International Red Cross. The vast underground operation provided shelter to anyone in danger—not just in Budapest but all around the country.

I was witness to one of these events on our farm in late summer, 1944, only a few months before the one-hundred-day siege of Budapest. Twenty acres of golden ripe grain waited to be cut by hand. Bad enough that my five brothers were off fighting at the front, but our entire area suffered from a dearth of able-bodied men for hire. To help Father solve this problem, one morning

41

at dawn, Uncle Ferenc arrived with ten Salezian brothers from the monastery about fifteen miles away.

"You must be crazy, Ferenc," my father said, "Anybody can see from half a mile away that these men are Jews. You want us all to be hanged?"

"You have no imagination, Gyula. Just leave things to me if you want your grain harvested."

"You cannot send these men out in the fields dressed like monks. They stick out like a sore thumb," my father objected.

My mother stood nearby, listening to them argue. Suddenly, she went into the house and, after a short time, returned with an armful of clothes. "We will dress them up as women," she said. "It will be less suspicious to see ten old women harvesting than a group of men who don't look like monks."

To everyone's great amusement, they took the clothes and dressed up, using scarves to cover their faces as much as possible, and my mother helped them to plump up their blouses. However, dressed up or not, their farming skills were terrible. I was supposed to teach them how to bunch the wheat and tie a straw rope around each one. But it was mostly a hopeless task, and my mother and I ended up doing this part of the work for them.

One very tall young man in particular, his hands lily white, was not meant for this kind of work. He claimed his name was Eric Goldberg and said he had just finished medical school. I went to Uncle Ferenc complaining that he was useless. "He must have had a nurse tying his shoes all his life," I said. "Put him in charge of carrying the water from the well. That's all he is good for." And so he did.

On the third day, shortly after lunch, three rangers showed up on horseback, trotting toward the large mulberry tree where the "workers" were resting. "Pretend you're asleep," Uncle Ferenc ordered. "You, Anna, go draw their attention elsewhere."

So I took the water bucket from Eric and started out to the well. The rangers followed me and asked if they could water their horses. "Yes, of course," I said.

"You have a large group of people in the field. Who are they?" one of them asked, pointing at the resting *women*.

"They are my mother's friends, and a couple are my aunts," I said, giving him a flirtatious smile. "What lovely feathers you have in your hat—most unusual." A while longer, I stood there joking with these men, fast running out of things to say.

Suddenly a gunshot rang out in the distance. The startled rangers gazed off in the direction of the sound then jumped on their horses, switching their rumps, and galloped off. A few minutes later, Uncle Ferenc arrived from the opposite direction on his bicycle. He hugged me and laughed. "We took care of them— you with your irresistible smile and I with my gun." This side of Uncle Ferenc I admired and believe exemplified his true self.

After that harvest, about three weeks before the siege of Budapest, an errant bomb struck Uncle Ferenc's apartment building, causing it to collapse. His wife, Anna, died under the rubble of their home. It was never certain who had been responsible, but Uncle Ferenc blamed the Americans for killing his beloved wife.

That event deeply affected him. I think perhaps he felt abandoned a second time. First, his parents died, and then came his beloved wife's premature death. Afterward, he was a changed man, moody and distant. We rarely saw him. With his increasing involvement in the Hungarian Communist Party, he and my father no longer saw eye to eye, and the estrangement between them grew.

October

It's funny how fate intertwines people's lives. Sometimes not once but twice.

I had hardly begun working for the Doroghys when the two left for Switzerland to stay with their son. They hadn't said much about him. I learned what I knew from a silver-framed photo on Dr. Doroghy's desk. Each day when I dusted it, I glanced at this slight man who appeared to be in his twenties and whose features seemed familiar.

The couple had been gone several days when the memory came to me. The man in the photo was Eric Goldberg, I was almost certain. I hadn't put the two together because the last name I knew him by was Goldberg, not Doroghy. I wanted to contact the Doroghys to confirm my hunch but decided that perhaps my inquiry would embarrass them, or perhaps that I shouldn't even know, and so decided against it. But perhaps Uncle Ferenc could answer my question since he had been responsible for bringing Eric to the farm. It was time that I visited him in any case to pass along my father's message and one of my own.

"I am disappointed in you, Uncle Ferenc," I said to him.

He raised his brow and regarded me with interest. "Why?"

"Because you work for a rotten regime. How can you? You, who always helped those in need and stood for justice."

He raised his arm into the air like a student asking to speak, but I refused to give him a chance.

"You went to Spain to fight for the freedom of total strangers, and now you are silent about the injustice at home."

Again he tried to speak. At this point, filled with emotion, I could only eke out what had happened to our farm in a whisper. "Is this your solution to ending poverty? Please, explain it to me. Hasn't my family worked for that piece of land? Don't you care? Or did you truly become one of them?" Suddenly I stopped.

His face was flushed, and his eyes had the look of an enraged bull. However, his voice was calm when he spoke. "I understand why you might be angry. Just the same, you are not being fair, Anna. I believe in justice, and I believe in Communism. True Communism is about a society in which people are not exploited but share in the wealth of the country. Of course, there are things I disagree with this government about, but I cannot control them; I can only control what I do. I am certainly not a Russian 'Stalinist.' Please remember that."

"Then what are you?"

"I am here for a purpose; that has to be enough for you." He paused, perhaps to see what effect his words were having on me. I felt skeptical and dissatisfied but said nothing and waited for him to finish. "I am very sorry about Gyula's property and about many other things that I can't discuss with you. At the right time, I'll discuss it with your father." He wiped his forehead with a handkerchief, suddenly looking tired and old beyond his years.

I felt guilty for what I'd said, but not sorry.

He changed the subject abruptly. "Tell me about your job. Do you like it?"

In telling him about my work, I mentioned Eric Goldberg; Uncle Ferenc confirmed that he was the Doroghy's son. "But why doesn't he have the same name?"

"To avoid persecution, Eric's father had started using the name Doroghy during the war, and afterward because everyone knew him by that name, he kept it instead of changing it back. His son had never changed his. So you see why their names are different."

<hr />

My life in the apartment was routine and uneventful. I spent a significant portion of my time reading, devouring the books on the Doroghys' shelves as I'd promised myself. I was especially fond of taking a book with me to the park.

The fall of 1947 featured exceptionally beautiful foliage tinted in every imaginable hue—an autumnal pallet on full display. Nearly each day I visited the park around noontime. Often, sunshine danced in the trees, and blue sky peeked through the branches. The yellow, scarlet, and orange chrysanthemums in the flowerbeds matched the colors of the leaves overhead, and little red squirrels made quite a show of frolicking in the park. It was easy to imagine all was well with the world.

On one such day in mid-October, I closed my book now and again, a rather dense tome titled *The Ethics of Aristotle*, taking time to drink in the serenity and surrounding beauty. I imagined fall as a lovely lady at the end of her youth dressed up to await the return of her departed lover. His arrival in spring would renew her soul and restore her youth.

A slight, frail, elderly woman drew me from my reverie. She stood beside a wheelchair-bound man and asked if she might sit down on the bench with me.

"Please," I said, turning back to my book to continue reading.

The woman adjusted the wheelchair so that the man, who I assumed was her husband, faced the two of us.

"Are you all right, dear?" she asked him.

He didn't answer her right away, but after a while he asked, "What are you reading?"

I didn't think he was speaking to me until he repeated the query. That's when I glanced at him and saw the man's lifeless eyes. "I'm sorry. I didn't realize you had directed the question at me. Aristotle. A section in one of his books titled, 'The Meaning of Virtue.'"

"Do you understand it?"

"I'm trying, but it's a little over my head."

"Would you read it to me? You can just continue from where you stopped," he said. "I've been blind for several years now, and my wife doesn't see well either. So I would be quite grateful."

That was how my daily lunchtime routine began, reading to Dr. Karl Német, a former math professor who'd been relieved of his position once his condition rendered him fully blind. When the weather didn't permit us to meet in the park, I read to him in the couple's crowded first floor apartment only three blocks from mine. In exchange for reading to him, his kindly wife, Margo, offered me coffee and cookies, and the professor provided discourse about whatever I was reading; he became a sort of teacher, which I badly wanted. It was a way for me to continue my education.

Each day walking home from my sessions with him, I felt happy—happy for myself and happy for the man's delight. Despite the turbulent political events swirling all around me, I felt that life could be beautiful after all. Perhaps I owed Aristotle a note of thanks as well. It had been serendipitous that I happened to be on that particular bench on that particularly beautiful day. How fortunate.

November–December 1947

American Legation in Budapest.

Stephen Koczak's telephone rang in his office. It was the Legation guard saying that a man insisted on seeing him. "It's after hours. What shall I do?" the guard asked.

"Tell him to come back tomorrow."

"He insists he cannot wait until tomorrow."

"All right, send him up, but tell him I have no more than ten minutes."

A few minutes later came a knock on the door.

A lean curly-haired man entered, his hat in his hand. "I am Elek Pikler, an attorney, coming to you with a request from Dezsö Sulyok's son-in-law. Apparently, your Colonel Jonathon Smith arranged to send some things to him in Vienna, but he claims the items are not what he was promised."

"How can this possibly have anything to do with me?" Working late again, Stephen felt annoyed that he had to deal with Smith's unfinished business. "Why don't you ask the Colonel?"

"Well, Mr. Smith is on vacation, and this man is threatening to tell things to certain agents if he doesn't get what he wants."

"So what does he want?"

48

"He wants to have his boat sent to him. It was promised to him by the Legation."

"A boat? What is the matter with the man? Isn't he grateful Smith saved his skin? Who was the half-witted person promising to deliver the boat?"

Twisting the hat in his hands, Pikler said, "It was Colonel Smith, and the boat is not so large. Only three feet long."

"Who has the boat now?"

"I do. It was left in my care, and I am very anxious to be rid of it. You see, part of the boat is made of solid gold."

"I see," Stephen said. "So you are saying that in these difficult times, the son-in-law of the former leader of Hungary's Freedom Party wants us to waste our time and diplomatic skills on his selfish errand?"

Elek Pikler's eyes carefully studied the floor. "Yes, I suppose so."

Stephen pretended to be turning back to the papers on his desk, before finally saying, "I don't like people not keeping their promises, so this once, I'll see to it that the damn boat is taken to Vienna." From out of the corner of his eye, Stephen watched the man back out of his office and close the door behind him.

Good riddance, he thought, already on to the next bit of work before going to spend the evening with Robin and his wife, Ethel, for a relaxed, home-cooked meal.

A few days later, Stephen was at the office feeling quite tired. The previous couple of weeks, he'd had little sleep. He'd made several trips to Vienna, smuggling more desperate people out of the country. Of course, this was not part of his diplomatic job, and it was not officially sanctioned by Minister Chapin, but Stephen couldn't in good conscience ignore the pleas of these people, many of whom would have faced death or prison sentences without his and Robin's help.

When he wasn't occupied driving people to safety after hours, he was traveling to and from Esztergom on business with

Cardinal Mindszenty. This evening he was expected to attend a reception Deputy Premier Rakosi was throwing for General Vorosilov, the new Russian commander installed to oversee the Soviet occupational army.

He yawned. Of course he would go. He loved his work, and part of his job involved attending these parties and receptions, which, in fact, were notorious for picking up valuable information. Besides, this would be Stephen's first event held by the real leader of Hungary and the country's Communist Party.

The man was an impressive political manipulator. In power since June 1 when he engineered the coup that forced Premier Nagy to resign while on vacation in Switzerland, Rakosi then managed to also rid the Freedom Party of its leader Dezső Sulyok and diminish the power of the Independents. The man was a force to be reckoned with. Shortly, Stephen would set aside his work to attend the event and get a close look at this feared man.

Eager to be finished but engrossed in one final task, Stephen didn't hear the knock on the door, and so was startled to find himself face to face with Pikler again. Holding his hat by the brim, Pikler kneaded it in his peculiar way, slowly turning it clockwise. "Mr. Koczak, we have another problem."

"What? Wasn't the boat delivered?"

"Yes, it was."

"Then why do we have a problem?"

Pikler looked around before pulling a chair close to Stephen, then started in a low voice. "I had two visitors late last night. My wife was already asleep. They were burly types, not to be trifled with. They came in and asked if I had a typewriter. 'Of course,' I said. Then they dictated the following letter: 'I, Elek Pikler, personally smuggled Sulyok and his family and his boat out of the country to Vienna with the collaboration of Stephen Koczak, a political officer of the American Legation.'

"'Sign it,' one of them said. The other one pressed a gun to my neck. What could I do?"

"So what do they want from you?"

"To spy on you. If I don't I'll be denounced as an enemy of the people and thrown into prison. I don't know what they'll do with you."

Stephen thought for a moment then told Pikler, "Well, find out and let me know."

Political receptions could be boring and required energy that Stephen had difficulty mustering in light of his tiring schedule, but duty called. The high-level Rakosi reception would be more interesting than most, and he wanted to gather information on General Vorosilov. If nothing else, he could always turn to Robin, who would also be there.

On entering the ornate and conversation-filled room, Stephen felt a few women's heads swivel in his direction. He was single, an eligible bachelor, apparently not too bad looking for he often gained female attention. To consort with Hungarian women was frowned on, but he knew Legation officers who indulged.

So far, Stephen had refrained, as much because of his non-stop schedule as from lack of interest. He hadn't met many Hungarian, or even American, women socially, nor did the ones he encountered appeal to him. His expectations and standards were high, maybe a bit too idealistic, he knew, and he'd be the first to admit his experience with women thus far had been limited—first by the intrusion of the war, and second by his dedication to his studies, and now by his career. He'd get around to it, he told others when they accused him of being a stick in the mud, but the entire matter would have to wait a little longer.

Representative Bodnar of the Smallholders Party approached him and offered to introduce him to the General. Stephen had already been observing Vorosilov. There was nothing particularly impressive about him—he was clean-shaven, had a trim strong figure and tight lips. Stephen and Bodnar stepped into the reception line. When their turn came, Bodnar introduced Stephen. Vorosilov's grip was firm. They briefly conversed in German. Then Bodnar led Stephen to a quiet corner and spoke in a hushed voice. "We'll see how long this one lasts. Stalin gets rid of his generals like that." He snapped his fingers. "Who'll be next?" They exchanged a few more words before Bodnar wandered off.

While thinking about Bodnar's prediction, Stephen noticed a man standing beside the General eyeing him. Nearby stood István Barankovics, leader of the Democratic People's Party. Stephen joined him. Discreetly directing Barankovics' gaze to the man alongside the General, he asked if he knew his identity.

"That's Colonel Ferenc Tóth of the AVO. I noticed him watching you."

"So it seems." Stephen took note of the colonel's features then studied the bald-headed Mátyás Rakosi, fully agreeing with a description he'd read in a *New York Times* article by Anne O'Hare McCormick: "He is an unprepossessing little man with small, shrewd eyes and the rude, authoritative manner of the stage Commissar."

He watched Rakosi's thick expressive eyebrows jump as he spoke. So this man was the scourge of Hungary and a foe of the United States. In person he didn't seem particularly formidable or dangerous. But public appearances were deceptive. Rakosi went on, lauding the General and Stalin, and thanking the Russian army for keeping order in Hungary. Applause was muted and an uncomfortable silence ensued. To dispel the quiet, Rakosi merely wagged his hand at the gypsy band, which struck up a lively tune.

Instead of returning home, Robin insisted on taking Stephen to an ex-pat party. As was his way, Stephen demurred, but Robin refused to allow him to go home. They drove along the river, the hills of Buda shrouded in darkness that disguised the ravages of war still so evident during the day. Buda was a place of undulating hills, villas, rose gardens, and the royal palace. The ornate Mathias Church, where kings once were crowned, watched over the city. To the unaware observer, the view seemed perfectly beautiful.

At the party, Stephen was struck by the difference between this social gathering and the previous one. This one filled with lively youthful people drinking, laughing, and chatting, the other officious and somber, with the exception of the gypsy band.

He felt Robin poke him gently. "Wake up, my friend. You're about to meet the prettiest Brit in Budapest. Over there between those two."

Stephen followed Robin's gaze to a tall woman with slender legs, beautiful olive skin, and a mane of long, dark, wavy hair. Robin pulled Stephen along and introduced them. "He's too serious for his own good, Joan. I'm putting you in charge of entertaining him, and keeping him from brooding or slinking home." Stephen rolled his eyes, and Joan laughed gaily.

Stephen spent the remainder of the evening in her company. Joan Robbins was vivacious and amiable with perhaps an overly toothy smile. After he left, he had to admit that she was neither bad looking nor bad company. He'd actually enjoyed himself, at least as much as he could at that late hour.

———◆———

Not long after this, on his way to the courthouse to observe the trial of two engineers who'd had the audacity to express their opinion on Russia's exploitation of the country's oil resources, Stephen ran into Joan. She invited him for supper. When he hesitated, her mouth turned into a pout. Not wanting to offend her, he agreed to go, though he warned her of his time constraints. "I'll have to be back in my office at seven for a meeting." It would be their first date.

A few blocks from the courthouse, the small restaurant where they ate overlooked the river. The fish soup and Hungarian strudel were much to Stephen's liking. Joan chatted away about her family and working for the British Embassy in an administrative capacity. He glanced at his watch as the time neared for his third meeting with Pikler. His mind wandered to what he might have to say. He hoped that perhaps he would learn what the AVO knew about him, and what they wanted Pikler to learn more of.

He had difficulty extracting himself from his date, who was loath to see him go, but after agreeing to see her again, she gave him a broad smile. "I look forward to it, Stephen," Joan purred and gave him a peck on the cheek.

By the time he reached his office at the Legation, Pikler was sitting nervously on the edge of his chair. He rushed to tell Stephen what the AVO wanted. "They are quite sure that you are running a large, secret service operation out of Vienna, and they want me to convince you to give me a job. You understand?" Pikler asked.

Yes, yes, yes, Stephen nodded. Looking into space, he drummed his fingers on the desktop. He was a little surprised they thought he was a spy, though not entirely. At least now he knew the reason for the AVO man's interest in him at the reception the other day. He took another moment to consider their options.

He studied Pikler. "We'll pretend to play their game. Tell them I am very impressed with your talent and that I'm willing to hire you, but only in Vienna." Stephen spoke each sentence distinctly. "Say that I need someone who is Hungarian and very clever. In return for doing this, tell them your wife must accompany you. Say that I only employ people who can't be blackmailed through family members who are left behind."

Pikler seized on the idea. "Ingenious," he said. In the next moment, the man once again began to work his hat with his fingers. "Will they agree to such a thing? They'll see through it, won't they? I don't know if I can lie. I—"

"You're a lawyer, Mr. Pikler—a good one, I hear. And presented in the right way, how can they turn down the offer? It's a perfect opportunity for them to think they're getting an inside view of the CIA. It's up to you, but I don't see any other way," Stephen said, indicating that this was Pikler's only option. He couldn't hire him to work in the Legation. The thing would get far too messy and complicated. "Agreed?"

Pikler nodded his head uncertainly.

"Come see me when you have news for me."

After Pikler left, Stephen sank deeply into his chair. It discomforted him to think that he was suspected of being a spy. Other than being part of the AVO, exactly who was this man Colonel Tóth? He'd get someone to look into it in the morning. And he'd speak to Minister Chapin. Get his perspective on what to do, if anything. He sighed. Another thing to add to his day. There weren't quite enough hours or days in the week to keep up with his lengthening list of assignments. And then there were the nighttime runs to Vienna, of which he'd completed at least half a dozen. If he was being watched, he worried about endangering the people he took over the border; perhaps he should stop, at least for a while. What else would the next few weeks bring?

———————•———————

The December wind rattled the window of Stephen's office. Though only late afternoon, it was already dark. He stood at the window overlooking the square where a young couple strolled hand in hand.

He was waiting for Pikler and feeling rather cross. He had tickets for the theater, and now he'd be late. Undoubtedly, Joan would be miffed if he didn't show up before curtain time. What the devil was his problem now? Only yesterday, Pikler had told him the AVO had agreed to let him take the position in Vienna and bring his wife. Everything had been settled, he'd thought, until Pikler called earlier in the day sounding frantic.

Finally the guard announced his arrival. "Send him up." Stephen started for the door thinking he might still get to the show on time.

Pikler arrived disheveled and out of breath, having run up three flights of stairs. "Here. Drink this," Stephen ordered, handing him a glass of wine.

The story that spilled out of Pikler was that his wife refused to leave without Jenő and Lenke.

"I didn't know you had children," Stephen said. "I would have told you to tell the AVO they need to go with you. Why didn't you say anything?"

"They're not our children. They're my wife's dogs."

"Oh, for heaven's sakes. Just go back to them and tell them the situation. Make sure you keep your nerve. You're almost free. Remember that." Watching Pikler retreat to the door, Stephen again hoped it would be the last time he'd see him.

December 17

My father was just returning from pruning some trees when he was startled to find Uncle Ferenc coming through the gate into the courtyard. Three years had passed since they'd seen each other.

Ferenc gave him an apologetic half smile but said nothing about their estrangement. "I've come to ask you to go with me to visit my parents and Anna's grave."

My father wondered why Uncle Ferenc had chosen this particular time to come. Perhaps there was something else on his mind. Ferenc had never been one to speak freely, keeping his thoughts and feelings to himself. Being circumspect and measured seemed to be part of his nature.

In the kitchen, he greeted my mother, commenting on the delicious smell of her freshly baked bread. "God be with you, Terèz. it is good to see you."

"God be with you, too," my mother answered. "What brings you here?"

He sighed. "My conscience. If you still believe I have one."

She didn't answer but bade him to have some food as she placed the bread and smoked ham on the table.

Just as when they were young men, the two ate in comfortable silence. Bread, ham, and hot green peppers. Ferenc spoke first. "I came to make peace with you, Gyula. I know we have different political views, but I love you just the same. You were good to me when I came to live with your family as a boy, and I will never forget that."

"Yes, Ferenc, but your comrades have not been good to me or my family," my father snapped. "Look what they've left us.

Almost nothing." His anger unleashed a flood of words. "You say the Communists are a party for the people. So, exactly which people are we talking about? We are the farmers who raise food for the country. Now what should we do? How will we live?"

"You need to know I don't agree with everything that's happening. Remember that when you think of me in the future, Gyula." His brow furrowed and his eyes drifted off. Then with a familiar half smile, he again asked my father to visit Anna's grave with him. "You loved her. You helped me bury her. Please come."

It was a long drive to the cemetery near Lake Balaton where the family was buried. Repeatedly along the way, he seemed on the verge of saying something to my father, but each time he stopped himself. My father ruminated about it later, but it wasn't until after Uncle Ferenc had died, or more likely was killed, that he understood what his cousin may have been trying to say.

They returned late in the evening. When my father invited him to stay the night, Ferenc demurred, saying he had to get back to Budapest.

"What's the rush?"

"Work summons me, brother." He patted my father's shoulder and started for the car. Halfway there, he turned, his voice slightly tremulous, and pointed at the old walnut trees. "Tell Pista and Father Imre they should dig up the grubs from under there." Once more he smiled his half smile, one that had often indicated some sort of concern. "And tell him not to say anything to his friend János Nyikos. Understand? He's not to be trusted."

My father pressed him to explain the cryptic message, but Uncle Ferenc said Pista would know what he was referring to.

———•———

When Uncle Ferenc returned to Budapest, I visited him and brought him some violets. Then too he seemed unlike himself. He asked how I liked my job, to which I said, "Not very much," and then he revealed that Dr. Doroghy had decided against returning home from Switzerland and was planning to sublet the apartment.

This came as a bit of a shock. Not so much that the Doroghys had decided to stay, but that Uncle Ferenc would know so much about their affairs. I discovered that Dr. Doroghy had been doing quite a bit of legal work for the Hungarian Communists, helping them negotiate commercial deals with other countries, which accounted for his comfortable lifestyle.

I don't recall exactly how the conversation veered toward a discussion of me being followed by the secret police, but in any case, he told me that as long as he lived here in Budapest, nothing would happen to me and that no one was "tailing" me.

"Of that I'm certain," he added.

"These days how can you be certain of anything?"

He turned his attentions to the flowers. "Thank you for bringing these to an old goat like me. Your aunt loved violets. She put them everywhere; she would have garnished my dessert with them if I'd let her." He chuckled at the memory.

"I want you to have something," he said. He abruptly left the room and returned with a small box. "I gave this to my wife when she was your age."

Lying on a pillow of fabric inside the box, I found the lovely engagement ring my Aunt Anna had always worn. "Uncle Ferenc, I am overwhelmed. I don't know if I should take it."

"Of course you should." He closed my fingers around the box, and before we could do or say anything else, the phone rang. His voice sounded pleasant enough as he told the person on the other end of the line that he'd be over in ten minutes.

I asked if I could stay to do a little straightening; his place was messy and in bad need of cleaning. "Of course, Anna. I'd be grateful. If you leave before I return, please leave the lights on."

"On?"

He smiled. "Yes. I like the place lit up when I return home."

That night Uncle Ferenc had an appointment with Pikler, in which the lawyer would explain the need to take his wife's dogs with them to Vienna. The situation amused Ferenc, Pikler later told Stephen.

"Those dogs," he said, "tell me, Pikler, are they made of solid gold like the keel of the boat you and Koczak smuggled out?"

"They are real dogs," he said, not bothering to refute the smuggling charge.

"Then let me see them."

Pikler whistled, and two sleek silver Vizslas trotted into the room. With a hand signal, Pikler stopped them. They seated themselves in the regal manner of their breed. "Here they are."

On seeing them, Uncle Ferenc gave Pikler the green light to take the dogs. "You will contact us when you arrive, understand?"

"Perfectly."

He scrutinized Pikler's face, an icy stare, which Pikler told Stephen made his skin crawl. "You'd better not double-cross us," Uncle Ferenc warned. "The AVO has ways of making sure. You know that as well as I do."

"I know."

Around the dinner table at my parents' home the day after Christmas, Father Imre said a blessing, his hands making the sign of the cross over the food. Pista's friends János Nyikos, the one Uncle Ferenc had warned our father about, and Sándor Tanács were also there to celebrate and eat my mother's delicious meal. After grace, the men could hardly wait to attack their soup.

Though the table was far from groaning with food, in those difficult times, we did well enough and considered ourselves lucky compared to those who went hungry in the cities. Living in the country enabled us to grow a few vegetables, have chickens and eggs, and generally have easier access to a wide array of food. For this dinner, we had chicken soup with dumplings, stuffed cabbage, and freshly baked bread sticks.

Except for the occasional sound of slurping, the soup was devoured in relative silence. Soup bowls were cleared, and talk turned to the land that had been expropriated from our family. Everyone lamented the fact, especially Father Imre who said, "I hope they left you the parcel with the old walnut trees?"

My father, who had passed Uncle Ferenc's message on to Pista, eyed the priest curiously. "I didn't know you were so attached to those trees," my father joked.

He took a moment to phrase his answer. "It's just that we all played in them when we were young." He glanced at János and then exchanged a look with Pista.

My father teased him. "That's the trouble with you priests. You're all so sentimental."

Jumping into the conversation, János Nyikos said, "Let's talk about something more interesting than walnut trees."

"Good idea," Pista said.

János turned to me. "How do you like Budapest? You've found a boyfriend yet?" he snickered. He had always annoyed me, so I brushed him off, rolling my eyes and giving him a disdainful look. Apparently that didn't dampen his curiosity about my life in the city. "Have you joined the Communist Party?" he asked.

"You know very well I would never do that. And for your information, I have the highly sought-after position of taking care of someone's apartment." I sat back, donning a smug look.

"Yes, a job that will end in a few months."

I cast a frustrated glance at my mother and lifted my chin defiantly. "I'll find another," I said.

"Maybe it's a husband you should look for, not a job, Anna," my mother said. "Why not come home when the job ends?"

"Mother!" I reprimanded her. "I am not ready for marriage."

She looked at me with a "mother knows best" expression. "There are worse things."

I grimaced at her. "Not for me. At least not now."

January 1948

On the second day of January, the Hungarian newspaper *Nemzet* lay on Stephen's desk, the front page covered with photos of the New Year's Day parade. School children and factory workers—everyone knew that many had been ordered to march—were carrying red flags and banners. The caption stated they were singing, "Glorious Victory for the People," in praise of Stalin for liberating Hungary.

Stephen shook his head. *Propaganda*, he thought. *Takes nerve to sell such lies to people suffering from the Russian and Communist so-called glory.*

At the bottom of the page, a photo drew his attention. The man looked familiar. "Colonel Ferenc Tóth Dies of Heart Attack," the headline read. The article stated that the head of the detective department of the AVO had died of an apparent heart attack at an event celebrating his promotion to head up Section II. Stephen knew this was the section known as "the butcher shop," a job not for the faint of heart. He recalled how searchingly the AVO man had looked at him at the reception for General Vorosilov. He couldn't help but be glad Colonel Tóth was gone. At least now he wouldn't be following him.

"Flowers for Stephen Koczak," a voice chimed behind him. It was Robin Steussy, holding a vase of red roses. "Just arrived. Thought I'd bring them up." He set them on the desk but teasingly withheld the small white envelope attached to the flowers. "I didn't know you were in love, man. Here I am, your best friend, thinking you'd tell me everything. So who's the lucky woman?"

Stephen grabbed the envelope and opened it. "Yours in friendship forever, Margit," he read and breathed a sigh of relief. This was code letting him know that Pikler, his wife, and those damned dogs had made it to Vienna.

Before he could explain any further, the door opened, and Joan sauntered in, her eyes hardening at the sight of the roses. Robin raised his brow quizzically at Stephen and said, "I guess I'll leave you two alone."

———◦———

I was in the Doroghys' apartment, hurriedly putting it in order before installing myself by the phone to call some friends and wish them a happy new year. I was in a wonderful mood, as I'd met an interesting young man who'd paid quite a lot of attention to me the previous night, a person I wasn't at all averse to seeing again. After my calls were done, I lifted the newspaper to glance at the headlines.

There at the bottom was the stunning news of Uncle Ferenc's death. After a long moment of paralyzing silence, the telephone rang.

It was my cousin, Misi, saying they'd received a telegram about Uncle Ferenc.

"Listen to me carefully. Tomorrow at eleven in the morning, you must go to his apartment. The police will be there, but you'll be allowed to take his personal belongings." He finished giving me instructions and told me when the memorial service would be held.

The following day, I appeared at Uncle Ferenc's apartment promptly at eleven o'clock. An elderly policeman opened the door and asked me what I wanted. I told him I was authorized to retrieve some of my uncle's things and showed him my identification. As if I was disturbing his routine, he grumpily allowed me to enter.

Only one step inside, and I was aghast at what I saw. The place had been ransacked, even photographs had been ripped out of their frames. I gathered the photos and some of the knick-knacks he'd liked. In his closet, the pockets of a few jackets had been turned inside out. When I began to sort through his papers, the policeman shouted at me to stop. "You may not touch those." He handed me a bundle of papers. "These are the ones you can take." When I began to sift through them, he told me to do it later.

"I prefer to do it now," I insisted stubbornly.

"Be quick about it."

Not trusting these people, I took my time examining every paper, making sure they hadn't included anything in the pile that could later be used to blackmail our family.

Misi arrived with a friend and a truck. They removed a few pieces of furniture, some clothes and pictures, and everything else I'd collected. "Anything you want, Anna?" my cousin asked. I wanted his old overcoat. He'd worn it often, and I decided it would be a memento of him. But there was another reason. He'd once told me it had a secret pocket in the belt. When I returned to his closet and pulled the coat off its hanger, I saw that the belt was missing. I was afraid they'd taken it. After a few moments of glancing around for it, I found it half-hidden beneath his bed. I snatched it off the floor and took it with me.

The memorial service was held the following day—a muted affair. Not many people attended, and the few who did were government officials, except my cousin Misi and I who represented his family. The words spoken by a man unfamiliar to us were lost on me. My eyes remained fixed on the closed coffin. Poor Uncle Ferenc, I thought. He fought for what he believed in only to have his life cut short, and after finding a scribbled note inside the belt, I felt fairly certain that his death had been at the hands of his *comrades*.

Hidden in the pocket of the belt, the note was folded into a small triangle and a God's eye had been drawn on the outside. The message was not addressed to anyone: "I have only a few hours left. I will have to drink it like Socrates had to drink the hemlock. They will say I had a heart attack."

The service came to a close. As was the custom, mourners lined up to lay a rose on the coffin. In this case, the roses in the basket were red, the color of the Russian flag. The color we'd come to associate with Communism. A color I now hated.

The rose I'd brought with me was yellow, Uncle Ferenc's and my favorite. He had given it to me on several occasions. Misi had cautioned me against placing it on the coffin. "They'll notice, you know."

I knew, but it was my only form of protest, and I couldn't worry about the consequences or what anyone would think, nor did I care.

"How can you be so stubborn?" Misi asked.

"I was born that way," I retorted.

When it was my turn, I felt people's eyes on me. I touched the rose with my lips and then laid it on the coffin over the place where I thought his heart would be. Tears piled up, but I fought the urge to cry—who were they to see my grief?

The news of Uncle Ferenc's death hit our family hard and deeply saddened us. Especially my father. After such a lengthy falling out, to suddenly have renewed the relationship, albeit tentatively, made it all the more difficult because of the things he wished he had said to his cousin.

His note reinforced our suspicion that his death had not been of natural causes, but rather politically motivated. And the way he'd behaved in the weeks prior to his death indicated he'd been worried, that he might have known he was in danger, and that he was tying up the loose ends of his life just in case anything happened to him.

The purge of those in the Hungarian Communist Party who'd fought with Tito in the Spanish Civil War, as my uncle had, or leaned toward Tito's brand of socialism was just beginning. Stalin came to see these men as a threat, and over the course of the next few years, they would be arrested, imprisoned, executed, or even murdered. Those who were lucky defected. Stalin wasn't about to allow Hungary to go the way of the independent-minded Tito. He was determined to keep his grip firm, and Stalin's man Rakosi didn't shrink from the brutal job.

A couple of years later in Austria, the Szulners, forgers who'd worked for the AVO, told me that a few days before Uncle Ferenc's death, they heard that the AVO had given Ferenc a visit and searched his apartment. They found letters from Tito's government. Gábor Péter, the ruthless head of the AVO, questioned him and this resulted in an argument between the two. Uncle Ferenc declared that he would retire. Péter grew furious. "You will retire when the AVO says so." After that, Uncle Ferenc was placed under house arrest until the party on January 1, purportedly given in honor of his promotion. And that was the end.

About a week into January, Mrs. Bokor, who worked at the Legation, entered Stephen's office looking worried. "I am in a difficult situation, Mr. Koczak," she said. "My brother escaped from Hungary and now his house is empty. A captain in the AVO paid me a visit the other day and said that the house is being declared abandoned property and the government is allocating it to him."

Stephen began to respond, saying that there was little he could do about it, but Mrs. Bokor interrupted him. "I can't afford to lose this house, so I lied saying the house has already been taken by someone in the American Legation. Mr. Steussy said you were looking for a place. Please, Mr. Koczak, I would be ever so grateful."

While it was true that Stephen was in search of a more suitable apartment than the room the Sisters of Social Services provided him, there were several reasons he preferred not to take this one, the main one being that he was afraid of living in a place that had the attention of the AVO. That's all he needed. Nevertheless, he pitied her and made the move.

———◆———

The latter part of January 1948 brought balmy weather, something that happened almost annually, and which almost always ended abruptly with an onslaught of cold weather and often snowfall. I sat beside a window on the express train to Nagykörös looking out over the fields, deserted except for birds and the occasional wild rabbit. Trees we passed swelled with the beginnings of buds, and a few crocuses even sent their leaves toward the sun. I loved riding on trains. They were a link to faraway places that I dreamed of visiting someday.

In my mind, I turned over what Julia had told me earlier that morning. The Interior Minister L. Rajk had banned some of the American films. *Well, I guess I won't be seeing Gary Cooper or Robert Taylor anymore.*

I hadn't let my family know that I was coming. I had decided to make the trip for two reasons: to fetch my journal and some letters I'd forgotten over the Christmas holiday, and with the pain of Uncle Ferenc's recent death still fresh, I wanted the comfort of family.

Taking the short cut, I traveled along the edge of town. The afternoon sun cast a honey-colored hue over the landscape. I whistled as I walked along, recalling some pleasant childhood memories.

Our pale yellow stucco house stood behind the bare branches of the trees. In the summer, the green shingled roof blended in with the leaves so perfectly that one might have thought the house had no roof at all. Grouped behind the house, the five tall walnut trees Father Imre felt so fond of provided additional shade from the sun.

As I walked down a lane with a canopy of poplar trees, appropriately called Tall Poplar Avenue, I fleetingly considered moving back. It wasn't what I wanted. For better or worse, my life now was in Budapest, and besides I'd never been that wild about the provincial outlook of the townspeople.

The land beyond the poplars had not been tilled by anyone as far back as I could remember. In November 1944, after the Russians had invaded our town, they forced a number of us to dig graves for the German and Hungarian soldiers they'd killed. I will never forget the horror I witnessed one day as I worked alongside my partner, a 16-year old boy named Tom, who was shot dead by a Russian soldier. Whenever I passed by here I said a prayer for him and the other soldiers who lay buried there in unmarked graves.

For a moment nothing seemed to stir, until Bodri loped toward me, barking and wagging his tail happy to see me, and shook me out of that unpleasant memory. I hoped he hadn't ruined my surprise arrival.

Together we completed the short trek home, mounting the steps to the front porch, which for most of my life had been my favorite place to play, read, and dream of travel. My mother appeared in the doorway, thrilled to see me approaching her. We ran to embrace one another.

Shortly thereafter, she begged me to attend a church concert with her that evening. It was a lovely affair, and I enjoyed just spending time with her. On our return, snow began to fall in large heavy flakes, and I spotted Father Imre coming out of the house. He waved to us but seemed in a hurry to join another man who sat on the bench of a horse carriage, the back of which was loaded with logs and branches. The minute the priest was seated, the horses took off, trotting at a rapid clip through the wide gate.

Inside the house, my mother asked what Father Imre had been doing here at this time of night. With an eye out the window, my father said, "He just stopped by to pick up some firewood to distribute to some of the poor in his parish. Looks like they'll need it." He and my mother exchanged a look.

Pista was about to step into the kitchen when my father shooed him out telling him to shake the snow off first. Pista stamped his feet and dusted himself off. "I predict the snow will be nice and deep by morning," he said mysteriously, moving to the stove and rubbing his hands together. "You know how I love that."

I woke up to a bright morning, the fields and trees covered in a deep layer of snow. The land lay quiet and motionless beneath the brilliant white. Only a black magpie atop one of the walnut trees interrupted the silence with its plaintive cry. I watched it spread its tail, then flap its pitch-colored wings and lift off into the blue sky.

The snow and a kitchen filled with the inviting smell of coffee and toasting bread put me in a playful, happy mood. I called out to Pista, inviting him to go for a stroll after breakfast. We grabbed our coats and scarves and were about to walk outside when half a dozen armed policemen on motorcycles roared through the gate, coming to a noisy halt a few feet from the house.

Pista retreated from the door, leaving me there as three of the men rose up the steps onto the porch, and burst into the house, their boots covered in snow. "We're looking for your son," one of them said brusquely to my father.

"Which one, I have five."

"Don't be funny. You know which one." He squinted at my father.

Pista stepped into the room. "Are you looking for me?"

"Is your name István Tóth?" The man's tone was harsh and it alarmed me.

"Yes, what do you want?" Pista said, showing little concern.

"Get your coat on," he barked, "all of you, you're coming outside."

"What's going on?" I demanded, but they refused to answer. Looking at my poor mother, I begged them to leave her here. "Why must she go out into the cold?"

The man slipped the rifle off his shoulder and gripped it threateningly. "I said, all of you." Another policeman grabbed Pista, tied his hands behind his back, and marched us all outside toward the walnut trees. There they secured my brother to one of the trees, grabbed shovels the other three had brought, and began to dig through the snow.

"What's this all about?" my father insisted.

"Ask him," one of the policemen said aiming his head at Pista. Pista shrugged. "I have no idea."

"When we find the guns, you'll have as many bullets in your head as there are guns."

My mother shivered in the icy cold, refusing to look at Pista. We stamped our feet and rubbed our arms, saying little. I started to go to Pista to warm him up, but the policeman wouldn't allow it. "You stay where you are."

After at least an hour of digging and cursing, they found nothing. They packed up and headed back the way they'd come. We heard them rev their motorcycles, then with a roar of engines, they were gone. I hadn't even noticed that mother had fainted. My father swept her up and carried her into the house, while I cut Pista loose.

"Was that true, Pista? You hid guns out here? How could you?" In that moment I was furious with him for endangering our family.

"No."

"Don't lie to me."

"Yes."

"How many, for God's sake?"

"Forty-two."

"Pista! I suppose that's what Father Imre was doing here last night?"

He nodded. It was clear that my brother would participate in the resistance efforts, risky or not. Though I agreed with their work, I felt differently once I knew the harsh reality of what might come to pass. Working with the underground was no longer an abstract concept and I was afraid of what might happen to him. "Please be careful."

"Don't worry. Whatever happens, I am ready. There will be a revolution. You'll see. We're working toward that, but to succeed we need guns."

I left Nagykörös with a terrible gnawing feeling of danger that accompanied me on the ride home and in the days to come.

February–April 1948

After thirteen weeks of reading to Karl, we had become a fixture in the park. I delighted in his company, our intellectual discourse and philosophical discussions, and the occasional delicious cakes and cookies his wife served us on days the weather prevented us from going outside. I savored each encounter all the more knowing that once my employment at the Doroghy's ended, they would come to a close. I'd have to find another job, one unlikely to afford me the luxury of these two hour midday visits.

On one such visit toward the end of January, I noticed that Karl was thin and not looking well.

"Are you ill?"

"I have cancer," Karl answered as matter-of-factly, as if he were talking about the weather. He probably noticed my expression of concern because he added, "You see, Anna, I am not afraid. When it comes, it comes. There's nothing we can do but to welcome death." His words reminded me of Pista's, and I wondered if I would be so brave in the face of my own mortality.

I didn't share Karl's philosophical attitude toward life. Perhaps in part it was due to Uncle Ferenc's recent death; now another man for whom I'd come to feel affection and, in a sense, depend on would be gone from my life. We were alone, and so I asked him how Margo was responding to the news.

"She knows I have cancer but not the extent of it. I don't want her thinking each day I might die. She is not good at handling such stress." Then he shifted the conversation to me. "Do you have a young man in your life?" Though he was blind, there was a searching quality to his eyes.

"Nothing serious. Not yet."

"Well, if you ever meet someone who is a philosopher, tell him I trained you for him." He was quietly laughing now and reached his hand out to me. "I wish just once I could see your face. I only see your soul, and that is radiant and kind, which of course is more important, though Margo tells me you are beautiful inside and out." He lifted my hand to his lips and kissed it.

The next time I saw Karl, in early February, he was in the hospital, almost skeletal and without words. It brought tears to my eyes. Taking one of his hands in mine, I collected myself and read to him. I felt a little squeeze. His eyes opened, staring into nothingness. His breath was labored.

Margo, so obviously distressed, was waiting for me outside the hospital door when I left. She handed me a note which provided the name of a woman, her telephone number, and her address. The accompanying message read:

"Dear Anna, Please go to this woman. She will continue teaching you French. Don't worry about payment—it is settled. With great admiration, Dr. Karl Német."

Margo and I embraced, both of us crying, and then she returned to the room. Later that afternoon Karl died.

When I arrived home, Valery, who managed the Doroghy's affairs in Budapest, was in the apartment and in her typically superior way informed me that on the last day of February, or thereabouts, an English couple would come to live in the apartment, and if I wanted, I could stay in their employ.

For whatever reason—most likely youthful impulsiveness and pride—I told her that I didn't. Of course I had no idea what else I'd do, but I planned to begin scouring the want ads, and felt certain that I'd have no trouble locating another position, perhaps I'd even become an assistant to someone, I thought.

Acting affronted and speaking very formally, I said, "It would have been more decent if you'd notified me of this on the first of February to give me more time to look for other employment. Why was that not done?"

"I assumed you'd be willing to stay. You could ask this couple for more money since they won't be absent as the Doroghys were. All you have to do is be a proper parlor maid."

"It is not my goal in life to be a parlor maid, but I'll take care of them the first day or two," I said assuredly.

"Suit yourself," she said.

After she left, I sat down and felt extremely sorry for myself. Uncle Ferenc and Karl's deaths, and now I had the task of finding a new job after having turned down her perfectly good offer. Good enough, at least until things in Hungary changed.

———◆———

Not long after Stephen had settled into Mrs. Bokor's apartment, she again came crying to him. "Oh, Mr. Koczak, please don't think badly of me, but the AVO man has come back and told me they would arrest me if I didn't turn the house over to him." Her weeping turned into loud, hiccoughing sobs. "What can I do but ask you to move out? Please don't fire me. Now, this job is all I have."

How was it, Stephen thought, *that he was always being saddled with these hard-luck cases?* Robin laughed at him, saying he was a magnet for such people.

"They can sniff a sucker a mile away." Though it was true, Robin wasn't much different and they both knew it. What was one to do in a country like this?

So he agreed and, by the end of February, would again be out of a place to stay. He couldn't go back to the Sisters of Social Services, that was certain, though he felt both affection and great respect for Sister Slachta. But where could he find a place on such short notice?

Shortly thereafter, a friend of Stephen's from Berlin—Károly Simon—arrived in Budapest and invited him to dinner at the home of his parents. Stephen arrived at Benczur ut 44 at seven o'clock. Over dinner, talk turned to his housing dilemma, prompting Mrs. Simon to exclaim, "Oh my, I have the perfect apartment for you. The people who signed a lease for it were ordered back to England so the owner is in the same predicament as you. They need to find someone straight away."

Though Stephen felt fortunate to have this opportunity present itself, he was also a bit apprehensive. He'd already lived in an area far from the city center, which had forced him to take cabs everywhere except to and from work for which the Legation provided a car and driver. The problem with taxis, besides the expense, was that cab drivers were often paid by the AVO to keep them informed of the comings and goings of various citizens. True or not, this had confirmed his desire to live closer in.

"Do you mind if I ask where it is?"

"Of course not. It's directly across the street from us. Number 41."

He was surprised and genuinely pleased. "That sounds perfect," he cried.

He had thoroughly enjoyed his evening away from work and catching up with an old friend. Before Stephen left, Mrs. Simon placed a call and set up an appointment for him the following morning.

"She sounds quite eager to lease the apartment," Mrs. Simon said. "I think you're in luck."

On his way out, he took a look at the building. It was similar to the Simon's, only a bit nicer and crescent-shaped with balconies and ochre walls. Both were four stories and featured courtyards. He liked the intricate, eleven-foot-high wrought iron fence and a tall linden tree that rose into the sky, adding privacy to those apartments with windows facing the street.

———◦———

It was the end of February and it had rained hard overnight. The branches of the trees were stained black; puddles had formed along the street. Even at eleven o'clock in the morning, the light remained dim and the sky dark with gray-bellied clouds.

I had finished inspecting the apartment and had found everything in order. It was my last day; the new tenant was expected to arrive shortly. A sense of nostalgia flooded through me, especially as I stood in the library where I'd spent so much time sitting and reading in one of the chestnut leather chairs.

Valery interrupted my reverie.

"I was looking for you, Anna," she said brusquely. "When the new tenant arrives, please usher him into the library. Then see to it that his luggage is placed neatly in the foyer. I'll take care of the rest." She glanced around, as she often had, looking for anything that was amiss. I resented the superior, haughty way she spoke to me, though I said nothing. I was not in a position to say anything. I was a parlor maid. Fortunately she was absent from the apartment most of the time, which suited me.

The doorbell rang not long after she'd given me her instructions. In the hallway, I glanced at myself in the mirror and adjusted a stray hair before opening the door. I found a man's back to me, gazing outside the hallway window at the rain that had started up again. Its percussive beat sounded against the windowpanes. I cleared my throat and he turned around. I recognized him almost immediately and felt my eyes grow wide staring at him. He was the man I'd seen in Uncle Ferenc's dossier—as handsome in real life as in the photo. Quickly I suppressed my look of surprise and replaced it with a courteous smile and greeting.

His army-style trench coat helped me recover from being completely taken with him—the item of clothing featured dozens of senseless pockets, not only in front but also on the sleeves. What on earth did he use them for?

Perhaps I took a beat too long before inviting him in, because Valery appeared, her voice irritated.

"Well, Anna, don't just leave our guest standing in the hallway." To the man, she said, a bit too sweetly, "Good morning, Mr. Koczak. Come in, come in."

"I'm afraid I can only stay a minute," he said, his tone polite but businesslike. "I've come to drop off my bags, and then I must get back to the office." Three large duffle bags stuffed to capacity lay at his feet looking like tired dogs.

Valery's face fell, as though she'd hoped to have a long chat with the good-looking American. His blue eyes seemed intense but kind. He was composed and clearly attuned to the situation. "I'd love to stay and get my things situated, but you understand—work beckons."

"Of course. Perhaps later," she said. "I'll have Anna take your things to your room and organize them."

He pressed his mouth into a polite smile. "That's not necessary. I'll do it myself. Thank you."

With that, he bade us good-bye and moved down the hallway to the stairs. He was barely out of earshot when she abruptly ordered me to take his heavy bags to his room.

I was to stay one more day and then would have to find another job. I hadn't done much about it in the few weeks since I'd known of my termination. Perhaps I'd thought all along that I would agree to work for the new couple, because spiting Valery really meant I was spiting myself. Once she'd told me that the new tenant would be a single bachelor, I doubted the position was appropriate for a woman as young as I.

However, the moment I laid eyes on Stephen, I couldn't get him out of my mind. I found myself wanting to stay and talking myself into and out of such a notion. One moment I had foolish romantic thoughts, and the next I simply imagined that it might be interesting to work for an American diplomat. Then again, what made me believe the decision would be up to me? Perhaps he had someone else in mind or wouldn't want me for other reasons.

That evening after he arrived, we introduced ourselves. Upon hearing my name, his mind seemed to go to work, but moments later the puzzlement on his face disappeared. He asked me to show him around the place. I liked his straightforward manner and especially his mesmerizing blue eyes. Still, I felt a bit awkward around him; plus, I wasn't sure whether I should act like a maid or someone simply showing him the apartment.

He looked around and seemed to like what he saw. He commented now and then and thanked me for putting his things away. "It wasn't necessary, you know." After the tour, I told him I would be leaving at noon the following day, that my job here had ended.

"Where are you going?" he asked, appearing unexpectedly distraught.

"I don't have other work, if that's what you mean. I live upstairs in the servant's quarters that used to be part of this apartment. So that's where I'm going."

He looked at me in a way that made me think he was trying to gauge what to say. Perhaps he had doubts, and for good reason. After all, I was the niece of an AVO man who'd had him followed, though I had no idea if he was aware of the connection between Uncle Ferenc and me.

Finally, he asked if I would consider working for him.

Without taking a moment to consider the prospect, and despite knowing how intensely my parents would object, especially my mother, I agreed. At least for the time, it solved the issue of having some income, I told myself. And as I'd daydreamed earlier, it might be interesting. I could always change my mind later.

Once he'd settled my employment, he dismissed me. The following day he announced that he'd be leaving for six days. "I'm going to Amsterdam to pick up my new car. I've been expecting it, but there was a delay. Finally it's here." He seemed quite pleased about it, and I realized that my routine—reading books and doing some light cleaning—at least for the time being would continue on as before. I had to admit slight disappointment though, as I'd looked forward to getting to know him and having someone around in the apartment.

While Stephen was gone, I sat down at the desk in the library to write my parents a letter. In this instance, I was happy they did not yet own a telephone. Telling them that I'd begun working for "Mr. Koczak, an American diplomat," was far easier through written communication.

I explained that my prospects for work weren't promising and that this would pay the bills. I added a few more lines asking about Pista and told them about what was going on in my life—not much—before signing off. I could already imagine the letter in return and the tone in which it would be written. "Not married? That is most improper. You are compromising your reputation as a respectable young woman. Unheard of, living in the same place with a bachelor. An American no less. We strongly urge you to resign."

Essentially, the letter that arrived from them expressed the sentiments I'd predicted. I put pen to paper to clarify a few points. "I'm not living in the same place, Mother. I'm on an entirely different floor and will remain a proper girl. I promise you."

My father's section of the letter stated rather cryptically that Pista had gone to help Father Imre for a short time. My uneasy feeling of our previous visit returned. What were he and Father Imre up to? Acquiring more weapons? His clandestine efforts placed him in great danger, but this brief note filled me with an even stronger sense that what-ever he and the others in the underground were up to would not come to a good end.

They closed the letter admonishing me to be careful with this American man, should I decide to stay, which, without saying it, they knew I would do.

———•———

The train to Amsterdam had been delayed for four hours. That plus the already long, two-day trip gave Stephen time to think. His mind wandered back to history lessons at Harvard, about the fate of nations determined by a single person or a pivotal battle. He worried about Rakosi and Stalin. About the increasing tension between the Russian backed government and the opposition. About Cardinal Mindszenty, the primary target of their slander and propaganda. About the increasing number of fugitives. What would the reaction and policy of the United States be? He sorted through various possibilities.

After a time, he turned his thoughts to having hired me. Had he done the right thing? I was Hungarian and a young woman, both of them strikes against me as far as the American Legation was concerned. In places occupied by the Russians, the Foreign Service frowned on staff developing close relationships with the country's citizens, no matter what the situation. And recently, some of the Legation men had caused scandals by having affairs; one of them—the infamous Colonel Jonathon Smith—had "courted" a Hungarian countess while her husband was a political prisoner. Stephen reassured himself he would refrain from an intimate relationship with me. He was not the type to stir gossip or embarrass the Legation. And, he vowed to have my background checked after he returned, so there would be no improprieties.

He passed the time reading newspapers filled with articles about the conflict in Palestine. Another mess, he thought. Reports and editorials favored the Jewish settlers, emphasizing that the Soviet Union had voted for the partition plan, ending the British mandate and establishing the state of Israel.

When he finally stood before his lustrous blue car, his very first, he could hardly contain his excitement. He ran his hand over the roomy Plymouth, which featured an extra long hood and lots of chrome—the bumpers, grill, ornament hood, running boards, and door handles. The vehicle shone and gleamed in the sunlight. He didn't mind in the least the two day trip driving back to Budapest. He was as pleased as if he were on his honeymoon. What didn't occur to him just then was that this handsome car would become the path to freedom for dozens of Hungarians.

———————⋄———————

I was brewing coffee and arranging rolls in a bread basket when Stephen came into the kitchen, as enthusiastic about his purchase as a boy over a train set. "Have you seen the car, Anna?" He spoke in Hungarian, as I knew hardly a word of English.

"It is beautiful, Mr. Koczak. The entire block has been in a fever this morning trying to guess whose car it is. When I went to the baker, half a dozen people stood around admiring it."

"Did you tell them it was mine?" he asked, alarm stitched to his voice.

"No, it's not my place to reveal such things."

"Thank you, Anna, I appreciate your discretion." Then he urged me to come and view it from the library window. I followed him into the room where we had a perfect angle on the Plymouth. He stood there, proudly staring at it, as if he couldn't believe he was the owner of such an elegant and coveted automobile. Though I admired it, I couldn't help noting the contrast between this expensive machine and the poor people of war-stricken Budapest. The car's price tag, about $3,700, was enough to easily house, clothe, and feed a family of four for an entire year.

Over the next few weeks, I learned about Stephen, and he learned about me. To my surprise, he didn't hesitate to point out my shortcomings as a housekeeper. He was meticulous, picky, and could be demanding. I didn't particularly mind as I was still new to this employer and still drawn to him, though at times I felt exasperated and found myself working hard to quell my temper. I thought most of his criticisms petty.

"What is this tray of ashes doing in my bathroom?"

"You left it there," I wanted to say.

Can you tell me if you see the difference in these two eggs?

The answer to the latter was obvious, but I answered with an attitude in my voice. "One of them is slightly harder than the other," I said.

"Slightly? Take another look. This one's hard as a stone. I like the eggs cooked soft, a happy medium between these two and of the same consistency."

I felt like taking one of the eggs and smashing it on his high forehead.

Another time, he asked why a button was missing from his overcoat, extending the button toward me. "Well, sir," I said, emphasizing the word *sir*, "it is not missing. You have it in your hand, so it must have just come off. Give it to me, and I'll sew it on."

Sometimes I wondered at his annoyance over minor transgressions, especially in light of the daily news reports on the radio and in the papers. Everyday, more people were arrested, held on trumped-up charges, tried in show trials, and sentenced to lengthy prison terms or even executed. The strain on the citizens could be felt. For many, in addition to not having enough to eat, they had to worry about what they said. The AVO seemed to have ears and spies everywhere; even children were known to tell on their parents for anti-communist sentiments and conversations they'd overheard.

At other times though, Stephen could be gracious and wonderful company.

"Come have some breakfast with me," he said on more than one occasion. Or, "Join me for some coffee." Or he simply wanted to carry on a conversation, as if he liked the break from work and the perspective of a Hungarian who wasn't required to maintain professional and diplomatic distance.

On such occasions I enjoyed myself. One spring morning in particular, I was watching the sunrays highlight Stephen's wavy hair. Feeling emboldened to speak freely, I suggested that while his Hungarian vocabulary was virtually flawless, his pronunciation was not. At first he was a bit miffed, but quickly managed to overcome his pride and requested my tutorial services, which I gladly gave.

Another day, I mentioned my father's concern that working for an American diplomat might draw the attention of the AVO to me. Based on Uncle Ferenc's folder on Stephen, I assumed he was still being watched, and being in his employ so was I.

I thought that this possibility had escaped him, though I was about to learn that wasn't the case.

He looked at me oddly after I said this. He studied my face and took his time probing my eyes. "Yes, that's likely true." He said nothing else. Later, much later, I learned that he knew of my connection to my uncle, a former AVO officer. He'd discovered it when he'd checked into my past. Despite the fact that I could possibly be a spy, a conduit to his affairs, he'd decided to keep me as his housekeeper, potentially endangering himself. But he had his reasons. Perhaps he'd decided that I was trustworthy, until he found out otherwise. After all, I could hardly help having had a relative who'd been part of the secret police.

May 1948

Jozsef Cardinal Mindszenty

One evening in early May, a little more than two months after he'd moved in, Stephen caught me in my favorite leather chair reading. I worried he might criticize me for it, but instead, he asked me to have a glass of wine with him and some of the cherry cake I'd baked, which he claimed was "heavenly."

"Tell me about yourself," he said.

"Where shall I begin?"

"From the beginning."

So I told him that I was nineteen, almost twenty, one of seven children—five boys and two girls—born near Lake Balaton, but growing up in Nagykörös, because my father had made a poor investment and became bankrupt. No longer feeling that his future lay in the town near the largest lake in Hungary, we moved to Nagykörös. I was only two. There, he was hired to oversee and run a large vineyard. By the time the war broke out in 1939, he had pulled himself together financially and owned about one hundred acres. Then I told him details of the war's impact on our family. "All five of my brothers served in the army. One of them, Károly, died on the Russian front at the end of the winter of 1941. My sister worked in Budapest, she is ten years my senior, but

84

returned here and is married. As for me, besides going to school, I spent a lot of time helping my parents with work in the fields.

"We also had to go to the canning factories to help with the production of canned and dried food for the army," I explained.

"On November 2 in 1944, my town fell into battle with the Russians. I was sixteen and afraid of being raped by the soldiers, which became a source of terror for all the girls my age. So I cut my hair and dressed like a boy. Before I knew it, I was ordered into forced labor with the young men.

"Our job was to dig communal graves for the dead German and Hungarian soldiers. First, we had to remove their tags and jewelry, if any, and turn it over to the Russians. Then, we had to roll the bodies into the graves.

"We worked in pairs. On the fourth day, even though it was cold, there was a terrible stench in the air from the decomposing bodies. My partner, Tom, couldn't take it and dropped one of the bodies. The head fell off and rolled in front of a Russian soldier, who started screaming at my partner, telling him to pick up the head. But Tom couldn't. He threw up. The Russian made the poor boy stand next to the grave and shot him. Then he motioned to me. I thought I was next. But he told me to turn around and walk. I did.

"Another shot rang out, and I was sure I was dead. But I was still alive, and I began to run. I ran home, afraid that he would come after me, but he didn't. Not that day or the next. It was as if the Russians lost track of who'd been working and how many of us there were. I never did go back, though every day, I feared they would show up."

He continued to pelt me with questions, which I took as a compliment. Next, Stephen wanted to know about life after the war. Another lengthy explanation ensued.

"We all missed about half a year of school, but in January of 1945, we started again, and life, at least for us young people seemed to return to normal. We studied, we had fun, we went dancing, and we had hopes for the future, even though the political situation was awful. We were waiting for our soldiers to return from wherever they were. And then, of course, the war officially ended in the spring of 1945.

"I would graduate from high school in 1947 and was to get married to a young engineer I'd become engaged to in the summer of 1944. He was a soldier and I waited for his return. But when he did, he didn't come to see me. Instead, he married a girl who, I learned from friends, was the mother of his three-year-old son."

Stephen interrupted my long explanation, wanting more details of this relationship.

"Well, there's not much more to tell. He came to see me a year later, and explained that he had been pressured into marrying her, but now he'd separated from her and wanted a divorce so he could marry me.

"I was furious that he would even suggest such a thing and yelled at him to go back to his wife and son and to raise him to be a more decent man than he himself was. That was the last I saw of him."

A smile formed at the edges of Stephen's mouth. "So you are unattached?"

"I suppose you could say that," I said evasively. I concluded my story, telling him what had happened in school that prevented my graduation and brought me to Budapest.

A frown creased his face. "The bastards," he said. I'd never heard Stephen curse, and it surprised me. But I could tell that this type of injustice outraged him, and from then on, he would allow a profanity to slip out when something happened that seemed more terrible or unjust than usual.

"You've had a difficult life, Anna. Thank you for telling me all this."

"No harder than most in this country. And it's not over yet, sir."

———◆———

And it wasn't. The ever intensifying situation in Hungary complicated Stephen's life on an almost daily basis. He was so deeply immersed in the multi-faceted and fast-paced nature of his work that it left him little time for socializing and relaxation. And though I understood these demands, to my chagrin, the time he spent at the apartment diminished as well.

One aspect of his official life at the Legation involved receiving Hungarian visitors, often desperate citizens who sought the Legation's help. After the nationalization of businesses with more than one hundred employees, they arrived with ever greater frequency hoping to secure a visa to the United States, which for the most part was a futile effort. On the one hand, there was the strict American quota on emigration, and on the other, even if they received one, procuring a Hungarian passport had become even more difficult.

A second duty of Stephen's was to prepare telegrams for the State Department reporting and analyzing political events in Hungary, including the Stalinist show trials against enemies of the state, the outcomes of which were predictable—coerced confessions by defendants, forced testimonies by witnesses, and forged or false documents. The US Information Agency often passed the information on to select newspapers, such as *The New York Times* and *The Washington Post* and then broadcast the content of the articles to the people in Hungary, citing the dailies as its source.

These broadcasts, though in accordance with the rules and stipulations of the Russian occupiers, infuriated the Soviets since they discredited the trials and made a mockery of them.

A third responsibility involved meeting with leaders of the various political parties and following the domestic state of affairs. Representatives of these parties requested assistance from the United States as well as reports and information on the US position on various issues. Stephen was asked by many: What will the United States do to force the Soviet Union to abide by the human rights clause of the Peace Treaty the Allies had all signed?

Regarding this, one day in a meeting with several leaders, Father Jánosi spoke out forcefully against the Cardinal. "The problem with the man is that he has the view of a provincial priest who doesn't understand the intricate web that ties the Americans, British, and Soviet Union to one another, a web that resists confrontation."

Of course, there was disagreement about his perception. Then, as if to prove his point, he went on to say, "And what about that silly letter Mindszenty wrote to your Minister about Colonel Smith and the Countess's affair? He should be discussing Hungary's problems, not spending time on the minor peccadilloes of Legation staff." He sat back appearing satisfied with himself. Jánosi's petty criticism surprised Stephen, revealing a side he hadn't known, and he took note of it.

Within the Democratic People's Party (DPP), there was also squabbling about what path to take in relationship to the Russians. Should they placate their occupiers by compromising on certain issues or stand up to them alongside Cardinal Mindszenty?

In one such meeting, the mayor of Szeged was present—a vociferous defender of the Cardinal's. "I believe it is essential that we take a stand, as the Cardinal has done. Compromise will only weaken our position. Can't you see the direction things are headed? Licking Stalin's behind will get you nowhere. We must stand up as Hungarians for what we believe is right."

Jánosi was piqued. "Are you saying that those of us who think differently aren't being Hungarian?"

"I am saying that you are either for something or against it. There's no middle ground. You'll see what will happen if we start to give in. It will be like a dyke in Holland. A small hole will soon crumble the wall of resistance."

Barankovics, the official head of the DPP, chimed in. "I think you are too judgmental, Mayor. Negotiating does not mean we are conceding. It means we are trying to tame the tiger to keep him from swallowing us."

That this statement came from Barankovics surprised Stephen. It caused him to wonder how much sway Father Jánosi held over the Democratic People's Party leader. Of course, Stephen knew the value of diplomacy and that it was a tactic necessary when countries dealt with one another, but, in this case, he feared that the mayor was right. Things did not bode well for Hungary, whether they compromised or not.

Perhaps what evolved into Stephen's most significant job was assisting Hungarians who had no choice but to flee the country clandestinely. Numerous times, he was the one to smuggle them out, despite the jeopardy of such operations. Even in preparation for these trips, some refugees were brought to a breaking point, raising the potential for interception. As part of the "train to freedom," Stephen often drove them across the borders of Austria or Yugoslavia at night when there were fewer guards. At the border stations, his anxiety peaked because of the real possibility that out of fright, the refugees hidden in the trunk of his car would tremble audibly or cry out. Minimally, discovery meant the passengers would land in prison and he would be expelled.

At the Legation, there emerged a peculiar form of communication between Stephen and Minister Chapin about these night excursions. While Chapin was fully informed of all of Stephen's official assignments, he avoided asking about his extracurricular activities, though, certainly, he was aware of them.

Stephen sometimes required my cooperation in these endeavors because people had to come to his apartment to begin their journey. It pleased me that he would ask for my help, as it showed that he trusted me not to turn him or my countrymen in.

Though he mostly assisted those who wanted to leave the country, on occasion he also helped people enter the country, as in the case of most foreign correspondents who were finding it increasingly difficult to gain entry. The Communists were limiting access because they had no interest in broadcasting their activities to the world.

Even without the risk of interception, Stephen knew that he was in danger. At a party given by the Countess Ilka, the mayor of Szeged cornered Stephen, telling him that his contact in the AVO claimed that they had stepped up their surveillance of him. "They are watching you very closely. Be careful."

This warning wasn't anything terribly new, except there was another man, not even someone who lived in Budapest, who knew of the AVO's interest in him. It was clear that he needed to be doubly careful not to endanger others, which included me. He worried about placing me in an even more precarious position than I was already in by virtue of working for him. It crossed his mind to let me go, for my own sake. But he was afraid if he told me the reason I might refuse. He knew how strong-willed and unreasonable I could be. He hated such dilemmas but promised himself to discuss the matter with Minister Chapin or Robin Steussy.

The following day he met with Robin and explained what the mayor had said. "I assume the same applies to you."

"I suppose that means we have to be more careful than ever," Robin said.

"Yes, I suppose so."

"Maybe we should stop making these runs?" Robin asked.

"Maybe."

"I know you won't," Robin said, "and I won't either."

"You are right." Despite the gravity of the subject, they both chuckled. "We can outwit them, my friend."

"That's for certain," Robin agreed.

For a time, they were both quiet, sipping their morning coffee. The low hum of office activity filtered through the door.

"Oh, yes, there's something else," Stephen said. Then he explained his thoughts about letting me go.

He regarded Stephen a moment then simply said, "Yes, perhaps you should."

June 1948

Just out of a meeting, Stephen's secretary informed him that a man, Father Pál Kender of the Democratic People's Party, had been waiting for about an hour to see him.

Father Kender arrived in Stephen's office and, without preamble, launched into a story about three of the party's representatives being tailed by the AVO. He claimed they would be arrested several days hence, the moment Parliament was no longer in session, when representatives no longer held political immunity.

"One of them is Congressman Kósa. He managed to outwit them and is now in the Jesuit house waiting for me to get him some help. It's too dangerous for us to keep him there much longer. The police come anytime they please and search us."

His story was familiar to Stephen. These stories of desperation were all similar with only a little variation. "What would you like me to do?"

"Perhaps you could let him stay in your apartment until we figure out something to do with him. They wouldn't dare search your home."

Stephen looked at him doubtfully. He'd never been asked to house a fugitive. Though, how could it be more dangerous than smuggling people over the border?

The man pleaded. "Mr. Koczak, he will be tried and hanged if you don't help."

"All right. Get Kósa to my house at one o'clock. I will meet him there." Stephen glanced at his watch and gave him his address. Father Kender thanked him and rushed out, as if fearing Stephen might change his mind.

Stephen picked up the receiver and called home, but the line was busy. He'd call again in a few minutes. Staring at the dial, he was reminded about static on the line he'd noticed the other day. He'd have someone check into it with the phone company. That the phone might be bugged had crossed his mind.

Instead of calling again, he decided to go home for lunch and wait for Kósa. As he walked out of his office, Minister Chapin called out to him, "Koczak, could you help me out?" he motioned him over and lowered his voice. "I have some people here—a protestant bishop and two others—and honestly I don't understand a word they're saying."

By the time Stephen was able to get away, it was nearly one o'clock. He worried what might happen if the man showed up unannounced at the apartment. Having dealt with a number of fugitives, Stephen had become familiar with the frantic and suspicious nature of their behavior. Anyone they didn't know, like Anna, was viewed as a potential conduit to the secret police.

The doorbell rang, and I wondered who it could be. I'd hardly opened the door when a tall, thin man, glancing nervously down the hallway in each direction, pushed his way inside and demanded to see Stephen. "Who are you?" I asked.

"It doesn't matter. Where is Mr. Koczak?"

"I don't know. I suppose he is at work."

"But he said he would be here." He gave me a wary look. "Who are you?" he asked again.

"I'm his housekeeper. My name is Anna." I invited him to sit down and wait for Stephen, but the man shrank back. His eyes searched the room. I went for the phone.

"What are you doing?" he cried.

"I'm calling Mr. Koczak for you."

"No, no, that's not necessary." His eyes darted back and forth.

I set the receiver back down. "Why don't I make you a cup of coffee and a bite to eat, then if Mr. Koczak hasn't arrived, you can call him?"

That seemed to suit him, though he followed me into the kitchen, pressed himself against the wall and kept his eye on me.

I felt sorry for the man. Clearly he was under some pressure or stress, and I imagined that nothing short of Stephen's arrival would relieve his anxiety.

He had just begun eating, shoveling food into his mouth as if he hadn't eaten in days, when a sound at the front door sent him out of his chair.

"They're coming for me. Please, where can I hide?" Squeezing himself into a corner, he looked as though he might die of fright.

Stephen entered a moment later and, instantly understanding the situation, he calmly identified himself and told Kósa that he'd spoken with Father Kender. "Why don't we sit down, and you can tell me what happened."

Kósa demanded that I remain within view so that I had no chance to call the police. Finally, he settled down in Stephen's bedroom, requesting the curtain be drawn across the window overlooking the courtyard.

He seemed about to launch into his story, when abruptly he stopped and looked at me. "Can I speak in front of her?"

"If you want her to remain within your sight, then I guess you'll have to talk in front of her."

I tried to remain as inconspicuous as possible and seated myself across the room.

"As you know, I'm a representative in Parliament," he began. "Ten days ago, two AVO men stopped me as I came out of the building and told me that they would be my escorts from that moment on. 'Wherever you go, we go. Whatever you do, we will be present. You are on the list to be arrested as soon as Parliament is out of session.' You see, my immunity from being arrested ends then," he explained. "They said they were going to follow me to make sure I didn't get any silly ideas of running away.

"They followed me like a shadow—to stores, to public bathrooms, to church, everywhere. At night, they stayed in front of my apartment. Twenty-four-hour surveillance in three shifts. You see, the only entrance to my apartment was on one side—my door and my windows all face the same direction. So it was easy for them.

"I went through hell trying to find a way to outsmart them. Then I remembered the story of the pig and the wolf. First thing every day, I attend church at eight o'clock. I continued doing so punctually. Every morning at seven forty-five a.m., I stepped out of the building to church. Always, they were standing there." His voice had risen in volume, as if he'd forgotten I was there.

Several times, as Kósa spoke, he abruptly rose, paced, and then stopped to make sure Stephen was listening. Then he quickly glanced around the room to make sure I hadn't left. Then he'd settle back into his story.

"'Good morning, Mr. Kósa,' they said and tipped their hats and followed me to church. I started watching them, what their habits were at night outside my door. They played cards, talked, usually until four or four-thirty in the morning, then they fell asleep for a while. Finally, I came up with a plan."

A shout from outside the apartment brought him to a stop. Eyes wide, he scrutinized me, then he lowered his voice and resumed his story. "Because the men on the night shift were so sure of my punctual habits, they allowed themselves to sleep until about six a.m. So today after making sure they were asleep, at about five thirty, I tiptoed past them on stocking feet and ran down the stairs. Then I took a street car to the Jesuit house, and Father Kender agreed to speak with you. He dropped me off here a little while ago."

Recounting what had taken place seemed to exhaust him as though he was reliving the entire ten-day episode. "I have a relative close to the border down south. If you can get me there safely he will take care of the rest. Mr. Koczak, if you could please take me there, I'd be very grateful."

Though I hadn't heard it before, Stephen was familiar with the story that spilled out of Mr. Kósa. However, in this instance, the blatant nature of the intimidation and threat seemed to startle him.

The telephone rang. Stephen picked it up and after a while said, "Could we postpone this until tomorrow?" Pause. "Well, if it can't wait…I'll be there as soon as I can." He turned to Kósa and told him to sit tight. He would take him, but Minister Chapin had an urgent matter he needed to attend to at the Legation.

Kósa trembled. He aimed his eyes at me. "What about her? Can I trust her? How do you know she won't call the police?"

Stephen fixed him with a serious look. "I trust her. That has to be enough. It's up to you whether you stay here or not." He waited for Kósa to say something, but he was silent. "All right then. I will take you after I return."

Before leaving, Stephen turned to me. "While I am gone, please don't answer the phone or the door. Do not let anyone in. Is that clear?"

"Of course it is, sir."

The minute Stephen was gone, I began to clean, unable to bear this man's nervousness. However, everywhere I went, whether dusting or sweeping, he followed me. His supervision was even more stressful than if I had just remained in the room with him reading a book. Just as I was trying to come up with a plan to calm him and give myself some peace, the doorbell let us know someone was at the gate. Kósa headed for the open closet and pulled me inside with him.

"Don't you dare open it," he hissed. In the next moment, he repeated the request, pleading like a boy. "Please don't let them in."

"I won't," I said, feeling quite sorry for him.

The bell rang again. And again. At least three more times. Then it stopped. I tried to imagine who it might be. No one was expected. I grew worried that it could be AVO men, but how would they know to find him here unless they'd managed to follow him after all?

I tried to convince Kósa that I could take a discreet look across the courtyard from the kitchen door without the person downstairs seeing me. "Don't you want to find out who it is?" But he wouldn't allow me to leave.

Then the phone rang. Kósa's face expressed alarm. He gripped my arm tightly. Finally, he allowed me to take him into the sitting room next to the library. The room had no windows; it obtained light from the library and bedroom through the wide doorways.

Once again, the doorbell rang, sending Kósa scurrying from one room to the other in search of a place to hide. Without realizing it, he opened the front door in the oak paneled foyer and ran out into the hallway. The door drew back of its own accord and slammed shut behind him.

Kósa was locked out. By the time I got to the door, he was knocking and shouting, "Let me in." He rushed inside, fell to his knees and started to pray in front of an oak panel which featured molding in the shape of a cross.

Then a key turned in the lock. Kósa was terrified. If the situation hadn't been so pathetic, I might have laughed. In walked Stephen, looking at the two of us, amused by the comical scene before him: Kósa kneeling and praying, and me standing nearby with a feather duster in hand.

It turned out that the person at the base of the building was my brother Pista—a surprise visit. I was so grateful to see that nothing had happened to him. In my apartment, I explained the situation, leaving out Kósa's name and his precise dilemma. To understand the import of what I was saying, Pista needed to hear no more than that the man was being hounded by the AVO.

After a bit of chitchat about what was happening back home—Margit was pregnant with a baby and some other local gossip—he came to the point. "Father is worried something will happen to you—first because of Uncle Ferenc's death; second, because of me and my work; and third, your bright move to work for this American diplomat."

Ignoring his reference to my precarious situation, I said, "Pista, you know why I have this job, and so should Mother and Father. Being someone's maid was the best work I could get. Anyway, the work's not bad. This is a nice house, being in the building where I live makes it convenient *and* safe, and he's gone much of the time, so I can read and do whatever I like, something not many housekeepers can claim."

"Even so," he said, "what he's doing is risky. Simply by living here, you would be considered guilty by association. And you could be arrested."

"You should talk about risky behavior."

"Yes, but I'm a man."

"Pista! How could you say such a thing?"

"Well, you are my sister. Is it wrong for me to worry about you?"

"Of course not. But Stephen is also very nice to work for. When he is home, which I already mentioned isn't that often, he can be quite good company. He's a very intelligent man." I laughed, hoping to put him at ease. "For an American."

Pista fixed me with a curious stare. "Sounds like it's more than just a work arrangement."

"I'm not stupid."

"Caring for someone isn't stupid," Pista said.

"Maybe so, but even *I* know there's no future in that," I said emphatically.

Pista's eyes grew more probing. "Sometimes we can't help ourselves. But I assure you that if you are in love with him, it will bring you sorrow." Perhaps he thought my vehement denial was an indication of the opposite, and maybe it was, but as often as not, I wanted to think of Stephen strictly as my employer.

"Listen to me closely, Anna. If this man Koczak has anything to do with hiding people or, God forbid, smuggling them out,

97

then you must move out of here. More than likely, the AVO is already watching him. They keep an eye on all Americans."

"Well, how do they even know I am working for him?"

"Don't be naïve. You know they can find out anything they want. If he's in their sights, they'll know everything about him soon enough. Bad enough you're related to Uncle and me, but this compromises your safety even more."

"I'll be fine, Pista. If I sense any problem at all, I'll let you know. I promise."

"And you'll quit," he said emphatically.

The following morning, I walked Pista to the subway, which led to the train station. Nothing more was mentioned about Stephen or the added dangers because of him and Uncle Ferenc.

------◆------

Not long after Mr. Kósa was safely delivered, a more difficult assignment arose for Stephen. Magda Szabo, an attractive Hungarian woman who worked for the Legation, arrived one morning quite upset. Not only had her husband, a lawyer who worked for the Department of Commerce, disappeared without saying anything to her, but there was also news of his disappearance in the newspapers.

Apparently trusting him, the government had sent him on a business trip to Paris under the surveillance of AVO agents stationed there. He was a "good boy" until the last day when he vanished. He managed to send her a note saying that he was on his way to Santo Domingo and would do everything in his power to find a way for her to join him.

The two had been married only a year, and Magda was very much in love with him. Naturally, she felt betrayed and feared that the political police would hold her responsible for his departure. Her fear was not unfounded. A key form of intimidation used to keep people from attempting to escape was to threaten those family members left behind with imprisonment, torture, or both.

Newspapers suggested that the CIA and the Legation were involved in the man's escape, and so Minister Chapin encouraged Robin and Stephen to find a way to get Mrs. Szabo out of the country.

A couple of days later, Stephen met with the minister to describe their plan. When he finished talking and waited for approval, Chapin stopped up his ears with his fingers and said, "Sorry, Stephen, but I have not heard a word. I don't have my hearing aids in." Then he stood up and left the room. Obviously Chapin agreed to what Stephen had laid out but felt it best to pretend no knowledge of the plan.

Together, Robin and Stephen told Magda that it appeared advisable for her to depart Hungary, and if she wanted to go, she must refrain from telling anyone. When they added that she would need to cut her hair, her hands flew to her head, grasping her hair as if it were her most prized treasure. The fear, as it turned out, was not so much about losing her long beautiful tresses, but that departure signified the loss of everything that was dear to her—her family, her home, her friends, her belongings. They would all be sheared away with her hair. She was clutching her hair as if it were the cord connecting her to life.

The reason for the cut had to do with Robin's wife's passport. By cutting her hair, Magda resembled Ethel. Hence, Ethel's passport would be used to smuggle her out. Not long after Magda trimmed her hair to resemble Ethel's, Robin and Stephen successfully delivered her to Vienna where she could begin a new life. They never heard whether or not she was reunited with her husband in Santo Domingo, but one could only hope. Magda's story was like that of so many refugees from Communist countries in those days—the saga of living behind the Iron Curtain, which continued in one form or another for four more decades.

Everyone was talking about the news in the papers. A group of catholic objectors had been arrested in Pócspetri during a demonstration against the secularization of religious schools. One of them had been accused of murdering a policeman and another for inciting the murder.

What the article failed to mention, because it based its information on government-issued news releases, is that a group of people had gathered in front of the city council wanting to know the decision on the resolution. Police came and ordered them to leave. When they refused, the police took out their guns and began beating some of the people. In the process, one policeman tripped, his gun went off and he mortally wounded himself.

Those arrested were beaten and a confession was extracted from the town scribe, who claimed he had shot the policeman because the parish priest had told him to do so. The two were tried and sentenced to death. As a result of these trials, the parish council had little choice but to pass the resolution to nationalize schools.

Stephen's schedule grew more hectic, especially with the departure of McIntyre, the CIA agent, some of whose work he had to take over. He also accompanied Minister Chapin on his frequent trips to visit the Cardinal in Esztergom and other clergy in their respective towns. Concern for the Cardinal's safety and a variety of other issues involving the church, especially school secularization, were heating up and sides were being taken.

In late spring, however, one of Stephen's trips to Esztergom involved a social visit in which he accompanied Minister Chapin's wife and her niece, Emily Clark. Though, at times, Stephen enjoyed the respite from his other duties, in this case, he knew that he'd been asked to escort these two women because Mrs. Chapin was in search of a companion for her attractive, well-educated niece, who was six years Stephen's junior and a Wellesley graduate.

Mrs. Chapin had been playing matchmaker since early after Stephen's arrival at the Legation. And though Stephen liked Emily, Joan was still in hot pursuit, which he didn't altogether mind, particularly when her attention didn't interfere with his work and suited his mood.

On a previous occasion, Mrs. Chapin had attempted to impress him with Emily by telling him that her niece was a descendant of the Clintons, a famous New York political family dating back to 1777, when George Clinton served as New York's first governor and later as the fourth vice president of the United States. A most suitable background for the wife of an aspiring young diplomat like Stephen was the message. He hoped that the subject wouldn't come up today, no matter how indirect.

The Cardinal showed the stress of recent events, but nevertheless, he maintained a cordial and friendly attitude toward his guests. He explained that the wine they were sipping came from his own vineyards. He kept the conversation light as he spoke to Emily and Mrs. Chapin, but later, with Stephen, he steered the conversation to recent events. "For a thousand years, we have had Christian education in the Danube valley," he said. "And now the Communists want to end it. I believe this may signify the beginning of the battle for our spiritual survival."

A vote in Parliament on the issue was scheduled for June 16. The Communists not only intimidated and harassed priests and members of the various political parties but also arrested, tried, imprisoned, and executed those who opposed them, prompting an exodus of politicians and clergy.

The holdout parties were István Barankovics' Democratic People's Party and Sister Slachta's Christian Women's Party. Though Barankovics and his party stood behind the Cardinal in opposing the school secularization bill, his friend and party member Father József Jánosi was urging him in the direction of compromise, claiming that this was the safest route. By giving in on this issue, they would save other freedoms.

As for Sister Slachta, she would vote against secularization no matter what. She was not afraid of the Communists or the AVO. At one point, for her brave stance, she was referred to as the only "man" in Parliament.

Fine pastries and coffee were served on the balcony overlooking the Danube. The Cardinal, chatting amiably, cut a striking figure— his aquiline nose, his intense but thoughtful gaze, his black robes gathered at the waist with a red sash, and the matching cap on his head. There was no doubt in Stephen's mind that the Cardinal was a force to be reckoned with, in particular, because his following came not through coercion but from the strength of his convictions and his genuine concern for the Hungarian people.

Afterward, Emily played several Hungarian songs on the piano, her fingers climbing and dipping over the keyboard, the melodies filled with joy and sadness, laughter and tears. Mrs. Chapin took the opportunity to whisper to Stephen.

"You know," she said, "I think it's just wonderful that you and Emily are both Catholic. It's so important for a couple to share the same values and religious outlook."

The music quieted, and for a moment so did she. Then in a low voice she added, "A party is coming up, and Emily needs an escort."

When Stephen accepted, she smiled happily, as though the entire reason for this visit had been satisfied.

Hungarian Parliament in Budapest.

On June 16, the newspaper headlines screamed that the vote for the secularization of schools had won. As predicted, only two parties—Barankovics' and Sister Slachta's—had voted against it. More concretely, passage meant that almost immediately 4,885 schools would be taken out of religious hands, 3,141 of them Catholic. As a result, nearly five thousand teachers, nuns and priests would lose their jobs. The larger implication, however, was that this vote signified the beginning of the end for people opposing Communism.

This outcome, largely decried and protested, gave the AVO's behind-the-scenes efforts to discredit and oust the Cardinal significant momentum.

I switched on the light in the dark empty room, singing the new love song I had just heard on the radio. Fixing Stephen's bed for the night, I spied a faint light from the library. Entering, I saw Stephen slumped on the loveseat.

"I'm sorry, I didn't know you were home," I said. "Is something the matter?"

After a moment's silence, he turned to me and asked me if I knew of a woman named Mária Blasko. He told me she was an artist and the publisher of a youth paper called *Sziv Ujság*.

"She told me a most upsetting story tonight at a party," he said. "Come sit down."

She had been walking along the banks of the Danube admiring the view of the bombed out ruins of the ancient palace on the hillside of Buda across the river's shimmering water. She had brought a pair of binoculars with her and aimed them at a flowering chestnut tree situated at one corner of the palace. It was covered in white flowers that aimed into the heavens like candles. Under the tree a young woman sat next to a man, her head on his shoulder.

It struck her how this peaceful romantic scene was in sharp contrast to the war that had raged here only a few years earlier. Hungarians had defended the castle, and bombs fell, burying men, women, and children beneath its walls. Mária pictured in her mind the terrible bloodshed and imagined that it had colored the river red, an image she would go on to paint.

When her eyes wandered back to the flowering tree, the couple who'd been there was no longer sitting in the same spot. Instead, two policemen held the woman's arms and were dragging her away. Then she saw the man. He was racing toward the river, chased by two other police. She could see the woman screaming.

She followed the man's flight through the binoculars. More police had gathered at the river, and the man had no means of escape. Then, at the last second, he ran into a building several stories high near the docks. She was relieved that he'd eluded the police.

Suddenly, he reappeared on the roof of the building. A policeman reached the roof seconds later. The man, perched along the edge of the roof, looked over his shoulder and then jumped, hurtling his body through the air with outstretched arms. The next instant he was splayed on the hard surface of the street.

I knew what Stephen was telling me with this story. This incident was emblematic of the world we were living in. Gone were the days when children played in the water when women gossiped as they washed their clothes along the river banks and when men fished from small boats. Perhaps I over-romanticized the past, but the contrast between then and now could not be overstated. It was nearly impossible for anyone not experiencing the breakdown of our world and the dangers that existed to fully appreciate what we were going through.

Minister Chapin and his wife had recruited Stephen for another outing, this time to Archbishop Czapik's residence in Eger. The hundred miles from Minister Chapin's home took nearly three hours, not because of poor roads, but because Mrs. Chapin and Emily insisted on making numerous stops to photograph the changing landscape and quaint towns they drove through.

The scenic route to Eger took them northeast, mostly along the foothills of the Mátra and Bükk mountains. At the outset, the drive proceeded through flat fields, then wound through undulating hills draped with lush green forests. The drive had a romantic quality, as it passed through the charming town of Gödöllo, famous for the baroque castle that was once the summer residence of Hungarian kings and queens. One could almost imagine royal entourages hunting in the surrounding forests. Among its most famous residents were Emperor Franz József and the Empress Mária Theresa.

Along the way, Emily and Mrs. Chapin chatted. Stephen sat, gazing at the scenery, his thoughts drifting to Emily. At this point, he'd seen her on several occasions. She was an altogether lovely young woman. Though the ride was slow, he didn't mind. It served as a much-needed break from work, and so for these few hours, he could take the time to relax.

Stephen couldn't explain to himself why he didn't take steps to claim her. He was fairly certain she was keen on him. And as Robin and others had pointed out, taking her as his wife would catapult him more quickly up the foreign service ladder. Yet, why was he hesitant? Wasn't he in love with her? Did that matter so much? He'd probably fall in love if they could spend more time together. But at the moment, he told himself he had to deal with Hungary's many problems, so for the time being, that would have to wait.

His glance fell on Emily. She seemed to feel his gaze and met his eyes, her expression sweet. Something told him that perhaps he should reach over and hold her hand, but reluctant to express affection publicly, his hands remained in his lap, and he shifted his gaze outside, watching the hillsides now covered with vine-yards, which meant Eger was nearby.

In contrast to Cardinal Mindszenty, Archbishop Czapik was indifferent to the times and enjoyed the benefits of his office. His staff served an extravagant nine-course midday meal, during which little of substance was discussed. Throughout, he charmed his guests and treated them with exceptional grace and courtesy, at the end bestowing them each with a gift—a beautiful porcelain dessert plate bearing the coat-of-arms of Eger and the Archbishop.

On the return trip, Emily snuggled against Stephen as much as etiquette permitted. She persuaded him to have a late supper with her, though he couldn't imagine eating after the sumptuous meal they'd just had.

"So we'll have wine and only a little to eat," Emily said, her tone coquettish, her eyes dancing.

It was later, while driving Emily home, that Stephen suddenly remembered he had promised to pay Joan a visit, no matter how late. *How can I be juggling two women*, he asked himself, *when I have enough trouble dealing with one?* Though he didn't relish going at this late hour, a promise was a promise. After kissing Emily good-night, he turned his Plymouth in the direction of Joan's home.

———◆———

The key turned in the door just as I was getting ready to meet Paul Varga, a young man three years my senior who was from my hometown. He majored in biology at the University of Budapest and had apparently taken a strong liking to me. He was terrific company, and I looked forward to seeing him.

Stephen came in, looking exhausted, saying he was taking a rest before going out again. "I don't feel well. Could you wake me in an hour?"

Though I sympathized with his apparent fatigue, it also irritated me that he assumed I should be there whenever he needed me and hadn't even been polite enough to ask if I had any plans. I was of a mind to tell him so, yet to his retreating back, I merely said, "Yes, sir." My tone was decidedly chilly.

He glanced over his shoulder, gave me a look, sighed, and then kept going.

Lately, Stephen had rarely been at the apartment for more than a few hours of sleep, and Saturdays, he often went into the office right after breakfast not returning until after I'd gone to sleep upstairs in my own quarters, which, appropriately enough, were once again inhabited by a servant. When he was at home, he often grew impatient and demanding. The times when he wasn't there in the morning, his bed still made, I preferred to think that he'd spent the night driving someone to safety. I tried not to take any of it personally, recognizing that among his many stressful tasks as a diplomat, one who cared deeply about Hungarians, spiriting distressed people out of the country had to be inordinately anxiety-provoking.

While on duty, I occupied myself reading, and when not, I mingled with a group of friends that included Paul and Julia, whom I'd neglected lately. Still, at times, I couldn't help hoping that Stephen would come home to break up the day's monotony and give me someone to talk to. Admittedly, I also wanted to get to know him better.

While he slept, I ran out to explain the change of plans to Paul. Along the way, I recalled several occasions on Sunday mornings when I'd come down for a cup of coffee and Stephen and I'd spoken for a short time. He'd describe Saturday evening outings to lovely cafés and restaurants, eating cake and drinking wine or tea, while the music of Mozart and Beethoven played in the background. I envied him, the life he led, understanding how my circumstances limited my own experience of the city and wishing that I could go to one of these places with him. I knew there was no point in that but daydreamed nonetheless.

The news of our aborted date annoyed Paul. "Perhaps you can come back after he leaves?"

"I'll try," I said, "but I can't promise."

When I returned home, it was clear that Stephen was ill. His face looked feverish and he coughed. He asked for an extra cover. I was concerned and brought him some tea. Hardly having set it on the bedside table, the doorbell rang.

"Are you expecting someone?" I asked.

He shook his head no.

When I answered the door, I didn't know who this long-legged woman was but guessed she was one of Stephen's paramours. I was about to invite her inside, when she strode in, her dark eyes barely glancing at me, seemingly acquainted with the apartment, as she rushed to Stephen's room. All I could hear was her rapid-fire English and cooing sounds. "Oh, you poor thing. Let me see if you have a fever, darling," and so on. Next, I was sure I heard the sound of kissing, followed by an agitated slightly raised voice.

Before I could make myself scarce, she burst out of the room, headed for the front hall, let herself out, and slammed the door shut.

I considered going back out to meet Paul, but worried about Stephen's condition. Then, again changing my mind, I decided to run out and further explain to Paul the situation and apologize for our interrupted date. He still wasn't happy, but I promised to see him the following day, which cheered him up.

I rushed home worried that Stephen might need me. But when I stepped inside, I heard her voice. She'd returned, so I went to my room and picked up *Pride and Prejudice*, thinking what a frivolous life some women led.

Awhile later, I was awakened by the ringing of my bell. I threw on a robe of light sea green velvet that had been sewn by a tailor and stumbled down the stairs still half asleep. Instead of finding Stephen alone, she sat there on his bed beside him. Stephen lifted his head enough to say, "Anna, would you call a taxi for Miss Joan Robbins?"

I stared at him in disbelief. This was why he woke me in the middle of the night? Furious, I extended the phone toward Joan, whose eyes pierced mine with an indignant, haughty stare. To Stephen I said, "Surely you didn't need to wake me just to call for a taxi?"

Stephen grabbed the phone from me.

This time, I swept out of the room in a huff, hearing my heart thudding in my ears and sensing their eyes drilling holes in my back.

Almost out of earshot, I heard Joan say, "How dare that girl be so sassy. You must reprimand her. It's the only way to keep them in line."

Seething, I shut the door to my apartment with extra force. That night I entertained thoughts of quitting, reviewing a variety of scenarios I might employ and then satisfied my anger by imagining the disappointed, sad look on Stephen's face when I left.

The following day, Sunday, I left to meet up with Paul and some other friends without stopping to see how Stephen was doing. Once outside, I felt as though I was being watched. Something prompted me to glance up at the tall ornate windows of Stephen's apartment, the ones facing the street. I couldn't be sure, but I thought I glimpsed his shadow at the glass, though when I looked up, it disappeared. A vague sense of pleasure pulsed through my veins at the notion of him watching me.

We ventured to the hills of Buda for a picnic, the same one where several weeks earlier, the lives of the man and woman who'd sat beneath the tree by the castle were so abruptly shattered—ruined like the castle itself.

Our picnic menu consisted of a wonderful spread of rye bread, goat cheese, smoked pork sausage, salami, tomatoes, and fruit.

For dessert, we had cookies filled with nuts, and of course we brought along some red wine.

I loved these occasional outings. They allowed me to enjoy life and to forget about my situation and my preoccupation with Stephen. For a time, I would get lost in our rambling conversations about literature, music, recent plays, and various other topics, anything but politics and religion, which were studiously avoided. Sometimes, we played Frisbee with a hard rubber ring or took long walks gathering wild berries.

We later stopped off at a small café where gypsy music was playing. The tempestuous music thrilled me, and I tapped my foot until Paul asked me to dance. Though I loved moving about the room with him, when he tried to steal a kiss, I was reluctant. I didn't want to lead him on, and he'd made it apparent that he would like more than just being good friends.

Walking home alone, I wondered if Stephen had ever been near the castle and thought that perhaps someday I would treat him to a real Hungarian picnic there. I began to feel badly that I hadn't at least checked on him to see if his illness kept him bedridden and that perhaps I ought to have brought him some tea and toast. Abruptly, his rudeness from the night before coiled into my mind, bringing to a halt this interlude of nostalgia. My anger returning, I decided that it wasn't my job to take care of him. Why should I bother myself on my day off? That task I'd leave to Joan or whatever her name was.

I was breathless after climbing the four stories to my room. I took off my coat, hung it up, and glanced around at the family photos decorating the walls, which I'd painted pale lavender. For the door, I'd chosen pale yellow with curtains to match. All of it was aimed to make the room cheerful. But somehow, I felt cheerless.

Moving over to one of the windows, I gazed absentmindedly out into the darkness and drummed my fingers against the windowsill. After arguing with myself and against my better judgment, I stole downstairs to check on Stephen.

I called out to him before entering his bedroom. Perhaps he wasn't even there and my worrying had been silly. There was no answer. About to turn away, I heard Stephen's voice call out softly.

His eyes looked feverish and the covers were pulled up to his neck. He looked miserable.

"What can I do?" I said, forgetting all the silly thoughts that had tumbled about in my head since the previous night.

"Can you just stay with me a while? Just sit. It will make me feel better."

"Wouldn't you like me to fix you something? Some tea or soup?"

He shook his head. "Maybe some water?"

I went off and fetched him a small pitcher, filling it with water, and then added a piece of bread to the tray. In the bathroom, I rummaged through the cupboard for a thermometer and some aspirin, finally finding them shoved all the way to the back behind some bottles of medication.

"Let me help you sit up." I placed my hand at his back, which felt sweaty to the touch, and gently hoisted him to a half sitting position then handed him the glass. He drank greedily, and I filled it back up.

"Here; take this," I said, pressing the tablet into his palm. He swallowed it with some effort. "You've been alone all day?"

He nodded.

"I'm sorry I didn't think to check on you earlier. I thought that Joan, uh, Miss Robbins would take care of you?"

"She stopped in briefly." He lay back down and breathed heavily as though talking exhausted him. "Could you read me something?"

I picked up a book of poetry and read the several pages of János Arany and Sándor Petőfi, two of Stephen's favorite Hungarian poets.

Measured breathing and a soft snore told me that he'd fallen asleep, and I could stop reading. I pulled the covers tight around him, smoothed his hair away from his forehead, and, without thinking, planted a quiet kiss on his cheek. His hand touched mine.

Gently removing it, I said, "I'll be in the other room if you need me."

———◦———

Once again, I was leaving my hometown and returning to Budapest. Both Stephen and I had been gone for a week, though he wouldn't return from Geneva and Rome until the following day. In Geneva, he had attended a reunion with classmates he'd met while spending six months there studying international affairs. Among other reasons, Stephen had gone to Rome to deliver a letter to the Vatican from the Cardinal. Stephen was not privy to its contents, but considering the circumstances, it was likely the letter dealt with the Catholic Church's precarious situation in Hungary and the Cardinal's hope for greater support from the Pope.

I found a seat beside an elderly gentleman, his face buried in a newspaper.

Generally I enjoyed the train rides to and from Nagykörös, taking time to gaze outside and allow my thoughts to drift. But that day, I was preoccupied with my sister's safety and, to a lesser degree, a story my father told me that involved the disappearance of our town's mayor.

The escape and disappearance of the town's mayor, Péter Boros, occurred two days before my arrival in Nagykörös. Apparently, Boros was arrested by four policemen. But on the way to the jail in Kecskemet, their vehicle was held up by several masked men, who freed the mayor, then stripped the police naked and tied them to trees on the main road.

"You can imagine their embarrassment the next morning as the women passed by on their way to work at the pipe factory." My father roared with laughter. "Those men are the joke of the town."

That wasn't what worried me. On the following day, two rangers came to the house questioning Father about it. They claimed he was the last person who'd spoken to the mayor.

"Well, if that's true," my father said, wearing a smile, "then he remained silent for an awful long time. Last time I ran into him was at the market two weeks ago."

They questioned my father a bit more, then, knowing they would get nowhere, they left, frustrated and suspicious.

Certainly I was glad that Boros had escaped; what troubled me was the fact that the police kept showing up at our house. Despite Pista's protestations, I knew they had him in their sights. They knew he was involved with the opposition but so far hadn't been able to catch him doing anything wrong. I feared that it would only be a matter of time.

The man beside me on the train turned out to be an old friend of my father's and a teacher in the Catholic grammar school I'd attended. Dr. Károly Szabo. He put his newspaper down, and we began to chat about the difficult and frightening time. I asked him where he was going. "To visit my son. He is a 'preferred guest' in the government hotel," Dr. Szabo said ruefully, meaning that his son was in prison. "You've heard of it I'm sure?"

"Yes, I'm so sorry," I said. "What happened?"

He explained that his son, a professor at the University of Szeged, was accused of forming a student underground movement on campus. Dr. Szabo pointed to an article in the *Nemzet*, which accused a group of students of beating a policeman to death in Szeged. Five young men were arrested. "The whole thing's a lie. I saw it. I was there."

Before we parted ways, Dr. Szabo told me that he too had been dismissed from teaching a few weeks earlier. All he did now was tend his small garden and his beehives. "The honey is the only sweet thing in my life." His eyes grew misty as he spoke.

In every direction it seemed that misery was piling up.

In the aftermath of the school secularization vote, Barankovics, as the leader of the Democratic People's Party, felt mounting pressure both from the Communists and the Cardinal. The Cardinal had been publically warned by the government to end his preaching against the secularization. It was very clear that the issue was one of communism versus Christian education. On the one hand, because Barankovics' party had supported the Cardinal and had voted against school secularization, Barankovics was accused of being a "Cardinal's man," a dangerous label. On the other hand, the besieged Cardinal now expected even greater support from the DPP to halt the bill from being carried out, testing Barnakovics' loyalty and bravery. And then there was Father Jánosi, who urged him toward greater cooperation with the regime.

When Stephen received a request from Barankovics to meet with him and Father Jánosi at the Jesuit house, he knew that the political leader hoped the Americans would stand more firmly behind Hungary's freedom and relieve him of the difficult position he was in. Only a country as strong as the United States could place meaningful pressure on Stalin.

The man was late. Father Jánosi and Stephen chatted while waiting for him. When he finally walked in, Father Jánosi exclaimed that he looked like he'd "seen death itself."

"I did," answered Barankovics and told them what had happened.

He had been walking along a major thoroughfare and came to a red traffic light where he waited for the light to change. Across the avenue he spotted a colleague from the DPP. There were only a few cars, but suddenly, one of them came barreling down the street at high speed. Two men emerged from behind his friend and gave him a shove that sent him flying into the path of the vehicle. There was a scream, a crash, and then the car sped away, leaving behind the twisted body of his friend who lay on the road, dead. The two men disappeared into a crowd of people drawn to the scene by the bloodcurdling cry.

The ambulance came, and so did the police. A suicide, they concluded. It seemed that no one had witnessed the incident except Barankovics, or if they had, they didn't dare say so. In fact, Barankovics admitted that he hadn't dared to say anything either.

As Stephen had suspected, Barankovics was hoping for more overt support from the United States. Unfortunately, Stephen could provide no assurances, though he very much wished he could. In that meeting, it also became clearer to Stephen that Father Jánosi had his eye on a more powerful position, but whether that was in the government or in the church, he couldn't be sure.

July 1948

"Oh, Mr. Koczak, how beautiful." I examined the leather hand-bag Stephen had given me. He'd made the purchase in Vienna on his way back from Rome. "Is it really for me?"

The purse contained several Revlon lipsticks and bottles of nail polish of various hues. I was thrilled. "How can I thank you? I've never owned anything like this and have been dreaming of using a fine lipstick since I was sixteen."

Stephen smiled as though he too was glad that his choice of gift made me so happy. He hadn't known what color of lipstick I might like and so had bought them in a variety of shades. Moments later, he left the apartment in a hurry telling me that he was having four guests over for supper at seven o'clock in the evening and asked if I handle it?

"Of course," I said. I knew such requests were part of my duties and therefore expected of me, nevertheless, his ability to switch so suddenly from treating me like a friend to dealing with me as a mere servant hurt.

The guests arrived promptly, though Stephen hadn't yet returned home.

I told them to make themselves comfortable and served them each a glass of port. The couple, in their fifties, was Mr. and Mrs. Vilmos Juhász. Accompanying them were their youngest son about sixteen, and their older son's wife.

Mr. Juhász seemed nervous, shifting in his chair, rubbing his hands together, and glancing about. Not so much different from Representative Kósa, the man Stephen had helped to escape a month earlier, though Kósa had been so anxious he'd seemed ready to jump out of his skin.

An hour passed, and Stephen still hadn't arrived. Finally, he phoned suggesting that his guests start supper without him and that he'd be home soon. This seemed fine with them. While I was in the kitchen, I overheard the young man say something about how young and pretty I was. "Ergo, she is Mr. Koczak's mistress."

"How shocking," his mother scolded. "Where did you learn such a word?"

His comment was insulting, and I was dying to correct him, but fortunately Stephen arrived, cutting my impulse short.

During this period, Stephen had more and more Hungarian guests over, and most of the time, it was clear that he was help-ing them out of the country. They arrived at all times of the day. Some assumed that I was American and struck up conversations in English, which neither they nor I understood. When they dis-covered I spoke Hungarian, they clammed up. It was distressing, but if I had tried to assure them that I was not a spy, I'm sure they would have been even more convinced I would turn them in.

A few stayed overnight, some only for a few hours, and when they left, Stephen often disappeared with them, returning home the next day tired, grumpy, and incommunicative.

Joan became a more frequent visitor too. She made herself at home, rarely missing a chance to give Stephen a kiss or hug when I was present. Unlike Stephen's other guests, she grated on my nerves, and I couldn't understand why Stephen liked her. She simply didn't seem like his type. There was nothing I could do but absent myself and hide in my room. If Stephen needed me, all he had to do was ring the bell.

Her presence made me uncomfortable and felt like an inva-sion of my territory. There was nothing rational about the feel-ing, and I tried to chase it away by being realistic, but emotions can be difficult to tame. Mostly, my attempts were unsuccessful.

One day Stephen invited me to attend a play. It was the first time I'd ever ridden in his car. The handsome blue machine rolled along the wide avenue and sitting there beside him felt lavish, I felt blissfully happy.

When we parked, I found myself wishing that Stephen would take my hand so that we could walk shoulder to shoulder. But no such thing happened. Instead, he began to hurry off, walking several paces ahead of me. When I tried to catch up, he seemed to walk even faster, never slowing down until we reached the theater, both of us out of breath.

Stephen smiled at me boyishly as he guided me to my seat. Though I was furious, I forced myself to return the smile. After the play was over, I could hardly remember what it had been about. All I could think about was giving him a piece of my mind once we returned home.

He surprised me when he suggested we stop off at the Moulin Rouge, a popular nightclub, for a drink. There, I began to enjoy myself, and my anger faded, though I was determined to reprimand his ungentlemanly behavior. Once we arrived home, he seemed very content, and I think he expected me to tell him how much I'd enjoyed the evening with him. Or maybe he thought we would discuss the play.

"Mr. Koczak," I said, emphasizing both words, using my most stern tone, "thank you for taking me out. However, I believe it would have been better if you hadn't. You walked three feet ahead of me as if I wasn't worthy of being with you, like some uneducated village man in front of his wife, because he thinks little of women."

Stephen gaped at me. Yet I continued.

"You should know that you are not obligated to entertain me. But if you ever do it again, I expect you to walk right beside me, as an equal, not as someone who is ashamed to be seen with me."

In the course of this tirade, I'd worked myself up, the heat had risen into my cheeks, and I was ready to burst into tears. Stephen grabbed my arm.

"Anna, I'm not ashamed of you. How can you say such a thing? I didn't mean to walk in front of you. I was afraid we would be late."

I refused to listen to what else he might have to say and ran out of the room and up the stairs to my own quarters. There I cried. I cried about being forced to do such menial work, about not being able to attend university, about not being able to be with Stephen as an equal. I did not want to be his servant.

— ◆ —

After this failed date, Joan returned with greater frequency. I steered clear of her as much as I could. One day, feeling restless, I walked along the once elegant Vaci Street. Now it looked drab. I avoided the American Legation by passing through Freedom Place. There I spied an office with large letters—IBUSZ, a travel bureau. A friend of my family's, István Halász, had worked there, and I thought I'd say hello if he was still there. I'd also pick up some travel pamphlets and daydream about traveling, despite the fact that international excursions were closed to all but a few privileged Hungarians.

The office was crowded with people, but I noticed István sitting at a desk. Not wanting to interrupt him, I sat down on a bench waiting for people to disperse. He was still a good-looking man in his late thirties. I remembered him as a young married man back from Paris, bringing his lovely but haughty wife, the Countess, to meet his parents, who were quite rich and owned a home a short distance from us. They spent summers in Nagykörös so that István's father, who'd had polio, could take the cure at the hot springs in our town.

I got to know his mother quite well. As a child of ten or eleven, I used to take them fresh goat milk and fruit, sent by my mother.

Mrs. Halász was a kind woman, who took an interest in me and sometimes came over to massage my mother's chronically aching back. I read to her, and she always asked to see my report card. Long before István had brought home the Countess, she asked me who I was going to marry.

"I will only marry a man who owns a sugar factory," I replied.

"Well then, I have to tell István to buy one by the time you grow up," she said laughing.

Apparently, his marriage ended in divorce some years earlier, about which I knew little more than that.

When the office had emptied of customers, I stepped up to the counter. István offered his assistance. I smiled impishly. "You don't remember me, do you?"

His brow furrowed and his eyes searched my face. "Hmmm." Then suddenly he remembered. "Anna! How wonderful to see you. What are you doing here?"

"I live in Budapest now. I thought I'd see if you still worked here. I've been wanting to pay your mother a visit to see how she is doing." I knew that his father had died right after the war and his mother had sold their house in Nagykörös to live full time in Budapest. "I spent so many wonderful hours with her."

"She's fine except for her eyesight. It's worsened over the past few years." He glanced around the near empty office. "I can take some time right now, and we can visit her. Would you like to go?"

"I'd love to!" I said, quite excited to see her.

We walked together, his arm wrapped around my waist, a gesture common among Hungarian friends, to his mother's apartment a few blocks away. Mrs. Halász was elated that I'd come. "István, tell me, how does she look? Tell me."

"She is beautiful, mother, like a swan." He smiled and winked at me.

"Let me feel you, Anna." I sat beside her and with her eyes gazing past me. She touched my face, running her hands lightly over my forehead, cheeks, nose, lips, and chin. "You are beautiful, but then you always were an adorable child."

We chatted a while, and I brought her up to date on my family, though only superficially, foregoing all the terrible events of the past year. She seemed tired, so after a while, we left and István invited me for a coffee at a café on Vaci Street.

In parting, he kissed my hand, as was the custom, but he took me by surprise when he asked that we meet again on Sunday.

———◆———

Five days after my twentieth birthday, a group of friends held a surprise party for me. It was a wonderful night of eating and dancing and forgetting about our country's difficulties as well as our own. For the evening, we were young again, healthy and full of dreams. We did what young people do. Over dinner, we spoke of what we imagined our futures to be.

When my turn came, I told them that if I could wish for something, it would be for something grand. "I want to go to Paris to study at the Sorbonne and eventually marry someone who loves me." I was quite serious in my delivery.

They laughingly teased me. "So who is this man you want to marry? Is he rich and handsome?"

I found myself blushing and took a long sip of wine to compose myself. I recovered and pretended to play along. With a secretive smile, I said, "None of your business." Immediately, I took another drink, a vision of Stephen's face in my mind.

After we parted, I took the bus then rode the underground rail and walked the last two blocks home. On this late July evening, the stars looked like bright points of light fastened to the sky. I gazed up at them, still savoring the evening and daydreaming about Stephen. Often, when I harbored such fantasies, I chided myself. *This, whatever "this" is, is nothing more than a schoolgirl crush.* As Pista had told me, "there's no future in it."

He was right, because even if my secret affection were to be requited, American diplomats weren't allowed to marry citizens of the country where they were stationed. If a diplomatic officer truly wanted to marry a foreigner, he had to resign first, effectively ending his career. It was a very clever way of enforcing this rule.

In the morning, I went down to the kitchen humming a tune. On the table, Stephen had left me a note: "Wake me at 8:30 and make breakfast for two." I immediately wondered who his guest could be, afraid of encountering Joan. She simply wasn't who I was prepared to see that morning. Or any morning.

I glared at the impersonal note and proceeded to crumple the piece of paper and throw it in the trash. I marched into the library, where he preferred to have breakfast and where he already sat peacefully reading the paper—alone. I composed myself before asking him what he'd like to eat.

"You know I always like the same thing. Or make whatever you want, it really doesn't matter. You are my guest today."

His announcement caught me off-guard. He must have sensed my thoughts and the need to explain. "I want to wish you happy name day. Today is St. Anna's day. My mother's name is Anna, and I want to at least be with one of the Annas in my life."

I prepared a variety of jams and fruit and fresh baked rolls, soft-boiled eggs, and coffee, which I arranged neatly on the table before taking a seat opposite him.

Rather strangely, he embarked on a philosophical discussion about God.

"What do you think of God? What is your notion of Him?"

I thought for a moment. "God is love. It is one of the only things no one can take away from you. He is the glue that helps make sense of life. He teaches hope and endurance. Without hope, where would we be? Especially in a place like my country."

"I like what you say, Anna. Already, at your young age, you are wise. Keep on believing that God is love. You are right. This gives you and your people hope."

"Perhaps this is why the Communists are afraid of religion," I said. "They want to squelch our hope for a better society and our willingness to struggle for it. God gives us strength and the willingness for great sacrifice."

He gave me an admiring look then checked his watch and stood up.

"Unfortunately, we'll have to continue this conversation later. It's time for me to go." He began to walk away, when he stopped and turned back to me. "Come, give me a hug and a kiss," he said. Then, as if realizing the implication of his words, he added, "Since I cannot kiss my mother, your namesake." Despite that, he held me tight for a long minute. "I'll try to come home at a reasonable time for supper," he called out before the door closed behind him, a sound that interrupted my happiness.

A sense of gloom and sadness enveloped me. I began moving toward the window to escape the darkness reaching for my heart and that of my countrymen. I heard a yellow thrush sing. The window was slightly ajar. I tiptoed over to it, hoping to see the bird. But it was nowhere to be seen.

Then very nearby I heard it sing again. Suddenly, the sweet thing appeared on an oleander plant where it stretched its neck and puffed up its chest like a fat opera singer. And just like that, my melancholy disappeared. Thanks to that little golden thrush, I was able to practice the French lesson I'd started taking thanks to the generosity of my friend Dr. Karl Német.

———— · ————

Though Stephen had promised to be home at a reasonable hour, he arrived after I'd eaten and had begun to pluck away on the strings of my zither, practicing for a youth program two weeks hence. For fun, I'd dressed in a regional costume from the Great Plains, where I'd grown up. He appeared at the entrance to the room without my realizing it and watched a while before announcing his presence.

"What are you playing?"

I told him the name of the song and that it was to be performed in a local show for middle-age children.

"Don't let me interrupt you. It's lovely. Keep going," he said. His gaze ran up and down my figure. Smiling, he added, "You ought to wear that outfit more often. It suits you. Authentic and beautiful."

After a while, we sat together on the sofa. He seemed very tired, and his eyes closed as we spoke. "Tell me a cherished memory from your early childhood. Please."

The story I told him was about the first day that Pista went off to school, leaving me at home without my favorite playmate. I was distraught. My sister tried to play with me, but without success. Finally, she had an idea.

She dressed me up in my best outfit, gave me a spoon and bowl of milk, then took me outside where we sat down beneath two mulberry trees and told me a story of an enchanted prince who had been transformed into a snake until someone redeemed him with a kiss. "Sometimes," she said, "the snake wears a diamond crown on his head." Her soothing voice continued until the story ended, and I'd forgotten about missing Pista. She had accomplished her mission and left me to play.

I gazed at the dewy grass which sparkled in the morning sun and allowed my imagination to roam. I saw myself as the girl who would restore the unfortunate prince to human form. A sudden noise drew my attention. Of all the strange coincidences, the sound belonged to a black snake weaving its way through the woodpile. The snake lifted its head and stretched toward my bowl of milk. I took the spoon, dipped it into the milk, and extended it to the snake, which actually drank from it.

The snake's head sparkled with diamonds, rubies, and emeralds like the crown of my imagination. He spoke to me and asked me to kiss him. I was enthralled and leaned in close, about to kiss the snake prince when my sister's bloodcurdling scream drew me upright. She was running toward me with a long stick in her hand.

"My God, are you all right?" she cried as the snake slithered back into the woodpile.

"Of course I am. He was the enchanted prince! Why did you frighten him away?"

I was so engrossed in telling Stephen the story that I hadn't even noticed he'd stretched out on the sofa with his head in my lap, until he asked, "Do you ever think of the enchanted prince?"

"Occasionally, though I'm no longer so fond of snakes. These days, I prefer a human prince, one with blue eyes, and he doesn't even need to wear a crown," I said coquettishly.

We sat there for a long time enjoying each other's company, exchanging only a few words. I dared to run my fingers through his hair. He moaned contentedly. That evening, he asked me to bring the zither to his room and sing him a song. A folksong about star-crossed lovers came to mind. Roughly translated, the lyrics go like this: "I would love you, but I may not, half the world stands between us. My heart is ready to break with sorrow." I'd just finished the refrain when Stephen fell asleep. I kissed his brow and went to my room, where I cried myself to sleep.

August 1948

On August 5, the headlines in the morning papers caught my attention. Apparently, László Rajk, whose name had become synonymous with the AVO, had been replaced as Minister of the Interior. He was reassigned to the Foreign Ministry, a position that wielded little power, and clearly represented a demotion, a move that was somewhat surprising since he had been known, according to a *New York Times* report, "as possibly the most uncompromising Hungarian Communist in high office and (who had) been purging Western-oriented groups suspected of disloyalty to the present regime."

The likely cause of his demotion was his link to Tito during the Spanish Civil War, like Uncle Ferenc. Not long after the reassignment, it became treasonous for Hungarian Communists to display any support for the Yugoslav leader. One by one, Tito's Hungarian comrades were eliminated from high government positions. Ten months later, in May 1949, Rákosi accused Rajk of being a "Titoist Spy," among other things. Though promised acquittal if he took responsibility for the charges, he was nevertheless sentenced to death a couple of months later.

In the afternoon, I received a message from Pista, delivered by a mutual friend who traveled quite often to Budapest from our hometown. In the brief note, he reminded me that Father Imre would celebrate the ten o'clock mass in the church at the Place of the Roses on St. Stephen's day, which was a couple of weeks away. He warned me against approaching Father Imre because he felt it wasn't safe for the police to see me speaking with him. I made a mental note of the message then tore it into pieces before burning it.

———◆———

A couple of weeks after receiving the note, Stephen and Robin went to visit friends in Berlin for a week. I took the opportunity to go home and help my mother string several hundred red peppers to dry. Though I wished to speak with Pista, he was away with Father Imre in Czegled. As it turned out, spending time with my mother was a great relief from my usual activities. No politics, no thoughts of anything but peppers.

I missed my train back to Budapest and had to take one an hour later. A few miles from the West Station, it made an unexpected stop. We wondered what was going on, but finally, it began moving again, creeping closer to the platforms in Budapest. We came to a stop alongside a freight train, from which emanated muffled cries for help, loud banging on the walls, then screams, and more pounding.

It was one of the so-called "trains of sorrow," the name given to trains that transported hundreds of innocent prisoners out of the country, mostly to Siberia. At times, we heard of people trying to break out and flee while at large stations, where they could more easily disappear in the throngs of people.

Passengers were impatient to get off of our train, but the doors remained locked. They too began to shout and beat on the doors. The train started up once more, moved a few yards, then stopped again, and this time the doors opened.

In the same instant, the door of one of the freight cars broke open and frantic people jumped off, mingling with the passengers of the train I'd just been on. The scene quickly turned into complete pandemonium with our train's passengers afraid of being in the middle of such an escape. How would the police know who was who?

I too was caught up in this whirlwind of human bodies running in all directions. I squeezed between them. After a few seconds, I'd emerged from the crowd only to have a hand grab my arm and push me up against one of the freight cars whose door was open. I kicked at the person, suddenly realizing he was trying to push me aboard the train, having mistaken me for one of the escapees. And then, with as much strength as I could muster, I bit his arm.

His grip loosened, and in the next moment, someone shoved me with such force that I flew face down. A heavy thump on my head caused me to lose consciousness. When I awoke, I was on the street outside the station, seated on a luggage cart beside an unkempt man with dirty hair and smelling of rotten fish. I tried to scream, but he clamped his hand over my mouth preventing any sound to emerge.

"Don't. I am not going to hurt you. The last thing you want right now is the police's attention." It was obvious he was one of the prisoners. His eyes pleaded with me. Then he added, "Besides, it was me who just saved you from being tossed onto that train to hell." He asked me for a comb. I reached into my purse and handed him a brush. Also, a paper napkin, clean and folded, to clean his face.

He motioned at my own face. "You need it more than I do." I realized then that my nose bled and my lip was cut. Blood had dripped onto my blouse.

"Do you have any money?" he asked. "I haven't eaten anything and could use a cup of coffee."

"I do, but we cannot walk into a restaurant the way we look. There's an outdoor vendor about two blocks away. Maybe he has something left." I was a bit wobbly, yet able to walk. The man looked much more presentable with his hair combed.

"What about your bags?" I asked pointing at the luggage cart.

"These aren't mine. The cart was there when I pushed you on top of it. I saw the guard grabbing you, trying to push you onto the freight train. For a second, he let you go, and I knocked him out and you too by accident, then I ran away pushing the cart with you and the luggage. Don't worry; the owners will find it."

"There are no words to thank you for my life. I can take you to a safe place where you could rest and clean up properly," I said.

"I have a place to go not far from here. My sister lives there."

The vendor was still open. I bought several sandwiches and two large cups of coffee. He inhaled the food and drank the steaming brew. When his hunger subsided, he told me that he had been put on the train four days earlier and had been in prison for a month before that for not turning his motorcycle over to the police.

"They took about fifty prisoners and put us on that train, providing only water and a piece of bread each day." He shuddered. "The train developed engine problems, which is why we were stopped. Two friends and I had been working on loosening the door hinges from the moment we got on. We waited to push it open until the passengers from your train started to come out, hoping we could disappear in the confusion. We were lucky." He shook his head and looked toward the sky. "Thank God."

At home, I cleaned the blood from my face and washed my blouse, then fell into an exhausted sleep. I woke up to hear the shrill noise of the bell ringing, having no idea what time or day it was. I could hardly make it out of bed. When the bell rang more insistently, I tugged a brush through my hair. It was already eleven in the morning. Still groggy, I took great care descending the stairs to Stephen's apartment. In the kitchen, without bothering to turn around, he said, "Where the devil have you been?"

"I had a bad day yesterday and I-I—"

He turned to see why I was stuttering. "My Lord, Anna!" he gasped. "What happened to you?"

He examined my bruised arms and swollen lip and insisted on calling Dr. Peti. While we waited, I explained the day's events. The train filled with prisoners, the man who escaped and rescued me, and how close I came to being dragged onto that cattle car. Stephen gazed off into mid-space absorbing my story and how representative it was of the tragic state of affairs in Hungary. He told me how frustrated he was that he could do so little about it.

"You do more than most Americans," I assured him.

"I suppose, but I wish the United States could put more pressure on Stalin."

"Why can't you?"

"The situation is delicate. Russia was our ally in the war, and we don't want to unnecessarily antagonize them." He stared at me, knowing what I thought of that.

"Fantastic. Your country supports a murderer, a man who suppresses human rights. I thought America stood for democracy and freedom."

"We do," he said, shaking his head. "Diplomacy is complicated. It's about compromise. You can't always have everything you want." He knew his excuses fell on deaf ears. Even he didn't believe them. This was the Foreign Service officer speaking.

Dr. Peti came and stitched up my lip. Stephen told me to stay in his apartment, that he would take care of me. That night, he offered to take me out of the country, but I was vehemently opposed. Under no circumstances would I leave my family and country. He seemed only slightly perplexed but soothed me, saying he understood. Soon after, I fell asleep with Stephen at my bedside.

❖

It could have been my imagination, but I felt a shift in our relationship after that. Now it seemed less formal more often, our interactions more intimate, even if they weren't all positive.

A few days after the frightening episode on the train, Stephen was reading aloud an article in the newspaper. I was still eating gingerly, though my lip had begun to heal. I listened, and when he had finished, I said, "Sir, you have to put the emphasis on the first syllable. Listen." I took the paper out of his hand and read the same article.

From the look in his eyes, I could tell he was irritated. After all, I was ten years his junior and pointing out his mistakes. There was the telltale coldness, the icy blue eyes that sometimes surfaced.

Recognizing his change in mood, I returned the paper. "I'm sorry if I was too blunt. I only wanted to help you polish your otherwise perfect Hungarian," I said, trying to flatter him. "You don't do that when you speak, only when you read. I can help you with it if you wish."

He pouted until the following morning when he asked me to read the papers aloud at breakfast so he could listen to my intonations and note the difference between reading aloud and our conversation.

Another day he asked whether he'd been a gracious host during a dinner party I'd helped him with. I didn't answer right away, which prompted him to demand that I be honest. "I won't get insulted," he added, though experience had proven otherwise.

"I don't know your customs, but according to ours, you were not very attentive to the ladies. You ought to help them with their chairs and remain standing until they are seated. You should also kiss the hand of Hungarian women when they arrive, like that lovely woman who was here." I described her to jog his memory.

"But she is the librarian at the Legation," Stephen said, impatience creeping into his voice. "I see her every day."

"Yes, but she was not the librarian here. She was your guest; plus, she is older than you and is used to proper Hungarian etiquette."

He turned away from me and pretended to study his coffee. "I didn't expect so much criticism," he mumbled.

"I am not criticizing you. It's not your fault that we have such antiquated customs. But it is your fault if you refuse to learn them."

I was amused by the sensitive look on his face. "It's not hard, nothing you can't learn in half an hour of instruction." Grudgingly, he again asked for my help.

I found myself becoming more relaxed, feeling free to sing and whistle as I cooked or cleaned, everything from old Hungarian folksongs to symphonies. Sometimes, I sensed that when he arrived home, these melodies or a mere touch of my hand wiped away some of the pressures of his daily life.

And as for István Halász, though we'd gone out a couple of times, my heart wasn't entirely in it. He neither owned a sugar factory, nor did he have the magnetic pull I felt for Stephen. Coincidentally, they did have the same name, István being the Hungarian name for Stephen.

———◆———

A few days later, Stephen had a terrible dream that he would tell me about a month or so later. In it, he was holding my hand as we strolled along a narrow path. Suddenly, a deep precipice opened up, and when we turned to retreat, the path had become impassable. He heard a voice ordering me to let go of his hand. He struggled to hold on, but I was slipping from his grasp. Screaming, I disappeared from view.

He woke up in a sweat, his heart galloping. It took him a moment to realize that what had just transpired wasn't real—that he'd had a nightmare. Nevertheless, anxiety clutched at him. He rang the bell to call me. When I did not come, he glanced at the clock, saw that it was late, and wondered where I could be.

Then he heard my irritated voice. "Yes? What is it?"

"I'm sorry," he said, "I just had a bad dream and—"

Not used to him responding so meekly when I was curt, I changed my tone of voice to a tease. "Oh, I see, now you're going to start waking me at all hours of the night after you've had a bad dream?"

I could see the surprise in his eyes when he noticed I was fully dressed. "You were out?" The question came out sounding challenging, a tone I was far more used to, though apparently he hadn't intended it so.

"Yes, I was. It was my night off, *Sir*. A friend took me out to dine and dance."

A pang of jealousy flared through his mind. "A male friend, I assume?"

"Of course, I don't go dancing with girls."

He wanted to but didn't tell me the specifics of the dream. But he knew it served little purpose. Perhaps he should ask me to leave, he thought. After I left, he lay awake pondering how he might present the situation. Should he be straightforward or pretend that he had to let me go? It would be easy enough to say that he'd broken Legation policy, and they insisted he obey protocol.

"I need a favor," Stephen told Robin.

"No problem."

"Well, you'd better wait until you hear what it is." Stephen picked up a pencil and wrote something on the pad of paper before him on the desk.

"Well don't keep me in suspense."

"In a couple of weeks, I'd like you to stay at my place to look after Anna while I'm in Italy."

Robin pretended to be shocked. "You're asking me to risk my reputation? Not to mention my marriage."

"But Ethel's away, isn't she?" Stephen said as though Robin had been serious.

"I'm not sure whether it's better or worse that she's out of the country. I can't wait to hear what she'll say. You know that tongues will be wagging here at the Legation." He grinned. "I suppose I'll do it. But you haven't told me why, Koczak."

"I'm afraid for her safety. I think there's less chance of something happening if you're staying there. This AVO thing has me nervous. Anyway, I'll just feel better knowing you'll be there to take care of things."

"A month ago, you were considering showing her the door for her safety. Now you want me to take care of her. Some reason you've changed your mind?" Robin teased.

"No, there's not," Stephen said defensively. "Anyway, what reason would there be?"

Robin's face took on a more serious cast. "Listen, old man, here's some advice. If you love Anna, forget it. For her sake and yours. Nothing good can come of it. And you know the Service won't permit—"

"I'm perfectly aware of that. Anyway, what makes you think there's something between us? It's Joan that's going with me, not Anna."

Robin arched his brow but said no more about it.

On our fourth date, István Halász invited me to his place so we could "speak more privately." My instincts told me to say no, but I was curious about what he had to say. His flat on the corner of Zoltán utca and Széchényi Rakpart overlooked the river. It was quite attractive and well appointed. I assumed that his former wife, the Countess, had been in charge of decorating, but I didn't ask, not wanting to raise any unpleasant memories.

István pulled out some photos of his other travel bureau in Rome, boasting lightly about how he managed to keep both offices going.

"What a dream Rome must be," I said, thinking of Stephen's impending visit and wishing that I could go there with him. I must have let out a deep sigh, or something that István mistook for affection, because the next thing I knew his lips were on my neck.

"A dream just like you," whispered István, his arms pulling me tightly to him.

My hands at his chest, I pushed him away. "István, I didn't come here for this."

He seemed surprised. "Then why did you come?"

In that moment, I wasn't entirely sure myself, but managed a quick retort. "Out of curiosity at how you men go about seducing a girl."

"So then let me show you the rest," he said confidently and quite ready to prove his words.

I lifted my chin and looked him in the eye. "I'm not like that, István. I'm sorry if you thought I was teasing you. But I really thought we were just friends."

He gazed at me with uncharacteristic earnestness. "In a few weeks, I'm planning to leave for Rome." He paused and took my hand into his own. "I want you to come with me, Anna. As my wife. We can live there safely without the Russians looking over our shoulders. What do you say?"

For a moment I could say nothing. I'd known that he liked me, but not like this. "István, you've caught me by surprise. I had no idea—"

He interrupted and went on as though I'd agreed. "We'll get married as soon as I can make the arrangements. You, the beautiful country wildflower will be the loveliest Signora in Italy." He smiled at the thought. "I may not have a sugar factory, but I've saved enough for us to live abroad, enough for the children we'll have."

His enthusiasm flustered me. "István, I have to say no. You hardly know me. How could you think that I want to be married?"

"You don't find me attractive?"

"No, no, it's not that. You're very nice looking."

"Could you not love me?"

"I think I could."

"Then what?" His eyes searched mine. "You're in love then? With someone else?"

"Maybe," I answered slowly.

"Does he love you too?" he pressed on.

"I don't know. I'm not even sure he knows I love him. He's from another world, another culture."

"Forget him, Anna, and come with me. You and I are made of the same fabric. I will do everything I can to make you happy."

I began to remove my hand from his, but before he let it go, he raised my palm to his lips and planted a kiss on it. "Please think it over. I'll be in my office waiting for you."

On my walk back to the apartment, I thought about what he'd just proposed. Why hadn't I said yes? It's what I would have advised any of my friends to do. He was in so many ways the man a girl would wish for—well-off, educated, handsome in his own way, and a decent man. Half of Budapest's women would gladly marry him. Of course, I knew what stood in my way, but I also knew the unlikelihood of such a union, no matter how much I might wish that it could happen.

Without even realizing it, I had reached my street and was only half a block from the apartment. A couple walked hand in hand. The woman stopped and kissed the man's cheek, and then they continued walking until they reached a blue car. The Plymouth. Only then did I realize the pair was Stephen and Joan.

I drew back in the hopes that they hadn't seen me and watched them until the car had gone. A sudden stabbing pain brought tears to my eyes. Though I felt terribly disappointed and my heart ached, the pain was real and quite unrelated to what I'd just seen. It emanated from the exact place where a few days earlier a dentist had extracted a tooth. I ran into the apartment to take some aspirin.

At some point after lying down, I lost consciousness. I fell into a delirious sleep in which I dreamt I was a bride hurrying to my wedding. The driver couldn't seem to find the church and kept circling the streets of the city, always ending up in front of 60 Andrássy Street. AVO men streamed out of the building toward the car. I panicked and tugged on the door handle to get away but it was locked. I screamed at the driver, begging him to let me go.

A voice that sounded far away made a sound like the rustle of leaves. "Shhh." My eyes blinked open to see a hand reaching out to me. I grabbed it and was eased out of the vehicle by Stephen, whose blue eyes smiled at me. "You're going to the hospital to get this fixed, whatever it is."

I managed a grateful smile. "Thank you."

The following day, when I came home, the first person I saw was Joan wandering around the apartment. Determined not to let her ruin my life, I nodded politely at her and left Stephen's apartment. Mounting the stairs to my own room, I suddenly became certain that I would say yes to István after all.

It was urgent that I let him know my answer, for it had been several days since he'd asked me to decide, so after a brief nap, I dressed with great care to make the trip to his office. Turning this way and that before the mirror, I felt satisfied that I looked quite cosmopolitan in the dress I wore only on special occasions—it was slate gray linen silk—and to compliment it, I put on my oxblood colored heels, with matching handbag and scarf. I thought he would be surprised that I no longer looked like a country wildflower but a city rose instead.

I went into the dresser drawer where I kept the ring Uncle Ferenc had given me. Its faceted stone dazzled on my finger—the perfect finishing touch. I could already see myself as the Italian Signora draped in lace and silk, with diamonds around my neck.

Before leaving, I stopped in at Stephen's apartment to let him know I would be gone for a while. Joan was in tears and Stephen seemed upset.

"Excuse me, Mr. Koczak." I gave him a moment to acknowledge me. Stephen's distress eased when he saw me. "I have an important engagement," I said. "I'll be gone for a couple of hours."

"You look like you're going to Paris or Rome, Anna."

"I just might be," I said, trying to sound casual and confident. Allowing my eyes to stray in Joan's direction, I saw that she was trying to compose herself. Stephen grinned. "You will be back, won't you?"

Without answering, I slipped out the door. I only felt a touch of guilt that it pleased me to see Stephen and Joan fighting. And that Stephen had noticed my outfit gave me a heady feeling.

Instead of taking a taxi to István's office, I turned in the other direction and walked a few blocks to the "Place of Roses," a lovely rose garden for which the square was named. Across the street, a tall church tower's shadow darkened a portion of the small park. I stared at the baroque style church, still under repair from war damage, and noticing that the door was open, I decided to go inside.

I wasn't in the habit of praying to God for advice. After all, God had the whole world to take care of, so why should he have to bother with my petty concerns? But the cool, peaceful sanctuary of a church had always been a good place for me to do some thinking, and I needed to think. Did I truly love István? What about Stephen? I listed the pros and cons of marrying István. Then I asked myself what logic had to do with love.

Instead of sitting down in one of the pews, I remained standing and took a look around. Eventually, I found myself drawn to a side altar dedicated to the Virgin Mary, the patroness of Hungary. A soulful painting of the young Virgin Mary touched me deeply. She was pregnant and stood alone before a gathering of angry men and women aiming accusative fingers at her. They were also shouting at József, obviously warning him what a mistake he'd made marrying this harlot. Just behind József, an angel leaned over and whispered in his ear as one of its wings shielded his eyes from the crowd. The other wing seemed to be pointing at Mary.

Despite everything, Mary seemed sure of herself and willing to accept God's command. Her face and being appeared ethereal—a young woman whose love of God enabled her to rise above the thoughtless hatefulness of the people.

Retreating to one of the benches, I bowed my head in prayer. It was to Mary that I emptied my troubled heart. I felt that she would know the answers to my questions. Lost in my thoughts, a sudden hand on my shoulder startled me. I gazed up into the eyes of a tall priest who asked if he could help. "You've been sitting here for nearly two hours."

"I've been here that long?" I asked. Then, still staring at the priest, I had the strangest feeling. It was as if I was looking into the understanding eyes of Uncle Ferenc. The priest could easily have been mistaken for his twin brother.

"I'm sorry to bother you, but we are closing the church." His voice exuded gentleness. "If you would like to go to confession, I can take care of it right now."

"No," I said softly, "I have nothing to confess. But thank you for being so kind."

It was ten minutes to four. If I called István, I might still catch him at the office. A public telephone was just across the street. I ran and dialed his number, but there was no answer. The same was true at his flat. In that moment, I felt as though Mary and the angel had in some way intervened, and I felt tremendous relief. Marriage to István was not meant to be.

"I'm sorry, István," I said and threw him an imaginary good-bye kiss as I knew he would soon be leaving for the train to Rome and another kiss to the rich Italian Signora in silk.

When I returned to the present, the sun had just dipped behind the buildings, and the square's thousand roses perfumed the late afternoon air.

At home, Stephen was alone, reading by the window in the library. He put the book down when I entered. "Are you all right?"

"Quite well, thank you," I said. Surprising myself, I added, "I just blew my chance of becoming a wealthy Signora in Rome."

Stephen gazed at me curiously. "Is that what you wanted to be?"

"Not really. If I had, I guess I'd soon be on a train with the man who invited me to marry him."

Absent-mindedly, Stephen brushed the pages of the book in his lap and stared past me, as if his thoughts transported him to some place both far away and deep inside himself. Then he rose and took my hand. "Sit with me. Tell me something about your dreams, Anna."

Without my usual reserve, I launched into how much I wished to go abroad, to Rome or to Paris. "I've often dreamed about going to Paris to study at the Sorbonne." In saying it a second time, I realized that this was a more significant dream than I'd imagined, one that saddened me because of the unlikelihood of its fulfillment.

He placed my hand in his and gave me an encouraging squeeze. This simple gesture filled me with the strength to continue. "I don't want to just study. I want to wear fashionable French dresses, elegant Milanese shoes, silk stockings, flowing scarves, and a dab of Shalimar." We both chuckled. "I want to see the ruins of Rome. The fountains and cathedrals. The Eiffel Tower. And I want to walk the narrow streets and wide boulevards with someone I love and who truly loves me for who I am." Suddenly embarrassed, I felt my cheeks flush. "Perhaps when you return from Rome, you'll bring back some photos and tell me all about it."

"Of course I will. But perhaps someday you will see it for yourself, Anna." His tone just then sounded as gentle as the priest's.

August 20, 1948
(St. Stephen's Day)

Over a year had passed since I'd moved to Budapest, and I was about to celebrate my second St. Stephen's feast day. The first had been exciting because I had the good fortune of being in the presence of Cardinal Mindszenty and hearing him speak, a memory I've treasured all my life. The second was exciting in a different way. Father Imre would preside over the mass, and possibly Pista would be in the crowd.

I remembered Pista's note warning me to be careful about publicly acknowledging him. I was afraid what this meant. Was he planning to commit some act of rebellion, and he wanted to protect me from guilt by association? Nonetheless, I hoped to at least to catch his eye. I yearned for my family and didn't want to miss a chance to see him.

Rising tensions between the people and the Russian occupiers were on display that warm, cloudless day. A number of churches where people congregated to celebrate St. Stephen's Day were surrounded by police to maintain order, though based on recent events their presence as often as not ignited trouble.

When I arrived at the square in front of the same church I'd visited a few days earlier, a dozen policemen armed with rifles guarded the doors of this mid-eighteenth century baroque style church, blocking entry. As a result, the square was packed with celebrants in their Sunday garments.

Father Imre emerged from the rectory leading four altar boys, who carried the various articles for the ceremony—two candles, a white cloth to cover the altar, a paten for the host, a tray of two pitchers, one with wine and one with water, and a chalice for the priest. They were walking in a processional toward the church.

Father Imre stopped at the base of the wide steps and gazed up at the police, who stood on either side of the double-wooden doors that were flanked by stone carvings depicting the life of St. Francis of Assisi. For a moment, the priest seemed to study the impressive carvings. Then, with purpose, he mounted the six stairs and at the entrance asked the police in a loud clear voice to allow everyone to enter.

Stone-faced, they pretended not to have heard him and continued to bar entrance to the church. A murmur rumbled through the crowd. Father Imre turned his back on the police and searched the area, then descended the same steps and set up a makeshift altar on a bench under a large acacia tree perhaps fifty feet or so from the front of the church.

This calmed the people and mass began in a quiet orderly way; that is until some minutes into the service when one of the policemen, plainly visible to the crowd, mocked Father Imre by imitating him when he made the sign of the cross.

This irreverent display incited a number of participants, causing them to shout and wag their fingers. One irate young man picked up a handful of pebbles and hurled them in the direction of the police, shouting, "Get out of here, you swine. How dare you insult the priest!"

The police responded by opening fire, the spray of bullets whizzing over the heads of the crowd, some striking the acacia tree whose branches shuddered and sprayed the leaves onto the priest, the altar, and some of the congregants. Though it was clear the police meant business, most everyone stood their ground, defiant and even daring them to step up the confrontation. Instead of a skirmish, silence greeted the police, giving them no excuse to make arrests.

Father Imre actually climbed on top of the make-shift altar so he could be better seen. "Anyone hurt?" he shouted. People shook their heads. A gentle breeze whirled the leaves around the square. I felt as if the hand of God was pushing them about and, through his presence, encouraging the people not to lose heart.

It crossed my mind that Pista might have expected something like this. I glanced about for him but didn't see his familiar frame.

Father Imre picked up where he'd left off. "My beloved brothers and sisters, almost a thousand years ago, our Holy King Stephen dedicated his new Catholic country to the Virgin Mary. He asked her to be the patroness of Hungary and laid down his crown and sword before her. Many times, this poor country has suffered at the hands of its enemies, but never did they close down our churches and schools.

"These leaves falling down on us are symbols of the tears of our Lady Mary. She is crying for us and with us, for the misfortune that has befallen our country."

As Father Imre spoke, there was a slow but constant stir among the worshippers. Almost unnoticeably, the men moved toward the church, creating a wall between Father Imre and the policemen. It took a moment for us to understand what was happening.

By the time the guards caught on that they were being surrounded, it was too late for them to mount a defense, short of shooting every man at close range. To escape, one of them pivoted and tore open the church door. The policemen piled inside. The air was thick with tension as the men chased after them and people shouted, "Get them."

Father Imre's voice thundered over the square. "Let them go in peace. Do not follow their example. We must not become like them."

The men abandoned their pursuit and emerged from the church, though the police remained inside. The men joined the priest in prayer. At the conclusion of mass, Father Imre, along with a half dozen men entered the church aiming for a peaceful resolution.

One of the men, I was fairly certain, had Pista's telltale sloping shoulder and head which tilted to the right, the result of a slight deformity he had from birth. I waited, hoping to have a chance to speak with him and Father Imre, but after about half an hour, I abandoned the thought and headed home. I longed to tell Stephen about what had happened and hoped he would be there.

Instead, I found a note asking me to prepare his suitcase for the trip to Italy and France, because he was leaving early in the morning, and to pack enough for two or three weeks. I knew part of the vacation he would be spending with Joan. I could hardly think about it. The only sign of affection was his admonition to be careful while he was gone and announcing that Robin would be staying at the apartment should I need him. I couldn't believe he hadn't even discussed this with me in person.

An overwhelming sadness seeped into me. I wanted to be the one accompanying Stephen, or at least be able to visit other countries. Perhaps I should have told István that I'd go with him to Rome. As long as the Russians and the Communists ruled Hungary, I would have little control over my destiny. I sat down in the chair Stephen usually occupied in the library and allowed the tears to fall. When I finally had enough energy to lift myself out of the chair and pull out his suitcase to pack the garments, the words "he's going with Joan" cycled repeatedly through my head.

***

On the morning of the twenty-first of August, Stephen was ready for his trip to Italy. His suitcases were neatly packed in the trunk of the Plymouth. After a few last minute phone calls and instructions, he was rolling along the streets of Budapest to pick up Joan and her brother, who had served with the British forces in Yugoslavia.

In Stephen's briefcase on the floor of the car were letters to the Pope from various church dignitaries. The message from Minister Chapin, Stephen had memorized. It would be exciting and a nice change of pace to be in Rome and Paris.

Joan nestled against Stephen in the front seat, while her brother sat in back, the three of them engaged in a lively conversation about current affairs. Joan's brother had recently returned from an official visit to Yugoslavia and was telling Stephen about the strained relations between Yugoslavia and Hungary and that travel in and out of Hungary had become severely restricted since July. Security had been so tight that it had taken him hours to cross the border. Some rumors even hinted that a war might break out between the two countries.

Joan tired of politics and changed the subject to parties she attended in Budapest and one she'd been invited to in Paris. "I've already made arrangements for you to be invited, Stephen. You will love it. Everybody is anxious to meet you."

Stephen felt himself stiffen and silently wondered why he'd agreed to go on this trip with Joan. Perhaps he would drop Joan off in Paris, let her party, and he would go on to Rome alone. The thought comforted him.

As they drove along their route through four different countries, the difference between the Western nations and Russian-occupied Hungary was marked. The countries under United States, British, and French control had begun to prosper, and it was evident not only in the level and quality of the reconstruction but also in the energy and behavior exhibited by the people. There was no fear in their eyes, Stephen thought. It was exhilarating, and by the time they reached Paris two days later, Stephen was less exasperated with Joan.

They visited museums and shopped for an evening gown for her. Her very British taste prompted her to choose a gown she could have bought in the middle of London. It irked Stephen, and he wasn't sure why. At one point, he left Joan trying on dresses and went in search of a bottle of Shalimar.

He enjoyed the party after all, running into a couple of men he'd served with in the army and meeting other diplomats. Toward the end of the evening, however, when Joan came to retrieve him from a group of older men and women and suggested they return to the hotel, several of the ladies congratulated Stephen. "What a lovely girl; we wish you all the best."

Stephen squirmed in his skin and mumbled, "Au revoir," took Joan's arm, and walked to their hotel.

"I have a surprise for you, Stephen," she said when they arrived on the floor where they each had a room. She took a key out of her purse and opened a door that led to a large tasteful room with one bed. "Our new room, darling."

Stephen stared inside. His suitcases had been transferred here. He hated surprises; he did not like things being forced upon him. Didn't Joan know that by now? Without saying a word, he picked up the phone, contacted the front desk, and requested their original rooms.

This prompted Joan to burst into bitter tears. Stephen tried to console her, reason with her, but she wouldn't stop.

"You don't love me," she wailed.

"I am not married to you," he said.

"What difference does it make? We love each other, and we'll be married soon, won't we, darling?" she asked with trembling voice and imploring eyes. "Say something, Stephen. Say you love me."

At last, he spoke the three magic words to pacify her and then went to his room, complaining of a splitting headache. There he received a call telling him he had a telegram from Rome. It was from the office of the Pope indicating that the Pope's schedule had changed, and he could receive Stephen two days earlier than the original time. It took Stephen only an instant to reply. "I will be there," his telegram said.

He sat down and wrote a note, telling Joan that he'd been ordered to Rome immediately and that he'd meet her there in six days. He felt tremendous relief at the turn of events. After only a few hours of sleep, he slipped the letter under her door and drove off through the quiet early morning streets of Paris.

He couldn't get over how pleasant it was to ride in his car alone—without Joan and without fugitives in the trunk. This was turning into the best part of his vacation. His eyes drank in the scenery. The cultivated fields, the charming villages, the roadside flowers, the distant mountains—all of it part of a beautiful world, one that he no longer took for granted.

He drove south through the Rhone valley toward Marseille and from there, he continued along the Mediterranean Coast into Italy to Rome, where a friend from the American Embassy invited Stephen to stay with him. After a satisfying Italian supper, their glasses filled with Lacryma Christi, a delicious red wine from Orvieto, they exchanged political views.

"I hope you won't be disappointed, Stephen," his friend said when he heard Stephen was meeting with the Pope and several Cardinals. "Politics are changing, even in the Church. The Soviet Union is a great power and there are people who feel cooperation is the key in today's political arena. Except maybe your courageous Cardinal Mindszenty. There are those in the Vatican who do not agree with him."

The following morning, Stephen was received by the Pope and four Cardinals. He delivered the letters he'd been entrusted with. Each one was first read by the Cardinals and then the Pope. One personal letter was read by the Pope alone.

They asked Stephen many questions about Cardinal Mindszenty and the American position on the Cardinal and his politics but communicated little to him on the position of the Vatican concerning Hungary and its Cardinal. He was told answers to his questions would be ready in ten days, just before he embarked on the return journey to Hungary.

Stephen left the dignitaries with a taste of disappointment. I might as well listen to Father Jánosi, he thought. They are singing the same tune. At the American Embassy party two days later, he had the same feeling. Hungary and its courageous Cardinal would not be supported by the Western Allies. They would be sacrificed on the altar of cooperation, as if they feared that Stalin would eat up the world if they dared to oppose him. It seemed that the ferocious Russian bear, growling and showing its fangs, was enough for America and Europe to shake in their boots.

Stephen attempted to explain his views, that Stalin could ill afford a confrontation—a serious confrontation—that he held a vast territory of discontented people, and all his energy was put into keeping them submissive. No way would he be able to effectively wage a war. He would back off if threatened.

An assortment of diplomats from various countries supported his views, but the British and some high-ranking Americans brushed aside his perspective. "You are too young, my boy, and too conscientious. If you want to be an ambassador, you have to learn to be flexible," said the British ambassador, half-intoxicated and patting Stephen's shoulder amicably.

That is what I am afraid of, Stephen thought.

With this event, his official chores in Rome ended, and he had one more day for himself before Joan's arrival. Part of that day he would dedicate to shopping for his mother and his housekeeper in Budapest—me. Without much trouble, he found a red coral necklace for his mother, something she'd always wished for. As for my gift, that took him more time to find. Eventually, he passed a store with fine-looking fabrics in the window. At first overwhelmed, with some assistance, he eventually chose enough material for two dresses.

He felt unexplainably contented and certain that the rest of his vacation would be pleasant in the company of Joan, who he no longer perceived as a threat, but as a pretty friend to see the sights with, chat with, and simply spend time with.

On the return trip home, all was well until the last day when the lush feeling of freedom disappeared the moment they crossed the border into Hungary.

September 1948

On a crisp, early September morning during Stephen's absence, in an effort to restore my sense of equanimity and peace of mind, I hopped on a train to join my cousins and other family members for the annual grape harvest. My Uncle George owned three acres of vineyards on the hillsides of Badacsonytomaj near Lake Balaton. It had always been a gay time for me. After all the hard work of the day, we would celebrate by eating and dancing and drinking last year's wine.

We were paired up—two young women with one man. The women picked the grapes into large baskets, emptying them into even larger containers with straps called *puttonys* that were worn as backpacks. The men and boys heaved their filled puttonys downhill to the house, dumping them into a huge vat about five feet in diameter, where older men and women stomped on the grapes, squeezing the juice out of them in the same method that had been used for hundreds of years. The grapes were then placed into a press and further squeezed until only the skin and seeds remained.

That night, the delicious aroma of roast lamb arrived along with a beautiful sunset and a light wind. Supper and copious amounts of wine from Uncle George's cellar were served outdoors, and afterward, the music and dancing began. My uncle played the zither with deft fingers and all the workers paired off to sing and dance.

Later in the evening, my cousin Misi pulled me aside saying that he wanted to tell me something important. He seemed worried. We walked to the lake and sat on a rock, our feet dangling in the small waves. It felt incredibly good to have the cool silky water kiss my tired, aching feet.

Misi glanced around as if making sure that no one was near enough to hear what he had to say. "Two days ago, the secret police came and turned our house upside down. They searched everywhere and asked questions about Uncle Ferenc. Why had he been here last fall and what had he been doing here. Mother told them he had visited briefly but spent a considerable amount of time at the cemetery in Saska visiting his wife's grave and cleaning it up."

The cemetery Uncle Ferenc and father went to months earlier was located about seven miles from Misi's home.

"Do you know what they were looking for?" I asked, worried they would descend on my parents' home next.

"No," he said. "I was wondering if you had any idea."

I shook my head.

Whatever the answer, concerning Uncle Ferenc's allegiance, it vanished with him on the day he died.

———— ◆ ————

I was slicing up a cake when Stephen entered the kitchen. He moved so quietly that he caught me by surprise. Though I wanted to, I couldn't conceal my delight at seeing him. He grasped my hand and pulled me into the library. On the table lay a rather large gift-wrapped package.

He nodded at it. "Open it up."

As I peeled the paper off and saw it contained not just one gift but several, I pressed my hands to my heart.

"From Rome! How gloriously beautiful." I ran my fingers over the smooth silk fabric and, with an expert movement, wrapped it around myself. It was moss green with abstract flourishes of pale yellow and lilac.

He'd brought me several other yards of silk—this piece lightly patterned navy blue—which I picked up and threw over my shoulder. Then he handed me one more gift—a bottle of Shalimar. I examined the bottle, opened it, sniffed its wonderful fragrance, and then almost deliriously happy, I dabbed a drop on my throat. "Mmmm. Delicious."

"I'm so glad you like it." He smiled delightedly.

"They are lovely gifts, but even better is the fact that you took the time to choose them so carefully for me." I said this without knowing that, in fact, Stephen had put in considerable time and effort picking out these items for me.

The following day as Robin was gathering his things from the apartment to move back to his flat, the doorbell rang. Stephen opened the door to find an elderly couple standing before him. "We are Mr. and Mrs. Taba, and we live in the apartment beneath yours," Mrs. Taba announced in a stern tone. Tilting her head to peer around Stephen, she continued. "We are here to speak to you about your housekeeper."

Stephen invited them into the library to sit down. Robin followed him. I was in earshot, though remained out of sight.

Her voice dropped a decibel, as if making sure no one else could hear her. "I do not know if you are aware that your young housekeeper betrayed your trust during your absence. There were loud parties, men of all ages coming and going at all hours. Women too. They came at night and stayed until morning. I'm sure you didn't give her permission to do such things."

Having heard these accusations I couldn't resist standing in the entryway at the far end of the library and listen in on Mrs. Taba, whose back was to me. "Mrs. Taba," he said, using his most polished diplomatic tone, "I will certainly look into this. I'm very grateful you told me the situation."

No sooner had they left than he came bounding back into the library and said to me, "I hope you have a good explanation for all this. You brought men up here?"

Of course, I assumed that Stephen would know this had been the handiwork of Robin, and his words to Mrs. Taba were meant to assuage her anger. I couldn't believe he actually thought I might do such a thing. I could feel anger rising to my face.

"Do you mean to say you believe what this woman said? Since I've been your so-called 'servant' you know that I have only a handful of friends, and you think that the minute you are gone I would organize a wild orgy? That's insulting and the most ridiculous thing I've ever heard." I gave him a fierce stare. "If you'd like to dismiss me, I'm ready to go."

Stephen was speechless and confused; he looked to Robin for help.

"I can explain," Robin said cheerfully. "It was me who had the party, not Anna. But I swear to you that this woman exaggerated grossly. I had one dance party and that was all." Robin came over to me and took my hand, but I brushed him off. I could see that he felt terrible, but I was so angry I couldn't speak. He apologized, saying, "I know I should have spoken up sooner, but I couldn't help enjoy the show a bit. I'm sorry, Anna. You behaved splendidly. How can I make up for this?"

I glared at the two of them without answering then turned on my heel and walked out. I was furious and hurt that Stephen would think so little of me. Stalking up to my room, I imagined never returning downstairs again.

However, when I finally did, I found a dozen yellow roses on the table. A note was attached, but I decided not to open it. I began cooking fish in wine sauce and plum dumplings. It was one of Stephen's favorite meals. I told myself I would behave civilly but keep things on a strictly professional level. No more gushing. Too, I thought I would show him what he would be missing if I left.

When Stephen came home, he immediately proceeded to join me in the kitchen. "That smells delicious," he said. When I merely nodded, he added, "Anna, you know how sorry I am. How can I make it up to you?" I savored the remorse in his voice.

I could feel his eyes on me as I moved about the kitchen. Finally, I leaned against the sink and looked at him sadly. "How could you have so little faith in me, Stephen? I thought you knew me better than that."

I think I surprised him by using his first name. His eyes wandered the room and landed on the pots cooking on the stove before he spoke. "Won't you join me for dinner? Please."

The vase of roses stood at the center of the table, and I added two white candles. He held the chair out for me, which made me smile. He was trying his best to be the gentleman I'd taught him how to be.

"Why haven't you opened the note?" he asked, looking at the small sealed envelope beside the roses.

"Oh, I thought they were for you," I said, though it wasn't true.

"Anna, it has your name on it." He handed it to me.

"Oh, I hadn't noticed." I took my time breaking the seal and pulling out the card. On it was written an apology and the words "With love, Stephen." Without even thinking, I planted a kiss on his lips, and before I could retreat, he held onto me and gave me a lengthy kiss back.

Though I didn't want to break the spell of the moment, I asked how he knew I loved yellow roses.

"Lucky guess." But his smile was mysterious, and I assumed there was more to it than that. Years later, I would learn that he'd been at Uncle Ferenc's memorial service and had admired my act of rebellion—placing a single yellow rose on Uncle's coffin.

The phone rang. As always, it came at the wrong time. I had a feeling this would interrupt our lovely dinner. Stephen insisted on not answering it, but I told him that he should.

He lifted the receiver to his ear, still clutching me tightly, but as he listened, his grip loosened and I slipped from his arms.

"Yes, I can meet you in ten minutes. I only have to pick up my keys. Yes, I know where you are." Stephen's shoulders sloped and his face looked glum. "Everything has to happen at night."

"Yes, things happen at night," I said, "—like love, fear, and mistakes."

He didn't say where he was going, which I recognized as a safety precaution. The less I knew the better. I would not be lying if someone, in particular the secret police, asked what he was up to.

When he left a short while later I overheard him repeating my words, "Love, fear, and mistakes. Yes, mistakes with a capital M. Let's hope this isn't one of them."

———◆———

At the convent, instead of Sister Slachta, a young sister awaited him. "Someone important is here to speak with you. He's waiting for you in our library.

"Who is this person? Do you know him?"

"I don't know him personally, but Sister Slachta said you can feel secure. He is in debt to her and would not dare to betray her or you, though I warn you he is a dedicated Communist."

The nerves in Stephen's body grew taut, and he grew fully alert. As he entered the library, he was astonished to see the editor of the *Party Journals* newspaper. He knew him superficially from the trials they had both attended when it was permitted, though they'd rarely spoken.

The editor, Iván Boldizsár, extended his hand to Stephen, who hesitated a fraction of a second before accepting it. Noting this, Iván said, "I am more afraid of you, Mr. Koczak, than you are of me, because if you reveal what I'm going to say to you and name me as the source, I will most likely be hanged. Were it not for my conscience, I would not have come. I came to see you because I know what kind of man you are."

Exactly what did this man want? Stephen wondered.

"Let me explain. During the war, Sister Slachta hid someone dear to me and her daughters from the Nazis. She gave them to the parents of Father Csertö, the Cardinal's secretary, and they took care of them for an entire year, treating them as their own family.

"I have learned that on Monday, Father Csertö is to be arrested. You must warn him to leave the country. Perhaps I am not a good man, but I love my family. My wife would never forgive me if I allowed Father Csertö to be arrested after what he and his family did for us.

"Let's assume you are telling the truth," Stephen said, "then tell me how you came to know this information."

"One of the AVO men who planned it told me."

"So not only are you a Communist, but you also have links to the AVO. What would stop you from getting the AVO to arrest me? Anyway, why should I stick my neck out for you?"

"I know it's much to ask, but please, help him. I know you have helped others."

Hearing this made Stephen uneasy, but he gave no outward sign of it.

The editor went on, "I know you have little reason to trust me, but I promise I will not betray you or the priest. Please. If nothing else, for my wife's sake."

"And if Father Csertö succeeds in disappearing, what will you do?"

"I will light a candle in the Cathedral for him, and then I'll do what I always do: publish some nasty articles about the young secretary of the Cardinal."

"One more question: Why wouldn't the AVO trace the leak about their operation back to you?"

"That is a risk I am willing to take."

Stephen finally agreed to see what he could do.

The man pulled a gray dress out of his briefcase and put it on. Next he drew out a wig, adjusted it on his head, and then extended his hand. "God bless you," he said and left, wearing that ridiculous disguise.

On Stephen's way out, he ran into Sister Slachta. "He is telling the truth, Mr. Koczak, I can vouch for that. I know Father Csertö often comes to the Legation on Fridays—that is tomorrow. I'll send him a message to be sure to be there by eleven o'clock."

Stephen assured the nun he would do what he could. He thought of mentioning what the editor had said about knowing that he'd helped others.

"The noose is tightening, Mr. Koczak. First they will compromise the men around the Cardinal and then him. This is their plan. I'm sure of it. We must do everything we can to prevent this from happening." Her brows knitted with concern as she fixed her gaze on Stephen. "Don't you agree?"

"Yes, I do."

The following morning, Father Csertö appeared at the Legation at the appointed time. Instead of his usual smile, his face was drawn.

"Good morning, Father, how was your trip here?" Stephen asked.

"Fine, fine. Thank you."

Inside the office, he bade the priest to sit down and declared he would tell him all about his meeting with the Pope. As a cautionary note, with his finger to his lips, Stephen indicated silence and placed a letter he had written before Father Csertö. To make it seem as though they were conversing, Stephen launched into a description of his trip to Italy, where he met with the Pope. In the letter, Stephen had simply explained that he had it on good authority Father Csertö would be arrested and that he needed to leave the country. Preferably right away.

The color had drained from the priest's face by the time he'd finished reading the note. With a steady hand, Father Csertö flipped the paper over and wrote that he would speak with the Cardinal once he returned to Esztergom.

The final line stated, "By tomorrow morning I will let you know if I need any help. Thank you, my friend."

Stephen lit a match and burned the sheet of paper inside a large ash tray.

On his way out, the priest told Stephen that he would send him some information about Santo Stephano in the morning. On Saturday, a booklet about Santo Stephano was delivered to Stephen's office. Inside on a bookmark were three words: "Greetings from Vienna."

Stephen sighed with relief. The priest was safe. A disaster had been averted.

Benczur Utca 41—picture taken in 1992. Stephen's apartment
is the three windows with the balcony from right to
left to the left of the doorway on the 2nd floor.

Anna's apartment—top floor—two windows to the left of the doorway.

That same Saturday, September 11 it was, I decided on the style of dress I wanted for the fabric Stephen had given me. I was preparing to leave when the doorbell rang. Assuming it was someone for Stephen, I was surprised to see a handsome, dark-haired man greet me and ask to speak to "Anna Tóth."

"That would be me," I answered. Studying his features, I could have sworn I'd seen him before, but I couldn't place where.

"I'm with the personnel department for the city of Budapest and would like to ask you a few questions."

"What is it you want to speak to me about?" I said and lodged myself in the doorway, blocking his view of the apartment.

"Your cousin Roza Papp gave me your name as a reference. She applied for a job in the city government. It's just routine; may I come in?"

Whoever he was, I knew that it was inappropriate for me to let him inside.

"Perhaps you can walk with me. I was just on my way out for an appointment with my tailor."

Mild disappointment flickered across his face. "Yes, of course. That would be fine."

"Wait here while I get my things." I closed the door and ran into the library to fetch the fabric I'd left there. I could not recall having heard anything about my cousin getting a new job, which made me uneasy. Of course, I could be wrong, and it was possible that the news simply hadn't reached me.

The feeling that I'd seen him before also bothered me. It was possible I'd seen him on the street or at the train station or any number of places, but something told me that my encounter with him bore some significance. A current of fear ran through me. Staring into the mirror, I adjusted a few stray hairs. Who was this man?

Returning to the foyer, I remembered Uncle Ferenc telling me never to let anyone see my fear and to have courage to over-come whatever difficulties befell me. I summoned my nerve and pulled open the door. The man was still there waiting. He had a photograph in his hand, which I noticed him slip into his pocket as I came out.

I started down the steps in front of him then slowed down to let him go ahead of me. A memory tugged at me. Who was he? I ran my hand along the smooth wood of the railing, trying to allow whatever thoughts lurked in my mind to surface. "What did you say your name was?"

"Lászlo Harsányi," he answered, turning around to face me.

Then it hit me. Uncle Ferenc's apartment building, the young handsome man mounting the stairs as I was leaving. He'd momentarily caught my eye. Uncle Ferenc had been expecting someone, presumably an agent of the secret police. Lazslo Harsányi had been this man. I was sure of it.

For a second I felt faint and leaned against the railing for support. What on earth did he want with me?

"Is something wrong?" he said, sounding genuinely concerned.

Gathering my composure I smiled and said, "No, no, but I should keep my eyes on the stairs instead of looking at you."

Out on the street, I asked what he wanted to know about Roza.

"It's just routine stuff," he said. "She gave your name as a reference." Reading from a document, he rattled off information such as her birthplace, age, and address. "Are these correct?"

"Yes, they are. Anything else?"

He began telling me how important it was to check out new applicants. One never knew about a person. They could infiltrate the government. He went on for a while. "Most importantly," he said, "do you recommend her?"

"Of course, I recommend her. She is my cousin." I would try to reach Roza later. It occurred to me that she'd never been to the apartment and wasn't even sure she knew my address.

The tailor lived close to the apartment, and we had just arrived. "Well, here it is. Have I answered your questions?"

He seemed disappointed that we'd reached our destination so quickly. "I hope this doesn't offend you," he said. "After all, we've only known each other for a few minutes, but I would love to see you again." He lifted my hand and brought it to his lips. "What do you think?"

I smiled, but said nothing. Then I turned away from him and entered the tailor's home. I felt Lászlo Harsányi's eyes on me until I closed the door.

As I made the return trip to the apartment, the image of the physically attractive Lazslo hovered in my mind and thoughts came and went. He had tried to gain access to Stephen's apartment; he had sought information about Roza; he had asked me out. The more I thought about it, the more obvious it became the reason for his visit was not about Roza. It was about me. But what did he want? I needed to find out as quickly as possible whether there was any truth to Roza's job application. If not, that would prove he had ulterior motives. Without her work number, I'd have to wait to contact her at home that evening.

On arriving home, eager to discuss the situation with Stephen, I checked the library, but he wasn't there. On Saturdays, after working in the morning, he sometimes spent the entire afternoon reading. So I decided to install myself in the library beside the telephone and distract myself by reading some Shakespeare. In a few hours, Roza might be back from work, and I'd try to call her.

At some point I must have fallen asleep, because voices in the hallway startled me. "Please, make yourself comfortable," I heard Stephen say, "I'll be back in a minute."

"Thank you, darling," answered a sensuous female voice I wasn't sure belonged to Joan, but I didn't wait to find out. Angry and frustrated, I moved silently through the apartment and managed to slip out unseen.

For the time being, he'd foiled my plan to call Roza because the only telephone was in Stephen's apartment. But it wasn't just that. How dare he bring strange women to the apartment when

I might be in danger? No sooner had the thought arisen than I realized how ridiculous it was. He had every right to bring home anyone he pleased, plus he knew nothing of what had transpired earlier in the day.

———•———

In the morning, I went to an early Sunday mass and returned reluctantly, knowing I might very well run into Stephen and the woman from the night before. No sooner had I entered than Stephen asked me to make breakfast for two. I dreaded seeing her, whoever she was, but I had no choice. When I finally entered the dining room, I couldn't believe that the woman who'd spent the night wasn't Joan, but rather the wife of a former Official from the Ministry of Education. I'd seen her photo in the newspaper a number of times. She sat glumly at the table showing the after-effects of too much alcohol. On seeing that I recognized her, her face flushed and she lowered her eyes in embarrassment.

Though I was hurt by Stephen's behavior, I tried to be rational, reminding myself that we were not a couple, and he had no obligation to me. Nor perhaps would he ever. However, it shocked me that he would bring a married woman, one so public, into his home to spend the night. It didn't seem like Stephen to flaunt social rules or risk embarrassing the Legation. He was much too careful. The only explanation was that he didn't know who she was.

Before I even reached the bottom of the stairs, a set of heels clattered down the marble stairs behind me. The Official's wife, still looking disheveled, swept past me without so much as a greeting or a look. A taxi awaited her.

Back in the apartment, I finally reached Roza. She informed me that she had not applied for any such job, just as I'd suspected. We chatted for a bit, and I then went to clear the dishes in the kitchen and found Stephen still sitting there.

I ignored him until he laid a hand on my arm. "You've got the wrong idea, Anna. Let me explain how this woman came to be here," he said.

I studied his face and waited for him to continue.

"Last night, some of my friends dragged me to a night club. Finally, at one thirty a.m. I was able to get away. I'd just gotten into the car, when a woman ran toward me and jumped inside. She cried hysterically saying she was disgusted with her life and was going to jump into the river if I didn't let her talk to me."

"This sounds very melodramatic, but I suppose I believe you," I said. "So what did she tell you?"

"She said that she had married a terrible man in order to save her brother from being arrested, that he was cruel, and that she could no longer stand it. When I asked her what I could do, she begged me to let her sleep at my place. I didn't have the heart to turn her away, and so she slept here."

Seeing my skeptical look, Stephen added, "Nothing happened between us. I swear." He looked embarrassed. "Do you believe me?"

"I'm not sure that it matters, but do you know who she is?"

"She mentioned her name, but I didn't recognize it."

"She is the wife of the former spokesman of the Ministry of Education. You can see her photo from time to time in the newspapers." I gave him a mischievous smile. "So you see you might be in for some trouble. If the doorbell rings today, I'll let you answer it."

We spoke a while longer—inwardly I'd forgiven him this indiscretion, if in fact there had been one—and then mentioned the encounter with László and his phony reason for approaching me. Stephen's ears perked up, and his brow knitted into a worried frown. "This is not good," he said.

We discussed the issue for some time, concluding that, most likely, László had been given this assignment to find out information on Stephen and possibly on Pista, as I'd thought. Perhaps even Uncle Ferenc may have played a role in their decision, especially if they'd done away with him. Perhaps they feared he'd revealed confidential information to me before his death, which might in some way compromise the government and the AVO.

If he contacted me again, we decided that the best course of action would be for me to play along, acting as though I had no idea of his connection to the AVO. If he asked me out, and we both felt fairly certain that he would, I should accept his offer and find out what I could. Refusing him might have consequences. By going out, I could string him along and forestall more sinister methods we both knew the AVO was perfectly capable of.

"Should this come to pass, and I pray it doesn't, promise you'll keep me informed. If his questions pertain to me and my activities, answer as evasively as possible, then talk to me about it. I will tell you what to say if it comes up again." He stared at his empty cup, thinking.

"You must be very careful about what you say, but whatever you tell him, make sure that it's true, so when he checks it out, he won't find out you were lying. Otherwise, you'll be caught in a web of lies, which will trip you up sooner or later. By being truthful, you will earn his trust, and perhaps it will even cause him to make careless statements."

I understood exactly what he was saying and nodded in agreement.

<hr />

I remember very well the next day, which was Monday the thirteenth of September. The baker down the street greeted me with a muted smile. "Miss Tóth, I must tell you something. A young man just stopped by and asked if I knew you. He asked what kind of person you are, whether you have a steady boyfriend, and whether you have a good reputation."

Of course, I suspected the man had been Lászlo, and it disturbed me that this tango had already begun. "Was he good looking with dark hair, maybe late twenties?"

"Why, yes, how did you know?"

I thought for a moment what I should tell the baker. Though he was a nice man, one never knew what turn of events might force someone to tell on others. "I met him yesterday," I said smiling, "and he seemed interested in seeing me again. Would you mind telling me what you said?"

"Nothing of any consequence—that you are a very nice young woman, but that I didn't know you well enough to know whether you had a boyfriend, and that from what I did know, your reputation was just fine." The baker looked puzzled. "Why do you think he asked a virtual stranger such questions?"

"I really don't know. But I will tell you if I find out." I turned the topic of conversation to the more mundane—the weather, business, and so on. I purchased some bread and went on my way, feeling pleased with myself. I'd been circumspect, but pleasant and had revealed absolutely nothing.

A voice from behind made me jump. "Miss Tóth." I released a small gasp and turned to find Lászlo grinning at me.

"You startled me," I said, recalling Stephen's advice to tell the truth and to try to act natural.

He apologized, a smile affixed to his face.

"How are you?" I said in a neutral tone.

"Fine, fine. Clearly the thirteenth is my lucky number."

"And why is that?"

"Well, I was just thinking about you. And here you are. How fortunate that we bumped into one another. May I join you?"

I'm not sure how I managed to produce a smile, but I did and nodded agreeably.

"You know, I haven't been able to get you out of my mind since I met you." His voice sounded sincere, but his eyes were probing. "Tell me you thought of me too."

I took a moment to think about the best way to respond. Not too eagerly and of course honestly. "Yes. How could I forget our encounter so quickly?"

He didn't seem all too pleased with my answer, but he plunged ahead. "Would you have some time for me tonight? We could go for dinner and then stroll along the Duna Corso."

"I'm afraid I'm only free on Sundays."

He persisted. "But six days is far too long to wait."

I affected a sigh. "All right, I will go on a stroll with you after dinner." We arrived at the gate to the apartment. "Meet me here at nine o'clock."

"I will be waiting for you, Anna. May I call you Anna?"

"Of course."

He kissed my hand and left. I watched his buoyant stride as he moved away from me. And so began my courtship with danger—with an agent of the AVO.

⁂

That same Monday morning at the Legation, Stephen requested the list of names of Hungarian AVO agents, and to his dismay, László Harsányi's name was among them. He went to the Legation file room to inquire if they had photos of these officers. "Some," he was told by the clerk in charge of the files. The man handed over a rather extensive file with photos mounted in order of last name. Stephen flipped through the pages and found him—a handsome young man of twenty-eight with dark eyes and black wavy hair. He looked neat, friendly enough, and sure of himself.

Stephen slipped the picture out of the file and told the clerk he had to borrow it for a few days.

"I'm afraid we don't allow these photos to leave this room, Mr. Koczak."

"This is an unusual case. I promise to bring it back."

Stephen immediately returned to his office to call me. When I told him I was going to meet László that evening in front of the house, he decided against telling me what he'd discovered. First, he'd take a look for himself.

A little before nine o'clock, Stephen sat in his car parked across from the well-lit gate of his apartment building. A few minutes later, a man came walking down the street. His wavy hair was slightly wet from a light drizzling rain. His raincoat was open. He stopped at the gate, waiting and glancing around. Stephen sank into his seat and pretended to look the other way.

When Stephen turned back, he could see his face perfectly in the light, and it matched the photograph in his hand. He watched me come out of the building and greet László, who bent down to kiss my hand, just as I'd taught Stephen was the custom among Hungarian men and women.

Stephen put the car in gear and slowly drove away. For a moment, he considered following us but decided against it. He wracked his brain for another way to handle the situation but could think of none.

Because of the rain, László suggested we go to a nearby restaurant called Gundel. "Let's make a run for it," he said, taking my arm and hurrying us along.

I'd only been to the stylish restaurant once before. On arrival, the head waiter bowed to László and asked if he'd prefer an intimate table or if he'd like his usual spot. "Intimate would be fine," he said and fleetingly glanced at me to see if I was impressed, or at least it seemed that way. I pretended not to notice, taking in the ornate surroundings instead.

There was no waiting. The head waiter invited us to come along. He threaded his way between the tables across the elegant room full of elegant people wearing expensive clothes. I couldn't help but wonder who all these people were, with their jewels and beautiful dresses and suits, when so many were struggling to put food on their tables and make ends meet.

My own dress, made of a mixture of gray silk and linen, was attractive though modest, and I wore no jewelry in contrast to the heavily ornamented women. Cinched at the waist, the frock showed off my figure, which at the time my friends often commented on, saying I was shapely, if not a little too thin.

Some of the women stared. In a large gilt mirror on one of the walls, I could see that Lászlo and I made a handsome couple.

We were seated at a cozy candlelit table for two. Our waiter arrived swiftly to take our order. Because we'd both already had supper, we only chose coffee and dessert, something called Rigo Jancsi—a round little cake with chocolate glaze. The waiter was about to move away, when Lászlo placed a stopping hand on his arm.

"We'd like a bottle of your excellent wine. The usual," Lászlo said with an air of sophistication—a man used to the finer things in life.

"Please don't get it on account of me," I interrupted, "I'm not going to have any this evening. I don't drink when I have to work the following morning."

Lászlo's mouth folded into a pout. "Just a little?"

I shook my head. Though I loved wine, I was determined not to drink a drop while out with this man. I had to stay sharp and couldn't risk a lapse in judgment.

While we waited for dessert, he asked me to tell him something about myself so he could get to know me better.

"Where should I begin? Should I tell you about my past or present?" I was testing him, assuming he'd have little interest in my past.

He thought for a moment, then suggested I begin with the present, and we could explore the past some other time. He touched my hand, and I allowed him to intertwine his fingers with mine. I indulged him for only a moment then pulled away.

Pretending not to know that he was aware of my present employment, I described my job as housekeeper for an American, though I didn't mention Stephen by name or what he did. Make him ask, I thought. "He is single and young, and sort of inherited me with the apartment," I explained. "I worked for a couple who'd lived there before him, and he asked me to stay on. There are few opportunities, and so I agreed." I examined his expression for any sign of surprise. "I hope it doesn't bother you that I'm a housekeeper, but unfortunately, I had little choice and so agreed."

"Not at all. The only thing that bothers me is that he is single and young and probably good looking too?" He arched his brow playfully.

"He is, but it shouldn't bother you. His life and mine run on different tracks. After all, he is American, and I'm Hungarian." I smiled sweetly at him, which appeared to have the intended effect.

"So what is this American's name, if I might ask?"

I told him, which produced little response, not even a question about exactly what this man did. Perhaps he thought he shouldn't probe too much and was saving the question for another time. Just as dessert arrived, he excused himself from the table. "I'll be right back," he said. "Feel free to start without me."

"I wouldn't think of it."

While he was gone, I noticed a few men paying attention to me. One in particular was quite brazen allowing as his eyes to sweep over me, blatantly lingering on the area below my neck. He seemed quite skilled at making a woman feel undressed, and I have to admit that, although I wanted to take it in stride, I blushed. After all, my experience with such men was limited.

A waiter arrived at the table and presented me with an envelope on a silver tray. He bowed and retreated. I opened it to find a card on which was printed a man's name, Samuel Gruenwald, his place of business, the Institute of Architecture and Construction, and his telephone number and address. On the back, he'd written, "I'd love to meet you."

I briefly glanced in his direction to find him shamelessly staring at me. The well-dressed pretty young woman who'd sat at his table was gone, probably in the ladies' room. He took the opportunity to throw me a kiss. It seemed that Samuel Gruenwald was the kind of man, despite being middle-aged with a receding hairline, who attracted women of all ages because of his wealth and station in life.

László reappeared. "Who was that man you were looking at?"

"Someone who apparently wants to meet me." I waved the card at him.

"Can I see it?" He reached across the table.

I drew it back and gave him a mischievous grin. "Of course not. It's private and none of your affair." Though I'd never led a man on, it seemed to come naturally. Perhaps it's one of those things that every woman learns to one degree or another.

"Well, I know that he is staring at you because you look so fresh and lovely, with raindrop jewels in your hair," he said poetically. What a masterful paramour. "Each piece of jewelry these women wear is most likely a gift from a different lover. You wear nothing, so you look like a virgin."

"Well, if that is a sign of virginity, I am one of the few who are here."

His eyes lit up. "I'm honored that you are with me. I am the envy of these men. What a wonderful feeling. Thank you."

Quite openly, I took a look at my watch and told him I needed to get home soon.

"Yes, we'd better leave before that man steals you away." He laughed lightheartedly. We drank our coffee and made short work of our dessert. As we wove our way between the tables back through the restaurant, I could feel Mr. Gruenwald's eyes at my back.

Fortunately, it was no longer raining. On our stroll to the apartment, I allowed him to link his arm with mine. Back at the gate, he asked to meet me the following Sunday afternoon for a matinee at the theater where John Steinbeck's *Of Mice and Men* was playing, and I agreed.

He kissed me goodnight on the cheek. I didn't object, though once he turned away, I wiped my face. A Judas kiss, I thought.

———•———

After seeing the play with László, he claimed the next few Sundays. In particular, we both enjoyed dancing—László was quite an energetic dancer, and it seemed to be his favorite pastime with me, perhaps because it was one of the rare moments I allowed him to have intimate contact with me—sweeping across the dance floor, cheek to cheek, his arm on my back, my hand in his. Often he whispered sweet nonsense in my ear and kissed me; occasionally, I returned his kisses. Sometimes, my mind wandered, and I found myself trying to imagine what it would be like to dance this way with Stephen.

We talked a great deal, but he put most of the significant questions to me when we were outdoors or during meals. When it came to the latter, I could tell it bothered him that I didn't drink, but I couldn't afford to lose my focus. So far, he'd revealed little despite his penchant for wine.

On one date at the end of September, he pointed out that I spoke freely about my past but the stories ended in 1945, the year the war was finally over. "It's almost as if the rest don't exist for you. Why is that?"

"Why, László, you never asked," I said with what I hoped was a disarming smile. "What would you like to know?"

"Everything," he answered.

In that moment, I decided to begin speaking about Uncle Ferenc. That way I no longer had to dance around the subject or wonder what he thought. I'm not sure whether that was a defensive or offensive move, but I thought it was quite clever. I told him that I hadn't spoken about those years because I had an uncle who had been a Communist and even became a colonel in the AVO. It was not something my family was happy about.

"After all," I said, "we knew what terrible things the secret police had done. Nevertheless he was very loving to me, and for the most part, I overlooked this aspect of his life."

Predictably, László's interest perked up at this, and his gaze grew more intent.

To avoid his scrutiny, I snuggled up to him and told him that I knew him as a little girl, and we frequently saw one another here in Budapest.

"It was tragic when he died. I miss him very much," I said.

"Being so close to you and involved in the government, he must have discussed politics with you?"

"Not really," I said. "With me he liked to talk about other things. In any case, he was a dedicated and very private man."

"Yes, I know," László said, before realizing what he was saying. "Why didn't you tell me you knew him?"

Flustered, he added, "I meant I can imagine that he was a discreet man."

———◆———

Stephen re-read the invitation from Mrs. Chapin. It wasn't customary to invite an officer of the Legation to tea, only their wives. He didn't really want to go, but it would be improper to refuse his boss's wife. He had a notion that her desire to see him married to Emily Clark was behind the invitation. Just as he liked Joan, he enjoyed Emily, but he simply wasn't interested in or ready for a lifetime commitment.

The Minister's wife was a charming hostess. As it turned out, they had a pleasant conversation about France and Italy, where they'd both traveled. Stephen was pleased they had mutual preferences for places and food, but more than anything, it relieved him that she hadn't brought up the topic of Emily.

"Oh, I almost forgot," she said, "recently, I met a lovely girl at a party at the British ambassador's residence. Joan Robbins, I believe. Apparently she went with you on vacation?" Her eyes were the epitome of innocence.

He'd dropped his guard entirely, and could feel the blood rush to his face. "Well, yes, we did travel together some of the time," he spluttered.

"I understand that you are now engaged?" She gave him a questioning smile.

Stephen couldn't quite believe what he was hearing, but this ridiculous assertion allowed him to recover his composure. "I can't imagine that Joan told you this bit of information."

"She didn't exactly put it into those words, but when I asked if the two of you were engaged, she smiled happily, suggesting she was," Mrs. Chapin replied in a neutral, diplomatic voice. "You look as though you're quite surprised."

Annoyed is more like it, Stephen thought. "I *am* surprised since it's not true. We are friends, very good friends, but we are definitely not engaged. I hope I haven't disappointed you?" This time he smiled.

"No, no. To the contrary. It's just that I am very fond of you. And so is Emily. I was hoping that the two of you might," she said, gazing at him confidentially, "well, that *you* might become engaged. She'll be back in a month." She looked at Stephen expectantly.

"I'm afraid I won't be engaged for quite some time. The time simply isn't right. In any case, my work is far too demanding for me to set up house and have a family. It wouldn't be fair to any woman, including Emily, who is very charming."

She was obviously disappointed, but the entrance of her husband rescued Stephen and cut short further discussion of marriage.

On his way home he recalled that in Paris he'd told Joan he loved her. It hadn't really been true, but he'd said it to placate her amid some dramatic outburst. He couldn't even remember the exact circumstances beyond the fact that she had been crying over something he had or hadn't done. He knew that it was a mistake to say such things frivolously and would make a point of being more careful in the future.

October 1948

I was staring at myself in the mirror, feeling quite smug. The dress the tailor sewed using the green silk Stephen had given me was not only fashionable, but it also fit perfectly. Preening before the mirror, I applied a bit of makeup and turned this way and that to make sure Stephen would be impressed.

The poor man had turned his ankle and was at home for the evening. I found him in the library where he sat by the window reading. After a moment, he put his book down and turned to me.

"Upon my word," he exclaimed, "you look ravishing. Come over here. Stand in front of me so I can see you better."

I was terribly happy that I was having the desired effect. At moments like that, I was sure that he cared about me, and I basked in his attention.

"In this dress you are of Paris—exquisite, fashionable, beautiful. I don't know what more to say." He sat there, his eyes roaming over my body. In contrast to Samuel Gruenwald's ogling, I didn't mind that he was undressing me with his eyes. I felt flush with pleasure.

He ran his hands over the tight silk bodice then lowered them to encircle my waist. The pressure of his touch was electric. I felt the chemistry flow between us. All I could do to stop myself from throwing myself at him was to step away and tell him that I wanted to show him the other one too so he could decide which he liked better.

After I returned wearing the second, a sleeveless flared dress in a dark shade of blue, he asked, "Will you wear one of these for me tomorrow night?"

"I would love to, but I am going out with László."

His gaze dropped to the book in his lap, and he seemed at a loss for what to say. I almost felt as though I'd broken the spell of the moment.

"Don't worry," I said, hoping to reassure him. "I wouldn't dream of wearing them for anyone but you." I went around to the back of his chair, where he couldn't reach me, and leaned over to give him a kiss on the cheek. "I don't know how to thank you," I whispered and then left.

I changed back into my regular clothes, and when I returned to his apartment, the doorbell rang. The last person I expected to see was Joan. And yet, there she was. She nodded at me and rushed past, acting as if this was her home with Stephen.

Seeing her there, I couldn't believe that only moments after Stephen had practically seduced me, she showed up. The situation was so inconceivable to me that I was too dumbfounded to even cry. I couldn't stand to be in the apartment another minute and fled upstairs to my room.

In mid-October, on my fifth date with László, he took me by train to the charming town of Szentendre, nestled among ancient volcanic hills along the Danube north of Budapest. I'd never been there, and was actually excited to go. It was a beautiful day, the sunshine embracing the autumnal countryside graced with trees of every hue.

From the train station, we walked the old narrow streets. Over the past fifty years, the many artists who came to Szentendre transformed the town into an artist colony. Homes were picturesque and many featured uniquely carved doors. The beautiful scenery had drawn a creative community, and it had become a destination for weekend visitors.

László and I wandered the hills to the summit where, looking north, we could see all the way to Esztergom and to the south, Budapest. For a while, we sat observing the scenery, watching the birds in flight, and listening to the chirp and buzz of insects. He seemed impressed that I could identify a number of birds simply by their song.

"Of course in Nagykörös that's nothing," I said. "We hear them from the time we are children and learn about the natural world that surrounds us."

"Still, I think it's quite an accomplishment and like hearing you talk about it." He reached for my hair and began to play with it. Though I knew better than to think about Stephen, especially after recent events, a few times, I couldn't help but wish that he, not László, were sitting beside me.

It didn't bother me that László was affectionate, because he was quite attractive, and had he not been an agent of the AVO, I might actually have fallen for him. Too, I knew I was in control of our amorous interactions and would allow things to go only so far. It was also true that I couldn't know whether he was putting on an act or that he genuinely liked me. Occasionally, I thought the latter, but even so, his flattery and tenderness mattered little—not when he had a job to fulfill, a job I often wondered about. Most likely it involved compromising me, taking photographs, and then forcing me to spy for the secret police. This practice was well known and many young women had fallen into the trap. It was critical that I not be lulled into complacency. First and foremost, I had to remember that he was an AVO man with a secret agenda.

When we gazed north to Esztergom, I asked if he'd ever visited.

"A couple of times," he answered.

Esztergom was not only the seat of the Cardinal but also a place filled with a thousand years of Hungarian history. During the time of St. Stephen, Esztergom was the capital of Hungary. The Cathedral was erected on the very spot where the royal castle had once stood.

"I assume you have visited the Cathedral and listened to one of Cardinal Mendszenty's sermons?"

"I am a non-practicing Calvinist," he said with a laugh, "not a Catholic, Anna."

"Many people listen to him who aren't Catholic, Laci."

"Since you are a Catholic, can you explain to me why the Primate has such strong opposition to what our politicians call progress?" He was frowning, as though he were truly attempting to understand this discrepancy.

I tended to avoid political discussions with him, but in this instance, I made an exception. "I believe he feels that his views conflict with those of the Communists. They espouse atheism; they are opposed to religion being taught in school; they are sending innocent people to prison; they are taking people's land and livelihood. The very things they say Communism stands for have been compromised. Aren't all these things true?"

The intensity of my voice seemed to surprise him. "I didn't know you felt so strongly."

My anger flared. "Well now you do."

He turned away, staring off into the distance. When he turned back, he said, "I hate politics. Let's talk of more pleasant things."

It surprised me to hear him say this so convincingly. Was he genuine about hating politics? He was enmeshed in politics. A part of me was desperate to confront him. To ask him whether he agreed with the current state of affairs, but it wasn't prudent, and I knew it.

We stood there a while longer, then I turned and called out to him, "I'll race you down the hill to the river!" Not waiting for an answer, I took off. I had quite a head start but also took pride in my ability to run fast. Lászlo only caught up with me at the bottom of the hill, or at least he let me think so.

"Got you," he said, picking me up and twirling me around. "Now I'm going to take you to my little house, one of those you like so much that looks like a swallow's nest. It's right by the river. Inside, a fine supper is waiting for us. I'll put on some soft music and light the candles," he said wearing a roguish smile.

My laughter had stopped.

"You will come, won't you?"

"Only if your mother is there."

"Anna, for heaven's sake, we are grownups." He shook his head, exasperated with me. "No, my mother isn't there." Then he sweetened his tone. "I just want to show you how much love I can give you."

Just short of batting my eyes, I answered in the most coquettish way I could. "It's all so tempting, Laci. The supper, the music, the candlelight. But I'm afraid of what comes after the supper."

"What are you afraid of? Don't you trust that I love you?"

"Of course I trust you. It's just that I don't trust myself." I smiled mischievously. "Anyway, love after five weeks doesn't always mean love after three or four months."

He seemed disturbed by my answer. "Three or four months? Why don't you just say it? You prefer Stephen Koczak over me. You prefer his caresses over mine!"

"Stephen Koczak? My employer? What makes you think he caresses me? And why would I be here with you if he was taking me into his arms?"

I'd never mentioned Stephen's name and wondered if he realized he'd just made a blunder. Perhaps he hadn't been given three or four months to lure me into bed and spoke out of desperation.

László avoided my look and was silent for quite some time. "I'm sorry," he finally said. "I am jealous. I couldn't bear to know you belong to someone else."

"Then why ask if you couldn't bear it?" Though I spoke harshly, I also found it confusing that he appeared so genuinely contrite. In a softer tone, I added, "Laci, I'm nobody else's. I don't want to be anybody's, not just yet."

A moment of doubt wormed its way into my mind. What if he wasn't pursuing me as an AVO agent, but simply as a man? That couldn't be, could it? Or had he fallen for me, despite his assignment?

One night, not long after the trip to Szentendre, we finished dinner at the Three Huszar and László called a taxi to take me back to my apartment, something he rarely did. When we got in, he told the driver to take the long way around, and I assumed it was his way of showing me that he wanted to prolong the evening. We were traveling along Andrássy Street toward Benzcur when all at once the cab rolled to a halt directly in front of the AVO headquarters.

The cabdriver looked over his shoulder at László, as if awaiting instruction, then exited the car.

My body tensed. I was about to leap from the car when László's hand gripped my arm. My heart pounded furiously. An instant later, I heard the trunk of the car creak open and then close with a loud thump. The cabbie slipped back into the driver's seat and set the vehicle into motion.

Shaking my arm, László asked me if I was all right.

"Yes, of course," I lied, prying my arm loose. "I was just thinking about the lovely day we had."

Never had I been so grateful to arrive at the gate before my apartment. "Next Sunday?" he said.

I very much wanted to say no, I wanted to run upstairs into Stephen's sheltering arms, I wanted to be rid of this charade. "Yes, that would be lovely."

Winding my way up the stairs, my imagination took hold of me. I was in the taxi again, and it stopped in front of 60 Andrássy Street. The cabdriver and László dragged me inside the building. They took me to a dark room, strapped me to a chair, and began plying me with questions.

I was sure that stopping there had been no accident. It was a subtle reminder of László's power over me. We both knew I wouldn't be able to refuse his advances forever. Playing along would have to end sometime, I just didn't know how much time they'd given him. The same was true for Cardinal Mindszenty, as reported in our Hungarian papers. Pressure and false accusations against him were mounting.

⸺•⸺

In the final week of October, I received a letter from my father. It worried me, since he rarely wrote letters. To my relief, the letter only stated that one of Pista's friends, Sándor Tanács, was coming to Budapest. My father asked me to please meet him on November 2, providing a street address and time. He also asked me to come home for Christmas, something I had planned to do in any case. The letter and the request left an impression, but not enough to worry me.

On the appointed day, I headed out to see Sándor and arrived promptly at the address in the letter. I was surprised to find that it was a wine and liquor store until I remembered that Sándor's father owned a pub in Nagykörös and that he was probably there to make purchases for his father.

We were both quite happy to see one another. After a brief greeting, he led me to a small apartment above the store where he was staying. The kitchen, living room, and bedroom were combined into a single room. Straightaway, Sándor offered to make us some coffee, which I gladly accepted, even though it was wartime coffee heavily fortified with chicory and aptly referred to as being "bitter as life."

The place was clean, but the furnishings had seen better times. The sofabed sagged beneath my weight. One large window facing south allowed in light—light that accentuated the need for fresh paint.

After he sat down and we'd caught up on one another's lives, Sándor handed me a letter from Pista and told me to read it, as Pista wanted a response that Sándor was to take back home with him. I was a little surprised to see that Pista used a childish code we had made up as young children, writing words from right to left, and starting at the bottom of the page instead of the top, a method which takes considerably longer to read.

Noosh, a friend of mine has seen you in a restaurant with an AVO man and told me to warn you about him. The agent's name is Lászlo Harsányi. My friend knows what he's talking about because he is one of our contacts inside the agency. It makes me fear for you.

If you know this man is keeping tabs on you, simply tell Paul that you want a 'gander' for Christmas. If you don't, then tell him you want a 'goose.' Please take care of yourself.

"So," Sándor said, "which do you prefer—a goose or a gander?"

"I want a gander, a very special gander. I've been wanting to tell my brother that since the middle of September."

After this rather cryptic conversation, Sándor lowered his voice to tell me that Pista was under house arrest for sixty days and also that he had been injured. "Two weeks ago, the police came to question him. Probably Pista was being stubborn, so they worked him over pretty badly and broke two of his ribs."

"What? Why haven't you told me this already? What did he do?"

"It's a rather long story, and if Pista hadn't gotten in trouble, it might even make you laugh." I suppose that I must have given him a troubled look because he said,

"It was the old gypsy judge's funeral. When the procession arrived at the grave, they found trash scattered at the bottom of it. The new judge grew furious, convinced that it was done by the Russian soldiers guarding their camp across the street."-

"Unfortunately, Pista was just across the way at the geese hatchery watching the funeral. During the festivities, some of the Russian soldiers started to call out to some of the gypsy women, who were further back from the grave and closer to the guards. This happened at the peak of the ceremony when the gypsies were shaking their fists into the air. The Russians must have thought the gypsies were threatening them and started to grab for their guns.

"In the next moment, the gypsies rushed over and attacked the soldiers, stripped them of their rifles, and at gunpoint forced them into a circle, tying them together and gagging them. Then the gypsies threw the rubbish on the soldiers and continued on with what they'd been doing. When they were finished, they left.

"A few hours later, when the Russians were changing guards at the gate, they discovered the soldiers, gagged and tied up. The local police were called in, and of course they couldn't find the gypsies. They went to the hatchery to find out what had happened, which is where Pista comes in. They accused him of having played a role in this and that his friends had been the ones who'd stolen the guns. They ransacked the hatchery looking for the stolen weapons, but found nothing. They didn't believe Pista had no idea where the guns were, so they took him to the police station and questioned him. When they didn't like his answers," Sándor hesitated, "well, then they beat him."

The idea that my brother had been beaten pained me, and I cried a little. Sándor patted my arm and told me that Pista was all right. "They let him go after keeping him overnight and took him back to the hatchery. They told him to stay in the hut where he and I live. So he's already finished two weeks. Only a little more than six to go." He regarded me a moment. "So you see, it would have been quite funny if Pista hadn't been hurt."

"I suppose," I said half-heartedly. A bothersome thought occurred to me, and I asked very quietly, "Sándor, does Pista know where the guns are?"

His look was circumspect. "What difference does it make, Anna?"

"Just tell me the truth. Please."

"Yes. But they are in a safe place. You don't have to worry."

Of course that's exactly what I did. *Dear Pista, what will happen to you?*

November 1948

By November, the slander campaign against the Cardinal had moved into full swing. The widely circulated Communist newspapers were filled with all manner of accusations, none of them true, or truth twisted to meet their objectives. The once thriving freedom of the press had been virtually silenced; most foreign reporters had either been sent home or had extremely limited access; independent news outlets had been shut down. Those who remained were considered harmless.

The level of discord in the capital placed renewed pressure on Stephen; ever more people were at the mercy of underground efforts to smuggle them out of the country to avoid prison or death. Given his dedication to funneling threatened citizens to safety, he often stumbled in at daybreak, exhausted and irritable. When I saw him in such condition, I felt terrible for him and offered him a cup of tea or coffee, hoping he could relax, and expressed my willingness to listen if he was in the mood to talk.

I worried about him, but he rarely spoke of his trips. It was dangerous enough to confide in anyone, but with me and my relationship with László, it was especially unadvisable. In any case, I could tell that mostly, he wanted nothing but to turn his attentions elsewhere. On occasion, he asked about how things were going with László.

In a recent such exchange, he'd surprised me by asking for intimate details about my outings with the AVO agent. Did he behave himself, or did he tend to be aggressive? After a few more questions, he came to the point, or at least what I felt was the point of this inquisition. "Do you like him? Does he kiss you?" His gaze was penetrating.

His question annoyed me, and I answered in a tone that indicated as much. "Didn't we agree that I have to pretend to like him?"

"Yes, but do you sometimes feel that you like being kissed by him?"

"What do you think?" I answered brusquely.

Stephen came over and pulled me up. He embraced me, and though I wanted nothing more than to fall into his arms and kiss him, I found myself struggling to escape.

"Why do you so often run away when I want to hold you?" he whispered the question in a tone that sounded both vulnerable and anguished.

I was trying to frame my answer when he added, "Tell me, Anna, because I do care for you."

"I suppose I believe you. But what will it come to? It frightens me to dream this way because one day, I will have to wake up. And the more beautiful the dream, the worse the awakening."

I waited for him to say something that would encourage me, but he said nothing. At least, he could tell me that if things were really getting out of hand with László, he would ferry me out of the country? He looked at me sadly then let me go.

The thought of escaping had been nothing but a tiny seed, and I knew I couldn't let it germinate even though Stephen had offered it before, so what hope did I have. And if he did offer it again, how could I possibly leave my family? My country? I couldn't stand the thought, and so I put it out of my mind.

———◆———

"I'm so tired," he said one morning. "Do you know I've had few good nights' sleep since I arrived in Budapest?"

"I'm sorry to hear that," I said. "I wish you could lead a more relaxed life."

Unexpectedly, he asked me my age.

"Why you know that, don't you? We celebrated it…on St. Anna's day. Anyway, I turned 20 in July."

"I will be thirty-one on the thirteenth of this month. I was already a big boy when you were born." He grew quiet for a time and seemed to be thinking back on his childhood.

"What did you do on your birthdays back in America?" I asked, wondering how much impact his Hungarian roots had in his upbringing.

Instead of answering my question he said, "I would like to celebrate my birthday with you, then I will tell you all about my childhood birthdays. It's on a Saturday. We'll celebrate right here at home with cake and wine. You will drink wine with me, won't you?" A rakish grin crossed his face, as he knew I refused to drink with Lászlo.

"Of course I will. I would love that. But are you sure that's what you want to do on your thirty-first birthday?" I asked because I thought that later on he might regret this impulsive offer; that in fact, he would end up preferring to celebrate with Joan and his other diplomatic friends, but I refused to let her name cross my lips. He was a big boy, and he'd asked me.

"All right, then it's a date. The thirteenth of November at six in the evening."

For the next week, I couldn't help the joy and lightheartedness I felt. Everything else was overshadowed—my grief and concern over Pista, even the Sunday date with Lászlo I would have to suffer through on the eighth. Fortunately, as it turned out, that day he didn't feel well, complaining of a headache, and he took me home early. He apologized, though of course, nothing could have pleased me more.

Shortly before the thirteenth, the weather turned cold and stormy. It seemed as though the wind blew all the leaves off the trees in a single night. The large chestnuts that lined the street were suddenly bare. The blustery weather shook the window panes like a madman. When I was forced to run the occasional errand, the chill wind ran its icy fingers beneath my coat and I couldn't wait to return home.

On the thirteenth, the day I'd so impatiently awaited, I didn't see Stephen in the morning. His bed had not been slept in, so I assumed he'd made another journey across the border. When would it stop? Considering the political state of affairs, I knew it would end only when Stephen left his post here in Budapest, which I suppose I hoped would be never.

During the day, while I baked a torte and decorated it, Joan interrupted my pleasure with several phone calls. "Where is Stephen? I haven't been able to reach him at the office. Please tell him that I want to celebrate his birthday, he promised." I pondered her statement but decided he couldn't be that fickle or forgetful. In her last call, she said that she absolutely had to see Stephen today as if I could produce him on demand.

So do I, I thought. *Today is my turn*. Still, a tiny alarm went off in my head.

By late afternoon, the wind was howling again, making the warm apartment all the more cozy. I set the table for two, with a vase of six red roses in the center and long-stemmed candles on either side. Standing there admiring the table, I spoke Stephen's name, rolling it around on my tongue, and saying it in Hungarian—István. I imagined a conversation in which I would use it.

Six o'clock was approaching, and I realized that my heart was beating faster than normal. Several times, I glanced out the window to check for his car. He usually parked on the street in front of the apartment.

About half past six, the phone rang. I skipped across the room to pick it up, only to hear that damn woman's voice again. "No, he is not here," I said. "I'll pass your message along." Though, of course, tonight I would do no such thing. It could wait until morning.

185

By seven o'clock, I alternately worried and grew angry. What if something had happened to him? Couldn't he at least call?

I waited another hour before picking up the phone and calling Julia, just for the sake of hearing someone's voice and distracting myself. I ran the risk of missing his phone call, but I simply couldn't stand wandering about the apartment alone any longer. She seemed glad to hear from me.

"You are so fortunate to find a man like László," she gushed, unaware of his connection to the AVO—something I wished I could confide in her, but of course that was impossible.

"Yes, just plain lucky," I said, glancing at my watch and again searching the street. To avoid any further talk of László, I steered the conversation to Julia's boyfriend, a topic that she never tired of.

"I don't understand what's taking him so long to propose," she said, releasing an exasperated sigh. "Perhaps I should just ask him myself?"

"Why don't you, maybe he's waiting for that?" I suggested distractedly. The truth was these conversations bored me. They were mostly the same. He did this, he did that; he forgot to do this, or was negligent about that. When would he marry her? Julia was not an empty-headed type, but lately she'd become obsessed with marriage to the exclusion of nearly everything else. She paid little attention to what was going on in Budapest, something we used to at least discuss.

"Anna? I'm talking to you. Didn't you hear what I said?"

"I'm sorry, what?"

"I have a date with a fortune teller. Come with me. Then we can both know what our futures hold." She giggled.

"No, thanks. That's one thing I don't want to know about— my future. Besides how can you believe a word those gypsies tell you?"

I began to worry that Stephen was trying to call and told her that I had to go.

"No, not until you tell me you'll go with me. Anyway, she's not a gypsy. I went once before, and everything she said came true."

"That's an even better reason not to go," I said. "Why should I be unhappy about terrible things that will happen later? Bad enough when it arrives."

"You are strange lately, Anna. What can be so terrible? Sometimes I wonder what's happening to you. You're always so serious."

"Well, these are serious times, in case you hadn't noticed."

"Agree to come."

Just to get her off the phone, I said yes.

The clock struck nine, and the phone rang again. I glared at it. Please don't let it be Joan. Closing my eyes, I thought, please let it be Stephen, and picked up the receiver. It was neither Joan nor Stephen. The voice at the other end was László's. He'd never called me on the phone, but had always set our dates on the previous meetings. Why was he calling?

"My sweet Anna, I couldn't resist talking to you for a moment. Do you remember what today is?" He waited a few seconds and when I didn't answer, he went on, "It's exactly two months ago that I first took you out. Do you have a few moments for me so we can celebrate? So I can give you a kiss?"

"You know I can't go out on Saturdays, Laci."

"But you're at home. Surely you're not on duty right now. It's late."

"Well, that's just it. As much as I'd appreciate a kiss, I've had a difficult day and am tired. I'll see you tomorrow. All right?"

"Good night, my love," he said. His voice had a nice quality to it. And just then I wished that he wasn't a member of the secret police, because my life would be so much easier if he weren't.

The wind rattled the windows and the room felt cold. I stoked the fire in the ceramic stove, then curled up in Stephen's favorite chair and read the play László and I would see the following day. *The Tragedy of Man* by Madács Imre.

I kept willing the door to open or the phone to ring, but neither happened. Again I worried, then thought he might have gone to see Joan after all. I found a hundred other excuses why Stephen hadn't come home, but couldn't find any for myself. Why was I still up waiting for him? It was nearly eleven o'clock. Five hours I'd waited. Ridiculous.

The following morning I found Stephen at home. Before I could say anything, he apologized for not having been able to come home until after midnight.

"I was stuck in Vienna and then Minister Chapin needed me to stop off at Esztergom. I can't tell you how much more I wanted to be here having birthday cake with you."

"That's all right," I said. "We can have some cake now." I brought out the torte and lit the candles on the table from the night before. "Happy birthday!"

"Thank you, Anna. How thoughtful."

"What did you do in Esztergom?" I asked, though most likely Stephen couldn't tell me.

He turned and gave me a quizzical look. It wasn't like me to pry in Legation affairs. But he must have decided I was trustworthy, because he explained that Chapin had been trying for some time to figure out a way for Cardinal Mindszenty to flee Hungary. "We've learned we can offer him safe passage to Rome. It would protect the Cardinal from harm and suit Rakosi's purposes at the same time. Having him defect would be the perfect solution."

"That sounds hopeful."

Stephen frowned. "Yes, it's a good plan, except that he refuses to go."

Though it surprised me to hear it, when I thought about it, I understood. This Cardinal had far too much courage. He wouldn't abandon his flock, even if it cost him his life. He was right of course, but nevertheless, it saddened me to think that he might go the way of my uncle. These men were truly evil. Suddenly, a fearful thought flickered through my mind. What about me? I was strong, but I imagined buckling under torture. I hoped that I would never be tested.

We spoke a while longer about nothing in particular—the cold, the holidays, and so on. "With Christmas coming, I'll have a little more free time," he said. "We'll make up for yesterday then, all right?"

"I'm afraid I'll be going home for Christmas. But I'll be back the day after. We can celebrate then?"

"Certainly. I look forward to it."

Noticing how haggard and spent he looked, I suggested he return to bed to rest. On my way out, I told him that Joan had called numerous times and insisted on speaking with him. Closing his eyes, he heaved a sigh. "Thank you."

———•———

On Monday, at the Legation, Stephen found a message waiting for him from István Barankovics, head of the Democratic People's Party. He insisted on the importance of a meeting, preferably at the Jesuit house so Father Jánosi could be present as well.

Though originally a supporter of the Cardinal, lately Barankovics had turned against the Primate, he had even been quoted as saying that Rakosi was "an excellent man." This shocked his political friends and enemies alike. Then rumors circulated that he was on such good terms with Rakosi that he was given a government car to travel around and persuade clerics in high positions to stop supporting the Cardinal. He used Father Jánosi's argument that the regime would be more compromising, less heavy-handed if the Cardinal wouldn't be so rigid.

Barankovics's defense of the Communist party did not sit well with members of his own party, so much so that he was asked to account for his actions. "Are you doing this as the head of the party or as a private man?" a party representative asked.

Surprisingly, he claimed to be doing it as a private citizen. Nevertheless, this created a major rift in the party. Stephen knew this was precisely what Rakosi wanted.

He was clever. He knew how to manipulate men for his own ends, especially those seeking power and personal glorification like Father Jánosi, and now Barankovics.

Stephen had heard no one enter his office, so was startled by someone's hands reaching around his head and covering his eyes. Even before the owner of the hands emitted a peep, he knew it was Joan by the softness and length of her slender fingers.

"Where were you on Saturday, Stephen? I waited all night for you," she pouted. "I had even organized a surprise to celebrate your birthday. And then the guest of honor fails to show." Her tone—sweet, hurt, and ever so slightly offended—was expertly calibrated to elicit guilt. She came around and sat on the corner of his desk, one high-heeled foot on the floor, the other swinging back and forth, her shoe dangling in the air. "Can you imagine how devastating it was?"

"Well, no, but I'm sorry. I was with the Cardinal. Besides, I don't recall having made a date with you. I certainly didn't know that you'd planned a party."

Joan stroked his face, then dropped her hand to rest on his desk. "You are so tiresome, Stephen. Why do you spend all your time with these people? All work and no play. That's you, love."

He was resolute. "This is my work. I came here to understand what's going on in this country, and that requires a tremendous commitment of time."

"Yes, yes. But we still need to celebrate your birthday."

"All right. You set the time."

"Tomorrow," Joan chirped. "I have it all planned out."

He glanced at the note he'd begun to write to Barankovics indicating he'd meet with him the same evening Joan had proposed. "Could we do it the following night?"

"You see, you never have time for me."

"Tomorrow then," Stephen agreed. "I'll change my other appointment for you."

Joan threw her arms around him and kissed him.

After she left, he wrote, "2:00 pm, Thursday, November 18," for his meeting at the Jesuit house with the two men.

———— ·◆· ————

By the time Stephen was on his way to meet with Barankovics and Father Jánosi, the birthday party, which had been sufficiently boring, had already receded to the back of his mind. Instead he was thinking about a recent letter the Cardinal had issued to the people of Hungary declaring that despite government attacks on him, he would not desert them.

> I am a representative of God, the Church, and my country.
> I occupy this office in service of my people. Next to the
> suffering of my country, my own suffering is nothing. I
> will not retaliate against those who accuse me, I will pray
> for a world of truth and love.

Stephen knew the letter had not been issued to provoke Rakosi and his regime, but rather to send a message of hope to the people. Nonetheless, the letter signaled the Cardinal's willingness to stand up to the Russians no matter what the cost. He was practically daring them to carry out the arrest that most thought to be imminent. He might be spared if he ended his outspoken opposition to the regime.

This was a problem for both the United States and the Russian-backed government. Rakosi did not want to make a martyr out of the Cardinal, and the United States did not want to appear as though they'd done nothing to prevent the Primate from being arrested and imprisoned. After this letter was made public, Minister Chapin had spoken to Stephen about his frustration with the Cardinal. "Why does he have to be so stubborn? All he has to do is leave the country."

Of course a top priority for the Legation was to protect the image of the United States, but in this instance, it annoyed Stephen that the Minister showed so little empathy for the people or even for the Cardinal. How could he fail to appreciate the Cardinal's tremendous strength of character for taking this stance? This attitude of Chapin's made Stephen irritable. To put himself in a better frame of mind, he parked about a block away from the Jesuit house so he could take a quick stroll before meeting the two men. Still, he found himself slamming the car door with extra force.

Inside the Jesuit house, while awaiting Father Jánosi and Barankovics, Stephen took stock of his elegant surroundings, which to his mind contradicted the basic teachings of Jesus Christ. Whatever happened to the vow of poverty? Aristocrats of the Church, Stephen mused. Perhaps this was, in part, why the Jesuit priests strove for power more than other orders.

Once the three were seated with cups of coffee served by one of the novices, it took little time for Barankovics to come to the point. In essence, he wanted to unburden himself of guilt. "I am only suggesting that the Church be willing to meet the Communist regime halfway. My policy is a policy of survival, not surrender. If Cardinal Mindszenty refuses, I am certain he will be arrested and the Church will lose its power and its freedom, what little there is left."

He glanced over at Father Jánosi. "It doesn't matter that others have said or thought the same thing, but I'm the one who will be blamed for the break- up of the party." He nodded worriedly. "I don't understand the Primate. We are only trying to protect him."

"What do you think the Cardinal thinks of your efforts?" Stephen asked quite directly.

Father Jánosi inserted himself into the conversation. "Mindszenty said he is sorry that István is so confused. As for me, he never liked me." He picked up his cup and drank from it. Then, slowly placing it back into the saucer and without looking up, he asked Stephen if he'd spoken to the Cardinal recently.

"Why do you ask?"

"We were hoping that if none of us can talk sense into him, perhaps you Americans can."

"I'm afraid the Cardinal is his own man and holds his own counsel."

He'd thought this was why they'd wanted to see him. To find out whether the Americans had had any luck convincing the Cardinal to leave. What Stephen also knew was that neither man wanted to be in a position to have to testify against the Cardinal, which, based on their recent actions, they would undoubtedly be called on to do. Such testimony would bring the wrath of a majority of Hungarians down upon them. And the only way out of their predicament was getting the Cardinal to flee or convincing him to genuflect to the will of Rakosi.

Stephen wanted to tell them that maneuvering in this political maelstrom was a dangerous business, but they would find that out for themselves. There was certainly nothing he could do for them, nor did he particularly want to.

He'd hardly arrived back at his office when a strange call came in. A man's muffled voice came through the receiver. "Sir, I am calling from a public phone. I am Vilmos Juhász's son. My father has received some terrible news. The secret police have signed a warrant to arrest Father Zakár, the Cardinal's secretary."

"Yes, I know he's the secretary," Stephen said, "but why isn't your father calling me?"

In a whisper the young man said, "He went to Budakeszi to hide at a friend's home."

Damned coward, Stephen thought. *What good would hiding do?* "So who gave him this information?"

"I don't know, he wouldn't tell me. But he did say that you are reliable and would help," the man's son said.

"Give me the address and let your father know I'll come to see him there."

"I do not know the address, and they have no telephone."

"How does he expect me to do anything without any information? And you—for all I know, you might not be Vilmos's son at all."

"I am his son all right. Let me call my mother, and I'll tell her to call you. Perhaps she knows the address." The phone clicked off.

Stephen stared at the telephone receiver before letting it drop into the cradle. Things seemed to be moving awfully fast. Most likely, the caller was telling the truth about the AVO having a warrant for Father Zakár's arrest, just as there had been one for Father Csertö. But he couldn't just run over to Esztergom to warn the Cardinal and his secretary without any details. He needed to find out if Juhász's information was accurate.

The phone rang again. It was Juhász's wife. She was hysterical. "Now calm down, Mrs. Juhász. Just tell me where I can find your husband."

"That's just it, I don't know exactly. I know the house, but not the address."

The whole thing seemed so ludicrous, it almost made Stephen laugh.

Stephen tried to maintain a calm voice. "So how do you suggest I locate him?"

She explained that she could provide directions and the name of the man with whom Juhász was staying. The one thing that sounded odd was why Juhász hadn't gone directly to see the Cardinal himself. She answered without apology, but with a tremulous voice. "He was afraid that the AVO might already be there, Mr. Koczak. He thinks it's not as dangerous for someone from the American Legation as it would be for him."

He didn't like the idea of going off to someone's home without having any idea what he might encounter. Nevertheless, he found himself asking for the man's name and directions and, not long after, was on his way.

Not unusual for November; a cold, penetrating dampness enveloped the countryside. About twenty minutes into the trip, it began to rain as if the heavens had burst at the seams. The road before him vanished. He leaned forward, attempting to see through the curtain of water. With the war-stricken roads still needing repair, and potholes made invisible by the pooling water, Stephen's precious Plymouth bounced around like a yo-yo. Fortunately, there were few other cars on the road.

He had to watch for the landmarks Juhász's wife had told him about, made far more difficult by the downpour. At last, he came to an intersection he thought matched the one she had described. After making a left turn, he soon found himself in the middle of cornfields without any houses in sight. Back to the intersection again.

The rain let up a little. In the distance he detected a glimmer of lights. As he moved toward them, a barely visible sign said Budakeszi. In town, he had to count streets. A left, then, three streets later, a right, seven more and another left. He had to knock on several doors before anyone was willing to help him. Probably they thought that with such a fancy car, Stephen was with the AVO.

Finally a man asked what he wanted.

"I'm looking for Alex Petri, a Lutheran minister. Do you know which house is his? It's important that I locate him."

"Are you from the police?" he asked.

"Don't be silly," a woman's voice said. "If he was from the police, he would know where Petri lives. Open the door."

After feeling assured that his errand meant no harm to their neighbor, they pointed out his house. As Stephen left, he smelled the aroma of food being prepared and remembered that he had told Anna he would be home in time for dinner. He wished he had called her. Another missed date. He didn't blame her if she gave up on him as being anything close to reliable. Yet, he also knew she was more in tune with his demanding schedule than most women would be. Joan, for example, mustered little patience for his erratic comings and goings.

By the time he knocked on the door, his socks and feet were soaking wet; he hated feeling cold, and that renewed his anger toward the spineless Juhász.

The minister opened the door and ushered him inside and deposited him near the stove to warm up. Juhász peered around the corner cautiously. After satisfying himself that the man standing there was in fact Stephen, he joined him at the stove.

Stephen took no time in getting to the point. "Tell me what this is all about, Mr. Juhász, and where you got the information."

"Iván, the man with contacts inside the AVO. The same one as last time."

It was true that Iván had been reliable last time. A man with a conscience. At least when it came to the clergy. Stephen briefly wondered how Father Csertö was doing now that he'd moved to Rome. Perhaps he would see him again should he make his way south. It still surprised him how little support the Pope was giving to Cardinal Mendszenty. Cardinals and Catholics were his flock. But then, the Pope had also tolerated Hitler, more or less. The whole thing baffled him.

"Get your coat and hat, we are going to Esztergom to alert Father Zakár."

"Oh no, Mr. Counselor, I cannot do that," Juhász protested.

"Yes, you can. And you will."

He returned a few minutes later wearing his hat and coat and had a black briefcase stuffed with papers. This briefcase went everywhere with the man, and in it were sixty-four letters of recommendation from "important" people. But what good would it do to have a missive from Otto of Hapsburg in Communist

Hungary? Nevertheless, he was quite proud of it, as he'd told Stephen in their initial series of meetings, a year earlier.

Before they left, the wife of the minister handed Stephen an earthenware jug of hot soup. "Take this for the trip. It is nice and hot."

Juhász sat hunched low in his seat. Stephen insisted he tell him every detail of what had occurred with Iván. "Around noon today, Iván asked me to have lunch. We met in a small restaurant on Rákóczi Street. He was speaking about things in general when suddenly he whispered the information about the AVO getting a warrant to arrest Father Zakár tomorrow. When I asked him what he wanted me to do about it, he said, 'That is up to you. It's none of my concern.'"

Stephen's voice rose with annoyance. "So you've wasted half the day getting this important message to Father Zakár."

Juhász's trembling figure sank lower into his heavy winter coat, to the point that his fur hat nearly touched the collar of his coat. Only his two large ears stuck out the side, very much like a pot with handles and a lid. Stephen could barely see the wretched man's eyes.

They arrived without incident at Esztergom several hours later. Stephen's watch said it was just past midnight. He had to do quite a bit of banging on the heavy iron gate before it opened and Father Zakár stood before them.

"You'll wake the Primate making such a racket. What do you want at this hour?" he asked.

"We are bringing bad news, Father," Juhász said. And before they'd even gone inside he blurted out the rest. "I was told by a very reliable source that you will be arrested tomorrow."

"We came to speak with you and Cardinal Mindszenty about what to do. As you can see, there's not much time."

Father Zakár did not react; his face was emotionless, as if the pronouncement had had little effect. Stephen tried to gauge what the priest might be thinking, when the man spoke up, "I will not wake up His Eminence if that is what you are asking me to do. He had a very difficult day and needs to rest."

Trying to assess the situation quickly, Stephen said, "I'm sure this is something the Cardinal would want to be informed of. It has implications for him as well."

"Nevertheless, I refuse to wake him. I'll inform him about it when I see him at prayers at five thirty in the morning."

"But that doesn't leave you nearly enough time," Juhász said.

"Time? I am not leaving the country, if that's what you two think."

"Father Zakár, I am certain that Cardinal Mindszenty would want you to be safe," Stephen said. "Nothing good can come of staying and being arrested. You know what they'll do."

"What can they do?"

"They will turn you against His Eminence."

"I'm not afraid of torture," he said with great certainty.

Intentions are well and good, Stephen thought. It was one thing to talk this way, another to experience it. The problem with such priests was that they carried Jesus Christ's crucifixion in their minds. He was the role model for self-sacrifice, but few are able to match his strength and will.

———◆———

At about the same time that Stephen woke up the next morning on November 19, shortly after nine o'clock, Father Zakár was being led through the doors of 60 Andrássy Street into AVO headquarters. Not long after, news about the arrest reached Stephen via a telephone call from Juhász, who had been informed by Iván. Apparently, several agents had apprehended the priest about two hours earlier just as he was leaving the Church of the Convent. And just as Stephen had suspected, Father Zakár had never briefed the Cardinal about his imminent arrest.

On November 20, the news was out about Father Zakár's arrest. It was rather vague citing anti-national activities. Nonetheless it managed to spread fear and concern about what would happen next.

Two days after Father Zakár's arrest, Cardinal Mindszenty sent out a pastoral letter that was read in Catholic churches throughout Hungary. The Cardinal's letter expressed concern for those forced to stand up against him. He assured his accusers that he understood they were not acting under their own free will but rather making a choice of Bread or Conscience.

It was a magnanimous letter that left us contemplating our own state of conscience and questioning those of our rulers.

After four days of interrogation and torture, from the nineteenth of November until the twenty-third, Father Zakár confessed. Not the truth, but what his interrogators forced him to say. He finally signed documents set before him, and on the fifth day, November twenty-fourth, they dressed the broken and humiliated man in his priestly robes. They told him that since he'd been a "good boy," they were returning him to Esztergom.

A decent breakfast, his first, was served to him. Hope lit up his spirit; his ordeal was over and he was going home. The car rolled along the Danube. The men in the vehicle with Father Zakár, different from those who'd arrested him, chatted with him quite pleasantly. Three more cars with nearly a dozen agents followed. The priest began to feel at ease and smiled at a few jokes they told, those proper for priestly ears.

"Did you ever have a sweetheart, Father?" one of them asked.

He remembered only vaguely the face of a girl he used to think was beautiful, but that was long ago, and he did not answer.

"I asked you a question," one of the men said, his tone suddenly harsh. Father Zakár began to shake.

"Let him be," said another policeman.

Father Zakár relaxed and wondered why all these men were wasting their time just to escort him home. Perhaps they wanted to apologize to the Cardinal about having kept him for so long. "It wasn't necessary for all of you to come. I could have taken the train," he said suddenly.

The men exchanged a glance. "We just wanted to be sure you got back all right." They all laughed, including the priest, though he didn't know what they were laughing about.

All the bodily abuse he'd suffered made it difficult for Father Zakár to walk. When they arrived at the Cardinal's residence, several of the agents helped him to his feet and guided him to the gate. The entourage of police and agents waited for the door to open.

The Cardinal had seen them arrive through the window and stood in the middle of a large room awaiting them. When the young priest stumbled through the doorway, the Cardinal extended his arms. To Father Zakár, he looked like a strong and sturdy cross that could bear his weight.

The Cardinal could see that his secretary wanted to run to him, like a child to its mother, but the poor man could not. Had it not been for one of the secret agents grabbing his arms, he would have fallen. After helping Father Zakár regain his balance, the agent held on to him, refusing to let him reach the Cardinal.

"Your Eminence, they brought me home. Isn't that nice of them? They even gave me some meat this morning." His eyes flitted back and forth, giving him the look of someone who was mentally disturbed.

Cardinal Mindszenty's tears welled up upon seeing this human wreck instead of the bright vivacious priest he'd known. "Let him go," he ordered the police and made a step forward as if to take him from them.

"You stay where you are." Four guns pointed at him. The lead agent ordered Father Zakár to produce the Primate's confidential files. For a moment the priest hesitated, his defeated eyes drifting to the Cardinal.

"Get moving," one of the men said, shoving him forward. With two agents at his side, Father Zakár shuffled along, his shoulders sloped and his eyes grazing the polished floor. He led the police to the chamber where important files were kept in a small underground vault. The police lifted it out and after briefly examining its contents removed every document it held.

The entire group returned to the large reception area. Guns had been put away. One of the men grabbed Father Zakár and pushed him toward the door.

"Where are you taking me? You said I could go home," he stammered. His eyes looked wildly about. "Please, I did what you asked."

"We did take you—it was a nice visit, wasn't it?" Then turning to the Cardinal, the agent added, "We are much obliged, Your Eminence. You have a well trained and cooperative staff. Thank you."

The Cardinal looked on, knowing he was impotent to stop these men's cruelty. He said a silent prayer and with his eyes tried to give Father Zakár the strength to survive his ordeal.

———◆———

Once again, it was date night with Lászlo. Each time we went out, I felt some combination of dread and curious anticipation—dread because I knew he wasn't simply dating me and curiosity because he always took me to interesting places.

This particular night, he took me to see *The Tragedy of Man*, a serious play about Lucifer criticizing God for the creation of man. What good had come of it? There was nothing but human suffering—war, disease, corruption, hatred, and so on. Nevertheless, Adam—of Adam and Eve—comes to the conclusion that man continues to have hope and the strength to overcome obstacles. We must try the best we can.

Indeed, I thought, *I must outsmart László and the AVO to avoid the fate they have planned for me.* One of the AVO's well recognized "recruiting" tactics was for an agent to lure a woman into a compromising situation, photograph her, and then use the pictures to blackmail her into working for them. The method was known to be quite effective. In the 1940s, the rules were different. That situation would be devastating to a young woman. I knew that I would do almost anything, even consider spying for these despised people, to avoid having such pictures spread out in front of my parents on their kitchen table. I knew that I had to be alert and clever—more alert and cleverer than László and his superiors.

Afterward, László suggested we go to the Moulin Rouge, the most popular nightclub at the time. Strangely enough, we were seated at the same table that Stephen and I had been the time he'd taken me there in July.

We discussed good and evil, God and the devil. László asked whether I believed in the existence of the devil. His question unleashed a torrent of emotion, and I answered without hesitation. "Look at life all around you—the greed, suffering, violence, envy, and endless betrayal committed by humans. What further proof do you want?" I fixed him with a penetrating stare, which I hoped conveyed that he was included in this group of detestable persons.

He squirmed in his seat, rescued only by the waitress who appeared at the table. He gave the scantily clad young woman a grateful smile. "Two cognacs, please," he was quick to say.

"Correction. One cognac and one raspberry soda," I said. "Unless, of course, you're planning to have two?"

László's face turned from slight embarrassment to annoyance. After the waitress left, he said, "Honestly, Anna, don't you think it's terribly provincial to order a raspberry soda in a place like this?"

"No, I don't," I said, smiling pleasantly. "In any case, I don't particularly like cognac, and I have to get up first thing in the morning to work. But to assuage you, I'll have a sip of your drink, all right?"

"All right, but on New Year's Eve, you have to promise me that you'll have a glass of wine to bring in 1949."

My mind grew alert and my thoughts leapt ahead. I saw myself with him that night; he would try to get me drunk, then take me to bed, and tarnish my reputation, just as he'd hoped to do when he'd invited me to his place in Szentendre.

"Well?" he said, jarring me out of my thoughts.

"Yes, all right, *a* glass of wine," I said.

Looking off, he appeared to smile with satisfaction. My stomach tightened. I tried to relax. The drinks arrived, and sipping his cognac, László asked me whether Stephen frequented this place.

I was a bit taken aback since we'd been there together. Did he know? Nevertheless, my response was curt, and perhaps even defensive. "How would I know? I don't ask him where he goes."

"Well, where does he take you when you go out with him?"

I peered at him with narrowed eyes. "Stop that nonsense. You know as well as I do that he doesn't take me out." It was one of the few times that I'd ever told an outright lie, and perhaps because of the play and the thoughts I'd had, I added, "And if you don't know, it's your fault; you aren't doing your job well."

László turned pale. "What job, Anna? What are you talking about?"

I let him squirm. No matter what he said, it would give away the fact that he was an agent tailing Stephen and using me to try to get information. At last, I took his face in my hands and planting a soft kiss on his forehead, I said, "Your job is to get to know me better. That is what I'm talking about. By now, you ought to know I always tell the truth." I smiled coyly.

On Monday I decided to go buy a doll for my niece Sára for Christmas. She was seven and had told me on my last visit that this was the only wish she had. I remembered being her age, and it made me happy to fulfill her childish dream.

However, as I walked through the streets, loudspeakers on top of cars broadcast the propaganda that the Communists had recently been pushing. "Comrades, we want to enlighten you so you are not kept in ignorance of the lies fed to you by the Catholic Church and particularly Cardinal Mindszenty. He wants to poison your minds with old-fashioned superstitions. He is selling out your own country to the Americans."

The announcements ruined my delight at running this errand. With them in power, there would be no getting into the spirit of Christmas. Suddenly, I hated these godless liars. They were attempting to ruin his reputation, though I believed that the more overt they were, the less the majority of the populace believed them.

I thought I felt someone touch my shoulder and turned hoping it was anyone but Lászlo. "Péter," I cried out, "how wonderful to see you."

He was a former classmate of mine and seemed a little surprised but pleased nonetheless by my enthusiastic outburst. He embraced me then asked what had brought me to Budapest.

"I work here as a maid to an American diplomat. I am not as lucky as you." Péter had gone off to the university a year before I was supposed to go.

His face darkened. "Well, my luck has run out. I was kicked out last week."

"Whatever for?"

"You know the story, Anna. It happened to you, too. Recently, all the students were asked to sign that same letter you had to sign. Those of us who refused to lie about the Cardinal were told two days later that we had to pack up and leave."

I felt terrible for him, imagining that his dreams were in shambles like my own. "Do your parents know?"

"Yes, my mother is heartbroken, and my father would like to kill those bastards. Forgive my language, Anna. They had their hearts set on me becoming a doctor. And I will," he said with determination, "but not in this lousy country. I want nothing to do with this regime anymore." He leaned close to my ear and whispered, "I'm leaving Hungary."

"How will you do that? It's so very dangerous." I thought of Stephen.

"I am not sure, but I've heard an American colonel will do it for a certain amount of money. It's probably more than I can afford, but I will get out, even if I have to take the road through the minefields. I promised myself," he said. I did not press him about who this colonel might be. The less I knew, the better.

We went to a small café to chat a while longer. Péter was excited as he spoke about going to Paris to the Sorbonne. Though I hoped he would succeed, I was also envious. At least he stood a chance of making his aspirations a reality, while I did nothing to further my interests. I remained trapped.

As I had wanted to do with Julia, I now wished I could confide in him about László, but once again, I knew I couldn't entrust anyone with this information. One never knew how or why such information might be passed on to the wrong people. Ignorance can have its advantages. After wishing one another luck, we went our separate ways, each of us in our own little universe of problems, disappointments, and obstacles.

The day arrived that I had to keep my promise of going to see the fortune teller with Julia. I continued to insist how ridiculous it was and told her I would not have my fortune told. She laughed and said that of course I would. "Wait until you meet her. She's amazing."

Exactly at noon, the proscribed time, we rang the bell of an apartment building on Harsfa Street. As if by magic, the door opened of its own accord. We mounted the stairs and entered a dimly lit room sealed against the daylight by heavy, blue velvet curtains. The only source of light came from numerous flickering candles. A childish version of the universe of stars was painted on walls a shade of blue even darker than the drapes. Each corner of the room featured one of the four symbols of the gospel—the lion, the eagle, the ox, and the angel. Finally, there was a lace-draped wooden table that had been turned into an altar. On it stood a statue of the Virgin Mary and in front of it were two candles and a crystal ball.

Sacrilegious, I thought.

"No, it is not. I am deeply religious," said a woman I hadn't even noticed until she spoke.

She caught me off guard. "How do you know what I was thinking?"

She indicated where I should sit. Although my intellect thought the whole thing silly, now I found myself intrigued. The woman did not look as I'd imagined. She was attractive, about forty, with graceful hands. She lit the candles, mumbled a prayer, and draped her head and body with a blue shawl. It almost seemed as though she and the statue on the table resembled one another. I shook my head. Now I was being silly.

She looked into my eyes and touched my hands. She took them to her lips and to the side of her heart, and then placed her own hands on the crystal ball. Her tapered fingers cupped the ball perfectly. For five minutes, she sat silent and immobile.

She spoke of my former engagement to a man who'd married someone else. She told me about the time an older man gave me another engagement ring. My uncle, I assumed. "And now," she said, "there are again two men in your life, neither of whom will tell you they love you."

"Why not? Can you tell me that?"

"I'm afraid they will not meet my eyes. They both have secrets."

"How do you know if they care for me if you can't look into their eyes?"

"I can see their feelings but not their reasons."

Her brow furrowed into a deep frown. "You are in danger. Be careful."

The certainty in her voice frightened me. "Are you sure? What kind of danger?"

At first, she seemed reluctant to say what misfortune loomed ahead, then she said, "Be careful of three bubbles in your drink."

This sounded ridiculous and absurd, the words of a charlatan, yet a vague sense of unease settled in the recesses of my mind. She refused to take my money, which further worried me, and she seemed eager to get on with telling Julia her much more pleasant future. Engagement, wedding, children.

Not long after the encounter with the fortune teller, Jenö Nagy, Julia's boyfriend, proposed, and a wedding date was set.

———•———

Back at the secret police headquarters on Andrássy Street, Father Zakár was deposited in a cell and left there. Agents read the files, sorted them into neat piles, and finally a bundle was sent up to the third floor where a forger awaited their delivery.

Mrs. Szulner's task was not so much to understand the documents' content but rather to become acquainted with the Cardinal's handwriting, which tilted in an unusual manner, and with the texture and type of ink that was used. This was an important assignment for her and her husband, Mr. Szulner, and would pay a nice sum.

She bundled the files, inserted them into a red folder, and locked it into a side drawer of her desk. A very orderly person, she straightened her desk just so, placing the objects into symmetrical order. Finally, she stood up and reached for her coat.

The following day, the two Szulners arrived at AVO headquarters promptly and early. So many documents required a significant amount of time, which she was being pressured to complete as quickly as possible. And because of this, both she and her husband's talents were enlisted. Mrs. Szulner was gifted, and her husband was accomplished enough that lawyers attempting to verify the authenticity of various documents clamored for his expertise.

That Gábor Péter, head of the AVO, had personally written the text to be substituted in the Cardinal's letters signaled the high level of importance and secrecy of the work. Not only this, but he would also supervise them.

Mr. Szulner nervously glanced at his wife several times during the course of the day, but she was intent on her assignment as though it were any other job, not the least bit concerned, it seemed to him, that this forgery could mean a noose around the Cardinal's neck. He would ask her about it on their way home, because this time, he was disgusted with himself.

After work, Mr. Szulner expressed his concern to his wife. "My dear Hanna, has it ever occurred to you that the Primate is probably the last obstacle to Rakosi's regime? Once he is in prison and sentenced, there is no one strong enough in the entire country to put up a meaningful opposition to the Communists. No other priest, no other politician, not even the leaders of the underground movement. And we are helping them to accomplish this."

She frowned.

He went on. "After they're rid of the Cardinal, we will be expendable too. Why would they risk having us two nobodies spilling the beans? Or blackmailing them? I don't like it, Hanna. I think we are in danger here. What's to stop them from getting rid of us after we are done?"

"You should have thought of that before," she spat. Mrs. Szulner was known for having a short temper and frequently demeaning her husband. "There's nothing we can do about it now. Don't ask questions. Don't give them any reason to mistrust us. Just do your job."

He hung his head.

"What do you suggest we do?" she said at last.

"I don't know, but this will take several weeks, so we still have time. I will figure something out," he said, though he looked anything but confident.

Then she made an announcement that shocked him. "I'm pregnant, dear."

December 1948

Though it was the last thing Stephen wanted to do after another grueling day, he drove to the Franciscan church to meet Vilmos Juhász, who had called earlier, frantic to see him. *Again*, Stephen had thought. He parked the Plymouth a distance away in front of a well-known restaurant and walked to the church from there.

He found it rather astonishing that the church was overflowing with worshippers, despite government rules and regulations that threatened churchgoers. He squeezed through the crowd and sat in a pew near the front.

Twenty-five monks knelt around the altar singing a melodic verse written for St. Francis. All but one sang. A small monk in an ill-fitting cassock only moved his mouth now and then. His dark eyes beneath bushy brows appeared to timidly search the pews. After the service, he sidled up to Stephen.

Convinced that this man was Juhász, Stephen was surprised to learn that he was not. "I am the Prior here. Let me take you to a back room, where Mr. Juhász is waiting for you."

Apparently, the reason for the overly large cassock was that he'd been delayed and had had to rush, and in the process had been unable to locate his own frock.

Barely greeting Stephen, Juhász in his usual dramatic fashion rushed to tell him the reason for calling. "I am in the gravest situation, a terrible great trouble. The AVO knows that someone was in Esztergom on November nineteenth warning Father Zakár about the arrest."

"How do they know it was you?"

"They know that the man looks like me. Who else in Budapest is so short and has such big ears?"

If the situation hadn't been so serious, Stephen would have burst into laughter. "Well, most likely there are a few," he said unable to suppress a smile. "Now what is it you want me to do?"

"I have to get out of this country. If they catch me, I'll confess everything. I am not a brave man, Mr. Counselor. If I talk, then you will be in trouble, and Iván will be in trouble, and scores of other people will also be endangered. You see, I must go."

"When is it you intend to leave?"

"In no more than two days. I dare not even go home. The Prior," he said, the first time acknowledging the man, and then settling his gaze on the head of the order, "he is kind enough to let me stay here until then.

The Prior nodded.

"My oldest son and I have a way out," Juhász said, "but we can't take women and children that way. Could you help my family, please?" he pleaded.

"I'll see what I can do."

After Stephen left, he pondered the circumstances. He already had passengers for the weekend—the wife, daughter, and son-in-law of Károly Peyer, the former leader of the Smallholder's Party who had fled Hungary right after the 1947 election because he'd been accused of spying. In the spring of 1948, fourteen of the party's members were put on trial and all received prison sentences. Peyer was sentenced to eight years in his absence.

It wearied him to think about how he could maneuver yet one more family out of the country.

———•———

At this same time, the defection of Finance Minister Miklos Nyáradi in early December launched a new round of blame, accusation, and shuffling of power within the Rakosi-dominated regime. The first casualty was Premier Lajos Dinnyés, of the

Smallholders Party, who was blamed by his party for allowing Nyáradi to escape: "(his) flight is a warning for the Government to be more cautious in appointing delegates for talks abroad." (*quotes are from articles in The Washington Post and New York Times)

Three days later, on December 8, the Smallholders Party asked Dinnyés to step down while their rhetoric had stepped up, with the party declaring that it would have to "purge its membership of 'bourgeois elements who are masking themselves as leftists'" and referring to Nyáradi as a "wretched traitor who joined foreign imperialists, deceived his own party, and became secretly an ally of the enemies of the Hungarian people."

It was clear that individuals and political leaders had to go to great lengths to prove themselves as true unadulterated Communists to avoid being thrown out of office or worse. The new Hungarian Prime Minister, István Dobi, wasted little time demonstrating his allegiance.

The entrance hall of the Opera House was buzzing with well-dressed, elegant people, something which impressed me because it was in such contrast to so many people one encountered in Hungary these days. I was excited to be here, about to watch a performance of Puccini's opera *Tosca*.

Lászlo was still in line checking our coats when a stout, balding man appeared at my side. "I have been expecting your call ever since we saw one another."

I must have given him a bewildered look, because he added, "I am Samuel Grunewald. I admired you at Gundel. Do you remember?"

After he announced his name, I did. "I'm sorry you were waiting for my call, but it's not my habit to call men who send their card to my table."

He smiled. "I like that. You have gumption. But I wish that you might change your habit? If you do, I will be honored." He leaned over and kissed my hand then left as unexpectedly as he'd come.

On hearing László's voice I knew the reason for his hasty departure. "How do you know Samuel Grunewald?" he said in an annoyed voice. "What did he want?"

It was interesting to hear the possessiveness in his tone. I wondered if it was real and, if it was, how I might use it to my advantage.

"I don't know him at all," I said. "I suppose you shouldn't leave me alone if you don't want me talking to anyone else."

"He acted as if you were old acquaintances," he grumbled.

"He claimed to have seen me at Gundel's," I said, adding, "I suppose it was the time when you and I were there."

László still seemed unhappy. I told him to cheer up. "I am here with you. So let's go inside and enjoy the performance." Just as I finished saying this, I noticed Stephen's colleague Robin reflected in one of the tall foyer mirrors. He appeared to be looking straight at me. Afraid he would come over, I grabbed László's arm and said, "Let's go. I don't want to miss a thing." I wasn't sure whether Robin had seen us or not.

As it turned out, that hardly mattered. Robin and two companions were seated directly in front of us. I wasn't sure how much he knew, but I couldn't believe this was happening. I prayed he wouldn't turn around to talk to me. During the show, Robin did in fact twist in his seat several times and glance around, clearly noticing László and me but saying nothing. I assumed that László also knew who he was, most likely, aware of all the American Legation staff.

During the intermission, László asked me why "this man" kept looking at me. "Don't tell me you don't know him."

To be on the safe side, I answered as honestly as I could. "I do know him slightly—he is one of my employer's friends. Would you like me to introduce you?"

"Why would I want to meet him?" he said.

When Robin turned around a few more times, I grew agitated, wondering what he was doing. I turned to see what he might be staring at besides me and László. There, about five rows back, sat Joan, the seat next to hers empty. She looked distraught. I imagined that she was unhappy because Stephen had stood her up, once again. I felt little sympathy for her plight.

After the last note of the opera, the crowd clapped and cheered. It had been a stunning performance. I made sure that László and I were among the last to leave. I did not want to run into Joan or find myself in an awkward position with Robin and his companions.

We stepped outside into a lovely wintry scene. Considering the accumulation of snow, it must have been coming down the entire time we were in the Opera House. We took the subway and then walked to my apartment the rest of the way.

A little to my surprise, László asked me to invite him up. "In such weather, it would be cruel of you to send me home." He held me tight.

"Oh, I think you'll be all right. Besides, there's only a few inches of snow. I have no doubt you'll make it to the subway." I lifted my face into the snow as it drifted to earth. "It's different for men, Laci. You don't have to worry about your reputation." I glanced at my watch. "After midnight—I have to ring the janitor of the building to open the gate. I don't need him to see me taking up a strange man."

Resigned to my persistent rejection of his sexual advances, he said, "All right, but how about going sledding on Thursday if the snow sticks?"

"I can't. I have to go with Julia to see her parents. She is getting married in February, and I will be the maid of honor." Afraid of getting him more upset, I promised to have dinner with him that evening. Two seconds later, I knew I'd regret my moment of weakness.

When the wife of the janitor opened the gate, she and László exchanged a look. It almost seemed as though they knew one another.

———◆———

Stephen was not yet home. At his insistence—"for your own safety"—I had begun to sleep in his apartment, not in my own quarters. I wasn't all too sure that it was a good idea to be separated by a single door, but he had no trouble getting me to comply.

I placed my things on a chair and went to the window to look outside at the snow. A tall figure emerged from the apartment building. It was László. He turned and waved to someone standing at the door. I knew that someone had to be the janitor's wife. So, my intuition was probably right. For a sum of money, she was probably spying on me and Stephen and supplying László with information.

In bed, waiting to hear Stephen's key turn in the lock, my thoughts were less than pure. I wondered why I didn't give in to temptation and just let Stephen know how I felt. Life could be short. Why should I be so prudent? Wouldn't I regret not having acted if anything happened to either of us—a possibility which seemed more and more likely?

I imagined a night of glorious lovemaking. Something I would remember forever. Stephen's key sounded in the door. He was home. I could hear his footsteps and knew his usual routine. But then, I heard him approach my room. His hand was on the doorknob. I dared not breathe, though my heart banged inside my ribcage. For half a minute he stood there, then I heard his footsteps retreat, and I could tell he'd gone to his room. I breathed again. This is how it would be; he would not come in.

After several days of sleeplessness, I decided to return to my own apartment at night. Upstairs, I found the door unlocked. Nothing was missing; everything was in order except the box in which I kept my papers and letters. It had been moved and the phone number of Gábor Farkas, Julia's brother, was missing. I knew right away that someone had gone through my papers, and most likely it had been either Lászlo or the janitor's wife. Fortunately, I kept nothing compromising in there. In fact, the only thing I worried about anyone finding was the list of addresses from my old classmates that I'd hidden in the secret pocket of Uncle Ferenc's coat.

Nevertheless, this break-in frightened me enough to send me back downstairs, where I discovered Stephen's apartment door was locked. He woke up to let me in and appeared both surprised and annoyed to see me. "What on earth are you doing up at this time of night?"

I explained the situation and then he scolded me. "Didn't I tell you it might be dangerous? What the hell are you going up there for at one o'clock at night anyway?" His eyes flashed angrily at me. It was the first time I'd ever seen him so furious. Instead of upsetting me, it comforted me to know the extent of his concern.

"Isn't your bed comfortable?"

"No, it's not that. I'm just not sure that we should be sleeping, well, so near one another."

"Are you afraid that I will come into your room when you don't want me to?"

"No, I know you won't."

He seemed puzzled until he looked into my eyes, then it seemed he understood. "Sometimes we are silly, Anna, wanting to do things we shouldn't. Everything has its proper time; otherwise, it is not right." He came over and kissed me on the forehead. "Go to sleep, and I'll try to do the same."

Of course, I could do no such thing and lay awake for hours, thoughts and emotions tumbling about.

The next day over breakfast, Stephen looked rather stern and told me to listen to what he had to say. "Don't let your emotions deprive you of your common sense. You live in a dangerous world; you need your wits about you. Emotions can be taken care of when the danger is over. Do you understand what I am driving at?"

I wasn't sure that I did, but without waiting for me to answer, he added, "I hope you haven't forgotten that I'm expecting five guests for lunch today at noon. Please serve something light and hot."

Perhaps switching subjects was deliberate, his way of turning my thoughts away from the emotional back to practical matters, but most likely it wasn't. In any case, the abrupt change had the opposite effect, almost sending me from the room. I managed to collect myself and told him I had not forgotten, that in fact it was the first time he'd mentioned it.

"It will be ready at twelve o'clock," I said coolly. I'm not sure he even noticed my reaction—so often was the case.

The men came, and as with many of Stephen's guests, they lowered their voices whenever I was nearby as though I were spying on them. This day, it annoyed me, and I was eager to leave. In a little while, I would meet Julia who would be trying on her wedding dress.

Julia's dress was beautiful. Her father had bought the fabric, a new French material called faille, in Paris for his only daughter. Afterward, I accompanied her to her parents' home for dinner. They now lived in a lovely house in Buda adjacent to Gellerthegy. Every room featured Persian carpets. The entire place bore an air of refinement I had rarely experienced, filled as it was with expensive furniture and objects. So this is what it means to be a Communist, I thought to myself. Earlier, Julia had said that her father was a Communist, "But otherwise, he is still a very nice man. You'll see."

Perhaps in these new surroundings, I expected her parents to have become a bit snobbish, but they were welcoming, genuinely pleased to have me over to their new home. Her father was still pleasant and easygoing, though at times, he came across as feeling more important than before. Over dinner, we reminisced about the first pen pal letter I had written her in 1939 and our first meeting in Budapest.

"I remember how excited I was waiting for you at the station," Julia said. "Then, when you arrived, I almost exploded with envy because of how pretty you were. Do you remember, Anna, how plump I was?" Talkative, Julia gave me little time to answer or even squeeze a word in. "After I saw you, I decided to go on a diet. Look at me now, I can wear a size eight dress."

Conversation went along in this vein for a while. While Julia's mother served coffee and cake, her father mentioned that if I was interested in changing jobs, he might be able to arrange one. I nodded and he went on. "I need an artistic, attractive girl to design indoor sets for films and such."

The job sounded appealing, but I was sure I'd have to sign a party card to even be considered. Before I could formulate the question, Julia's mother said to her husband, "What happened to Irene? You just hired her a few months ago."

"The boss promoted her to his department. He likes pretty girls. So I need someone by the end of February when we start filming again. What do you say, Anna? Are you interested?"

"This boss of yours, what does he do with pretty girls who don't want to be promoted?"

"He makes a bit of a fuss, but if they are firm about it, he leaves them alone." He gave me an appraising look. "I'm sure you could handle him. I think you'd be perfect for the job. How about it?"

"Of course I could handle him, but…"

"But what? You're not afraid to quit your current job, are you? Just tell your employer you want to do something more with your life. Come on February first to sign a contract. You'll meet Mr. Grunewald; he's the head of the company. He likes to welcome our new employees. You'll start on the fifteenth."

"Mr. Grunewald?" I asked. "Mr. Samuel Grunewald?"

"You know him?"

I gave him a sphinx-like smile. "You could say that."

On my way home, I turned the idea over in my mind. Of course, there was the issue of that damnable party card, and even though the position sounded attractive, I doubted that I could bring myself to sign it.

When I entered the apartment, I thought I smelled Joan's perfume wafting in from the kitchen. Remembering that I hadn't done the dishes, I thought I should hurry up and get them out of the way, but wasn't keen on encountering Joan. I was about to go in when the phone rang and rescued me, at least momentarily, from what I knew would be unpleasant.

It was László, calling about our six o'clock dinner and saying he would be delayed by an hour. "Is that all right?"

"Yes, of course," I said and hung up.

Stephen entered the room just then.

"I suppose that wasn't for me?"

"No, it wasn't. I have a date with László this evening."

"Well, before you leave again, I want to show you something."

I followed him in the direction of the kitchen, knowing what was likely to come, though I hoped I was wrong. Joan was there and I greeted her. She looked upset and ignored me.

Pointing at the dishes in the sink, Stephen said, "You left the kitchen in a total mess, Anna. When Joan and I wanted to have a cup of tea there wasn't a single clean dish. How do you explain that?"

I felt my face flush with anger. "It's hardly possible there wasn't a cup or a dish since we have service for twenty-four. As a matter of fact, I saw that you left the used tea set on the table for me, Sir."

"Joan was very upset."

"Why was Miss Joan upset? This is not her kitchen, and she doesn't have to clean it up. I was about to do it when I got the phone call."

From Stephen's look, it seemed he knew he'd made a mistake berating me this way in front of Joan, with whom I could tell he was already upset. Now he was also irked by my impudent response. To regain control over the situation, he asked me to make supper for two. "Joan is staying a while."

I fought to control my emotions. Every inch of me wanted to lash out. Had he forgotten what I'd just told him—that I had a date with Lászlo? I formed my thoughts and without a tremor in my voice said, "In case you don't remember, you gave me the afternoon and evening off. I am going out after I finish cleaning up the kitchen. Anyway, it will be much cozier for you two without me." I smiled at both of them. Directing myself at Joan, I added, "You can leave the dishes. I will be home by nine thirty."

Joan was clearly taken aback, and Stephen looked as if I'd just slapped him.

———— ◆ ————

As soon as I laid eyes on Lászlo, I could tell something was wrong. He seemed very out of sorts and lacked his usual enthusiasm on seeing me. He took me to supper at the Three Huszar, a place that catered to young adults and served fine fish, one of Lászlo's favorite foods. He ordered filet of sole in wine sauce and so did I.

When it arrived, he was so preoccupied he didn't even seem to notice. I placed my hand on his. "Wake up, Laci, before your food gets cold."

"I had a difficult day today. I almost lost my head and hit someone."

"You? You wouldn't hurt a fly!" I watched his expression.

"I didn't, but I almost did."

"This morning someone gave me some good advice, László. It went like this: 'Don't let your emotions deprive you of common sense.'"

"Yes, that is good advice," he said, but his tone was filled with doubt. He began to eat and tried to be light-hearted, but underneath it laid a current of misery. "I'm also upset because I can only stay for a couple of hours. Work," he said disgustedly.

"It's rather late to be working, isn't it?" I said, hoping he might say more.

But he only grumbled in agreement.

I didn't discover until much later that László had been pressured by his boss that very afternoon. The piece of paper they'd taken from my apartment had been a train ticket stub to the town of Vác, where a friend of mine, Gábor Farkas, was in prison. I had written his prisoner number—2751—on it. László had checked it out and discovered it belonged to Gábor, who was serving six years for beating up his boss and calling him a stinking Communist. The reason for the attack was that this man had molested Gábor's wife. Once László reported it to his superior, Ernö Szücs, he insisted László find out my connection to Gábor.

But this wasn't the reason László had wanted to strike Szücs. As László was leaving, his superior had demanded to know why he hadn't made any progress getting me to bed. Then winking at László, he said, "I met her once at her uncle's apartment. She was, well, how should I put it? A girl I would love to get my hands on." He paused to let the words sink in. "You were given this assignment, Harsányi, because of your sex appeal. Doesn't she find you desirable?"

He released a sardonic laugh. "Damn it, László, get her into bed. You're being paid to compromise her, not date her. Am I being clear?"

László could do nothing but nod. He had indeed developed feelings for me.

"We have other methods for getting her cooperation. If you're protecting her from that, then get it done." His tone was severe and uncompromising.

Eventually, László came around to probing me about Gábor Farkas. "Have you ever been to Vác?"

When people spoke of Vác, they could either be referring to the town or the prison. I wondered how to answer the question. "Why yes, have you heard that I was there?"

"No, no, I just thought you might like to go there. It's a quaint old town."

"To satisfy your curiosity, I've been there twice to visit an acquaintance in the prison." I went on to tell him that the man had been punished for a slap and that I thought the punishment far too extreme for the crime. I did not, however, tell him my friend's name. I thought I'd make him work for the answer. In a pretense of showing him my lack of concern over our conversation, I turned my gaze to one of the paintings of the famous Huszar, the Hungarian cavalry of old, which lined the walls. The place really was quite attractive. Its cherry wood panels gave the room a pleasant reddish glow. Along one side of the small dance floor in the middle of the long rectangular room was a violin quartet playing traditional Hungarian music.

"What is his name?" he said, trying to sound casual.

I fixed him with a cool smile. "Gábor Farkas. He is the brother of my friend Julia. Satisfied?"

I suppose since he'd gotten what he wanted, he turned on the charm. "I'm sorry, darling. I didn't mean to question you. I was just curious whether I knew him, and I don't. Put a lovely smile on your face and don't be cross with me."

Over dessert, László informed me that he wouldn't be able to see me the following Sunday but that he would call in case his schedule altered. "You know how much I miss you when we don't see one another. In any case, I don't see you nearly enough. And don't forget that you are mine on New Year's Eve."

Pretending that nothing unusual had happened between us, I said, "Why who else would I be going with if it isn't with you?" Though, of course, I wished I were spending the evening with Stephen. I was growing tired of the charade and wondered if it would ever end.

On the way home, my thoughts turned to the offer Julia's father had made. Perhaps all my problems would go away if I just signed the card avowing that I was a communist and took the position, which would allow me to leave Stephen's employ. Would the AVO continue to hound me then?

At home, as if to confirm that this would be my best course of action, on Stephen's bedside stand rested a photo of Joan, smiling happily. I felt as though she were telling me to get out of Stephen's life and hers. Looking at it more closely, I was pleased to see that her slightly protruding teeth marred her admittedly attractive face.

For some time, I mulled over László's miserable state that evening. Could it be due to a case of conflicted emotions? Sometimes, I had the very distinct impression that he had real feelings for me. There were moments when I saw in his eyes the kind of longing that exists between lovers, not just someone who wants to take advantage of a girl. I had times too when my own feelings softened. But I always reminded myself that he was not to be trusted. If this was a vulnerability of his, could I take advantage of it?

On the other hand, perhaps his distress resided in the fact that he hadn't succeeded in reeling me in, and his superiors were pressuring him. I decided most likely it was the latter.

———◆———

On December 19, László took me to Gundel's restaurant again. He ordered roast duck served with chestnuts and baked cinnamon apples for both of us. It was one of his favorites and mine as well.

His mood was quite different from our previous date. He seemed relieved as though something had changed. Best put, he surprised me with what he had to say. And I couldn't make up my mind whether I should believe him or not.

He began the conversation by confiding about a dream of his.

"I've always wanted to go to Paris," he said, looking intently at me, "to live there for a time and perfect my French and, who knows, maybe even stay there." His face was serene, as serene as I'd ever seen it, and his eyes lifted to the ceiling as though he were imagining such a future.

He leaned in close and dropped his voice to a whisper. "If I decided to leave Hungary, would you come with me? Would you be willing to tie your life to mine?"

I didn't know how to answer. Should I simply say yes, in which case he would know that I'm either interested in or considering leaving, which of course was forbidden and punished if one isn't successful? Or should I waver, saying something noncommittal but not bruising his ego? Or should it be a simple, flat-out "no"?

In the end, I told him that I'd never given any thought to leaving my country, neither alone nor with anyone else. "But ask me again when you've decided," I added, gazing into his eyes with a look that indicated I would consider going. "You know that I like you very much."

He seemed happy with my answer, as equivocal as it was. I knew enough about people to understand that sometimes people in love hear what they want to hear, and it seemed this might be the case with him. Then again, I couldn't be absolutely sure that he wasn't just fishing and this supposed dream of his was bait.

"I would like to make it happen soon, Anna."

We were eating in silence, enjoying the succulent duck, when he steered the conversation in another direction. "Do you know what you need, Anna? You need a diamond on your finger and a gold necklace around your neck." He smiled, and I smiled back. With the wave of his hand, he motioned for the musicians to come to the table. He requested a series of my favorite Hungarian folk songs about love, romance, and desire. For a time, I forgot about our complicated entanglement and simply enjoyed the music. László tapped his foot to the rhythm of the melodies.

Later, I thought about this man taking me away to live in the City of Light. He was handsome and attractive, and perhaps I would come to love him. I'd often imagined Stephen smuggling me out, but so far, he'd given me no indication that he would. So why shouldn't it be a secret agent? Maybe he really was in love with me. There was something dangerously romantic about it.

The thought nagged at me on and off for several days. Finally, a few days before leaving for Nagykörös for Christmas, I revealed what had happened to Stephen. His answer was curt and told me nothing I hadn't already thought of. "He may have fallen in love with you, Anna, and his offer is sincere, or maybe he's just testing you. The question is would you go with him if he was sincere?"

Indeed, would I?

I went up to my room where I'd been reading a novel about spies. In it, the spy, a man, inserts a drug into a chocolate bonbon. The woman eats it and, losing her good judgment, allows the man to do with her what he wants. Afterward, she is blackmailed, and to save her reputation, she agrees to be a spy. Of course, at the time, such stories abounded. Uncle Ferenc had given me the book and said that it was based on a true story.

Suddenly, loud shouting drew me back to reality, and I ran to the window. There I witnessed the horror of the police dragging away a man in handcuffs. I recognized him. A shy, rather large man in his thirties. He shared the fourth floor with me. We knew each other little, having only exchanged polite greetings.

Rumor had it he was a homosexual—an orientation very much frowned upon at the time. If he was and it was known, he would have been unable to find a job. Nevertheless, I wondered if this might be the reason they were carting him away. More likely though, it was something political.

I scurried downstairs to Stephen's, actually afraid I might be next.

Just as I arrived, the telephone was ringing. It was László. "Anna, darling, I just found out that I'll be free for four days at Christmas. I would love to invite myself—that is, I wish you'd invite me to go with you to Nagykörös. Don't you think it's time for you to introduce me to your parents?"

The thought mortified me, even with the possibility that László loved me. I would never impose such a risk on my family. The wolf at the door was all that Pista, or any of us, needed. Think fast. "Well, it would be nice, but I'd really have to consult my parents, and I don't think there's enough time for an exchange of letters. Perhaps another time? In any case, I'll be back on the twenty-seventh, so we could celebrate then."

I was lying. I would be returning on Sunday, the twenty-sixth, the day I'd promised to be with Stephen. Time away, I hoped, would help me gain perspective, allow me to recover my good judgment, and finally come to a decision about my future.

Mobs of people crowded the train station in Budapest. The one I'd planned to take was filled to bursting, so I took the express train, which arrived half an hour earlier than the other. Not expecting anyone to pick me up then, I took the bus to the middle of town where there was little evidence of Christmas—only the nativity scene outside our Catholic church and a few candles lighting up the dark windows. The townspeople commonly felt there wasn't much to celebrate. It seemed to me that the lightly falling snow was trying to cover up their misery.

I walked through the deserted streets with a vision of Stephen's lovely eyes to warm my heart. My oldest brother Míhály lived around the next corner. My sister-in-law was at home. "Oh, dear," she said, "you just missed Sára and Pista. They left for the

train station a short while ago to come get you. He was so looking forward to surprising you."

Soon Pista and Sára came back, the little girl's face bathed
in tears.

"I'm sorry, Sára, I had to take a different train. The other one
was full."

"She cried the entire way home," Pista explained. He turned
to our niece. "You didn't want to believe that your auntie had
probably taken another train, did you? You see, I told you she
would be here."

Sára's little head bobbed up and down. "Come and give me
a kiss," I said and knelt down. She came to me slowly, her chin
turned down, a pout on her lips. We embraced and then I took
her over to my suitcase. "Let's see what's inside, shall we?"

"All right." Her eyes took on an eager curiosity.

I pulled out a large box and gave it to her. Her blue eyes lit
up as she reached for it. Her small hands unwrapped the paper
carefully. She saw there was a card, which she opened and read
aloud in her childish voice. "To my sweet Sára, from Aunt Anna."

When she saw the doll, the smile that spread across her face
was the best gift I could have had. It's a memory I'll always treasure. She clutched the doll to her heart and sat down beside me.
"Thank you, Auntie," she said, hugging me and then the doll.

She sat that way for a while, and I asked why she wasn't playing with her.

"I am," she insisted. "I'm telling her how much I love her."

I was so moved by her innocence and sweetness that tears
welled up in my eyes. Though the day I purchased the doll was
ruined by my encounter with poor Péter after being expelled
from the university, this made up for it a hundredfold.

She and I played together for a while until I left for my parents' home with my brothers, catching up on the latest news
and gossip.

"Can you believe that my own father-in-law would send the police to harass me over hiring a man who doesn't have a party card?" Míhály grumbled.

It was outrageous, and I said so. In my mind there was only one word for that man, and that was bastard. He'd taken our family property and now was forcing my brother to act against his will. What kind of man did such things? A heartless and cruel one.

"Why should I hire a blasted communist, when I'm not one?" Míhály complained.

"You will be soon if you want to keep working," said Gyula. "I had to pick up my card last week. That or get fired!"

"You can't be serious," Pista said. "You are a communist now?"

"Easy for you to talk. You don't have four children who need food three times a day." Lászlo and Gyula jumped on Pista for not understanding their plight.

"But not you, sister," Pista said, turning to me.

I glanced away. "No, not me." I couldn't let him know that I'd actually been contemplating such a thought. The temptation of the job with Sam Grunewald's film company was still dangling out there. What a different life I would have.

"Yes, yes," our two brothers chimed in, "neither of you know what you are talking about. That's because neither of you have any problems."

At that, Pista and I exchanged an arched glance. Together we answered. "You are right, we have no problems."

———•———

Of the six siblings, Pista and I were the only ones unattached and so spent a great deal of time together over the holiday. In our walks along the snow-laden lanes, we shared numerous secrets. This Christmas, I had one other goal: to dissuade him from placing himself into the eye of danger by continuing to work with the underground, despite my support of their efforts.

On one such morning, we walked down Poplar Avenue away from the house. The frozen snow cracked beneath our feet. Two black crows sat on a branch. Ever lively, Pista picked up some snow, packed it tightly, and launched a snowball at the crows. The birds took flight, complaining noisily as they flapped their dark wings and disappeared into the wintry, gray sky.

"How long before they catch you, Pista?" I asked.

"I don't know, Anna. Three months, maybe four. If I'm lucky, maybe more."

I hadn't expected such a frank response, and it frightened me. With great concern, I asked if he fully understood the ramifications of being arrested and imprisoned by the AVO and what that would do to our parents. He shrugged.

I tried another tack. "Have you thought of escaping from here and going to the new world, brother? You are young and have a long time to live, if you aren't foolhardy."

"Listen to you. Someone so young and already you've lost your idealism? You sound like our parents."

I boxed his arm. "I don't want you hurt or killed."

"We can't all run away. To save one's own life isn't always the answer to the problems we need to solve."

"If you're in prison for life, that won't solve anything either, will it?"

"No. All I know is that I must keep doing what I'm doing. What about you? You've got the AVO on your back. Does Stephen know?"

"Yes, he knows."

"What does he suggest you do?"

It took me a moment to answer. "He hasn't suggested anything other than to play along." Hearing myself say those words aloud confused me. I'd thought them and yet had made excuses. What *was* he thinking? He'd saved so many people. Why hadn't he at least spoken to me about the possibility of saving me? I didn't want to think that it was a reflection of how little I meant to him.

"What do you mean he hasn't said anything? Doesn't he know what the AVO does to women? They make them suffer all manner of humiliation—"

"You don't need to tell me; I've heard."

I cut the walk short, saying that I didn't feel well.

On Christmas Day, I placed a few gifts I'd brought on the table. At that time in Hungary, Christmas was strictly a religious holiday, not a commercial one. Most people did not exchange gifts. Only children received a present or two. Most of them Stephen had bought at the American PX in Vienna and insisted I give to my family. They were small luxuries like coffee, cocoa, chocolate bars, vanilla, and saffron, all virtually impossible to get at the time. He also sent several cartons of cigarettes, which in those days cost a small fortune and were a big hit. I also gave my father a pipe, the kind he liked but could not buy in Nagykörös. After opening his present, he puffed away contentedly, an image I carried with me in the difficult time that was to come.

Only my mother looked sad time and again. I wondered if she was feeling ill, but she claimed that she wasn't.

Christmas Day found Stephen in Robin's car about to embark on a trip to Vienna to fulfill his promise to Vilmos Juhász, who, along with his eldest son Feri, had found a way out of Hungary with the help of the Jesuits. The previous day, Stephen had helped Mrs. Juhász and the other two sons, and now was about to transport Vilmos's daughter-in-law Gizella and her two young children out of the country. One was a two-year-old and the other a baby of only nine months.

Additionally, he was taking an older woman, a Mrs. Szláv with a complicated history. Her daughter had been the mistress of a powerful publisher, and when she left to marry a cousin from England, he accused the mother of having engineered this marriage and even threatened that he would have her arrested. Stephen wasn't certain this would come to pass, but these days, anything was possible.

He knew he was taking a rather big risk. If ever he'd needed luck it was this time, because of the young children. There was no telling what they might do.

He took off sometime in the early afternoon. Though normally he restricted his illegal border crossings to nighttime, this day, reasoning there would be less supervision on the holiday, he chose daylight. On the way to pick up his passengers, the car developed a strange noise, but then it stopped, and he forgot about it.

His first stop was Gizella and the young children. They piled in with only a few belongings. Gizella's face was tear-stained. Her eyes clung to the house where she and her family had lived, a place she couldn't have imagined leaving as little as a few months earlier. Stephen could feel her deep sadness, and it upset him to see her so forlorn.

His greatest concern, however, resided in getting them to safety, and this relied on keeping the two young children quiet. She told him that before they reached the border she would administer sleeping pills to them. It wouldn't be a bad idea for Gizella and Mrs. Szláv to do the same, he thought, knowing there was always the possibility that someone would panic.

A short time later, the elderly woman joined them, recoiling at the mere sight of the babies. "What if they scream at the border? We'll all be caught!"

Stephen explained the plan, but as they drove, she continued on about it until Stephen warned her to stop. "There's nothing to be gained by this behavior. So unless you want to get out, I need you to behave respectfully toward Mrs. Juhász. If I'm not worrying about it, neither should you."

She grunted and turned her face toward the window. They'd come to the outskirts of Budapest. Stephen had come to know that often at this point, people reacted differently to this journey. Some cried, some were completely silent, lost in their thoughts or refusing to acknowledge their circumstances, others blabbered on, angry or simply nervous and taking it out on the people in the vehicle.

Stephen had a few well calculated spots along the way where he usually changed the position of the "cargo" in his car. By the time he ushered everyone into the large trunk of the vehicle, the babies had received their medication and appeared fully asleep. There was some arranging and re-arranging before they were settled in the trunk where it was cold and dark and the surface hard and uncomfortable.

Everything went smoothly until shortly after they left the last town before the border. A loud bang and the sudden sliding motion of the car elicited several shrieks from the two women. "Quiet!" Stephen barked as he brought the car to a halt alongside the road not more than a hundred meters from the customs checkpoint. "Let me see what's going on."

He jumped out. A flat tire. "Damn!" In a low voice he quickly explained the situation to his passengers and reassured them that all would be well, despite the fact that four guards were advancing toward the vehicle.

The noise had obviously prompted them to investigate what was going on. Just before they arrived Stephen cautioned the women to remain absolutely still. He was as prepared for such a situation as one could be, but he could never count on how others would react. Nevertheless, he felt more irritated than nervous.

Within moments, the men had reached the car. Stephen greeted them, one of whom recognized him. "Ah, Mr. Koczak, what seems to be the trouble?" Then noticing the problem he said, "We'll fix that in no time. Just give us the jack."

"I'm afraid I've borrowed this car from a friend, and he forgot to give me the key to the trunk." He shrugged helplessly. "I do have a spare in the backseat though." Stephen had the forethought to always place a tire there for an occasion like this.

They looked inside and pulled out the spare. "Don't worry. We'll get a jack from town," the guard said pointing in the direction from which Stephen had just come. One of the men ran back to the border station, jumped on a bicycle, and rolled speedily toward the village.

An icy wind blew over the Austrian mountains and swept across the land. Stephen, well aware that much hinged on his ability to act nonchalant, lifted a bottle of cognac from the front seat and offered it to the remaining three men. "Sorry, I have no glasses."

One of them laughed. "So much the better. This way no one will see how much we drink. You first, sir."

Stephen drank from the bottle then wiped it clean and handed it to the next man. The bottle went around a few times, Stephen taking care to allow very little alcohol into his mouth. He refrained from gazing at the back of the car; he could only pray that the trunk remained soundless. By the time the fourth guard returned on his bicycle, they shouted, "Hurray," obviously feeling the effects of the cognac.

Stephen glanced at his watch. Over half an hour had passed. He couldn't help but worry how the women and two children were holding out. Soon enough though the man returned, the guards exchanged the tires, and on Stephen's way through the guard station, one of the men handed him a cup of steaming coffee. "You can bring us the cup on your return."

There was some relief in having made it through this checkpoint, but there was still the heavily patrolled crossing at the Austrian border, after which he would stop at a safe distance to release the passengers from the trunk. He thought about the many times over the past seventeen months that he'd faced this ordeal. His confidence had grown with each crossing, but one could never fully relax. There was always the unexpected, as there had been that day.

He'd learned, however, that guards varied tremendously, from those who were suspicious, cautious, and alert to those who gave his documents only a cursory glance. He imagined the guards, like the people in Hungary, fell into several camps: those who were staunch Communists, those who for the sake of their jobs went along with the regime, and those who lay somewhere in between. The problem was he could ever know which of the three he'd encounter.

Eventually they made it to Vienna, and he deposited the two women and two babies at the Press Club, where he always stayed. He was greatly relieved to be rid of Mrs. Szláv, and began to relax. As he often did, he joined a group of reporters who bombarded him with questions about Cardinal Mindszenty. Is he in danger? Will he be arrested? If so, when? What will happen then?

That night, their questions annoyed him. He'd come to know the Cardinal and not only respected but liked him. He was deeply concerned about his welfare and felt frustrated there was nothing he could do. He wished the United States would take a more aggressive stance, but that was unlikely. His answer was curt: "I imagine it is only a matter of days until he is arrested."

"How do you know? What information do you have?"

"You don't need information. Just use your brains, your eyes, and ears. That is what I do."

———— ◆ ————

On the morning after Christmas, when I was about to leave, my mother burst into tears. She hugged me as if she would never let me go. "I will never see you again," she cried aloud to the consternation of our entire family.

234

"Mother, I will come home in a few weeks, all right? Of course you will see me," I said, trying to reassure her.

My mother heaved a trembling sigh and dried her tears. She held me at arms' length and took a good look at me then embraced me once more and kissed me good-bye.

Though my mother's outburst upset me, once I was ensconced in my seat on the train, my thoughts turned to Stephen, and all my misgivings about him disappeared. I simply couldn't wait to spend the rest of the day and evening with him.

———◦———

That same morning Stephen started back to Budapest. At the border, two of the men who had helped him fix his car were on duty. Stephen returned the cup, and in the process, one of the guards tilted his head slightly and aimed his eyes in the direction of an attractive woman. "Be careful," he whispered. "That girl over there, she's from the AVO. She's here to keep tabs on you."

Stephen gave him a nod of thanks. Only moments later, the young woman approached Stephen with a bright smile. "Are you on your way to Budapest?" He nodded. "I missed my ride, a misunderstanding, I'm afraid. Would you be kind enough to take me back?"

Stephen felt the guards watching him as he formulated an answer. "It would be my pleasure. I'd love some company, especially with an attractive woman." A few minutes later, they were on the road, taking a route that passed through Ezstergom. Originally, he'd thought he might stop to see the Cardinal, but now that was impossible. Still, he decided to stick to his initial plan.

As they drove through the town, on nearly every street corner, police stood menacingly beside their motorcycles. He turned to the woman and asked her what was going on. "Is there a procession today?"

She shook her head. "I don't know."

The answer became apparent when he saw three, large American Hudsons followed by a dozen police on motorcycles. There was only one government agency that used these expensive cars in Hungary—the Ministry of the Interior.

Stephen slowed the car to watch them make their way into town. Turning to the young woman, he declared, "The AVO. They are going to arrest the Primate of Hungary."

Her eyes grew wide. "How do you know?"

"What else would they be doing here?"

After dropping her off at the Nemzeti National Theater in Budapest, where presumably someone was meeting her, Stephen sped off to the Legation, where a number of his colleagues awaited him. He had not been mistaken. The Cardinal had been arrested and taken to 60 Andrássy Street. They gathered in a meeting room to discuss the situation.

I arrived back at the apartment at two o'clock in the afternoon as I'd promised. The chill in the air indicated Stephen hadn't been home for some time, so I made a fire to create an inviting atmosphere.

On a tray, I arranged baked goods I'd brought from home, humming to myself in anticipation of Stephen's arrival. The clock struck three, and I washed my face and arranged my hair. To keep busy and push away the fear that he was once again detained, I began to tidy the apartment.

It was dark by the time the telephone rang and shook me out of my thoughts. Part of me worried about picking up the phone for fear that it would be Lászlo, not Stephen explaining what was holding him up. I had convinced myself that he would be home at any moment. My fingers touched the receiver, debating whether to answer, when the ringing abruptly stopped.

I went to the window and glanced outside. Nothing but bar-ren tree branches, an empty street, and the streetlight that shone into the window. I drew the curtains closed and turned off the lamps. Now there was nothing but the dim light from the stove. I kept the fire burning as I waited for the key to turn in the lock, for the steps to sound in the hallway, for the door to open and close, for a hand to touch mine, for a voice to welcome me back.

Long ago Christmases visited me in my solitude. Those before the war had been full of joy, laughter, candlelight, trees decorated with candies, and the scent of home-baked cookies and honey cake mingled with fresh pine.

As I waited for his footsteps, I couldn't forestall thoughts about what would happen when, at some point, he finally went away, and I would be left behind. Would there be Christmases in the future? In this dark mood, thoughts of László and the AVO hovered around me in the silent room.

It was almost midnight when Stephen arrived home. Only when he entered did he remember that he'd promised to celebrate Christmas with me today. His mood was anything but festive.

"Why are you sitting on the floor, Anna?" he asked, lowering himself to the floor next to me. But I had neither the energy to move or answer. He stretched out on the floor and put his head in my lap. I could see that he looked tired and anxious. He made a subtle reference to his activities the previous night. As always, I couldn't help but forgive him and feel admiration for the danger he continued to place himself in.

"They arrested Cardinal Mindszenty today." His tone carried sorrow and defeat. "I was coming back from Vienna. On the road just outside Esztergom, I saw the AVO cars pass me. I knew they were going for him, and there was nothing I could do."

What we had predicted for so long had come to pass. What could I say? At least now I knew where he'd been and why he had been detained, though the reason for it couldn't have been worse. I began to stroke his face.

"Don't stop," he said.

"But my hands are rough, not soft," I said.

"Your hands are strong and warm and reliable. I love the touch of them." He took my fingers and kissed them then placed my hands back along the side of his face.

We were silent for a long time. I wanted to ask a multitude of questions about the Cardinal's arrest and what would happen now, but I didn't want to disturb the moment, nor did I want to remind him of the day's events. Eventually, I told him to go to bed. "I'll turn down the covers for you."

As I went about my task, he asked me, "Why do you sometimes sleep in your room upstairs? Aren't you afraid? I don't like you being up there alone. You know I've asked you not to go up there at night."

"I'm not afraid." I gave him a kindly look. "Good night, Mr. Koczak."

The Hungarian state-controlled papers and radio news were filled with the Cardinal's arrest, calling him a traitor, an American collaborator, a bad influence on the country, an enemy of the people. Twelve other persons were also arrested, accused with collaboration. Three of them were priests, the other nine lay people.

However, just before the Cardinal saw that he was about to be arrested, he had written a short note to his priests, to the church, and to his countrymen, and word of it circulated. The note read as follows:

> I did not take part in any conspiracy. I will not resign my office as Archbishop. I have nothing to admit and will not sign anything.
>
> And if I do, that will only be the result of the human body's frailty and I declare in advance that it is "nothing—and invalid."

This event shook our country from one end to the other. Though the Western world carried the news, their outrage seemed to end there. Even the Pope in Rome did nothing. It was our hope that the Americans, the French, the British, and others would send help in the form of soldiers to liberate this innocent man.

It was anticipated that some of those who had been arrested would be turned into key witnesses against the Cardinal. The American Legation officials, particularly Minister Chapin and Stephen, were named as having conspiratorial dealings with the Cardinal, which of course, in some sense, was true.

An atmosphere of fear permeated the city, and it threw fresh light on my own precarious situation. It suddenly became far more likely that as Stephen's housekeeper, I might be called to condemn him and reveal anything I knew about Stephen's illegal activities. Claiming ignorance was little deterrence to the AVO's ability to garner information, as evidenced by Father Zakár's torture in which he divulged everything he knew and everything he didn't. This likely included Stephen's offer to smuggle Father Zakár out of the country and his frequent meetings with Stephen, in which he passed on sensitive information about Hungary's political and economic dealings, material Stephen had turned over to Minister Chapin.

———— ❖ ————

Stephen's anxiety had ratcheted up considerably, and he insisted I stay in his guest room. "I don't want anything happening to you in the middle of the night. They can't arrest you here, you know that. I have no control over what happens to you outside this apartment, so at least do me the favor of listening to me about this. All right?"

I agreed, though he and I both knew there was little he could do about my pending date with Lászlo on New Year's Eve. Several times, I considered feigning illness, but I knew this would hardly spell the end of my dealings with Lászlo or the AVO; in fact, it might worsen my situation.

————— ◆ —————

On the afternoon of New Year's Eve, I moved about the apartment, dreading and resenting the evening. I was resentful, because it meant I couldn't spend it with Stephen. A bouquet of fourteen roses was delivered to the apartment. Seven yellow and seven red. With a look of disgust, Stephen handed me the accompanying card which read: "For the fourteen lovely Sundays you've spent with me. Love, Laci."

After reading the note, I had the urge to sweep the roses off the table.

With knitted brow, Stephen asked, "When are you coming home tonight?"

"I don't know, but I'm going to try to make it soon after midnight."

"Please, please be careful," he said, wearing an intense look of concern. He explained that if anything happened, I should contact him at the Legation where he was duty officer until midnight. He planned to come home immediately thereafter.

My weakness for roses didn't allow me to throw them away quite yet, and so I took them upstairs to my room and studied them, wondering if Lászlo had sent them at the prompting of his heart or for purely professional reasons. I wanted to believe he wouldn't go through with his assignment because he cared. And sometimes, I even felt sorry for him. His was an unnerving job, just as for me it was an unnerving game. The stakes for both of us were high.

Whatever he had to do, time was running out, and I worried that tonight he might strike. I had to be more vigilant than ever. After all, he'd insisted I take a drink. Unlike in the past, I was filled with anxiety.

From the closet, I pulled out my new, black lace dress lined with silk. My arms and shoulders remained visible through the lace, which I thought made me look more glamorous. I wanted to disarm László, to make him think I had fallen for him. Looking in the mirror, I felt pleased. Too, I liked appearing more sophisticated and worldly than I was. As a finishing touch, I pinned one of the yellow roses onto my dress.

László picked me up in a taxi, something he rarely did. He explained that he wanted to protect my feet from the freezing cold and that because a taxi would be difficult to get after midnight, he wanted to spoil me now. Without taxi service, we'd be taking the subway.

He'd hardly finished talking when the taxi stopped before a door that bore neither sign nor appeared to lead to a restaurant. Though I couldn't help wondering where he might be taking me, being on a charming street called Hunyadi Square, I couldn't imagine he had any sinister intentions. Hunyadi is wedged between Chengery and Vörösmarty Streets, not far from my uncle's former apartment.

As it turned out, a small sign I'd failed to notice announced the name of the restaurant: "Vörösmarty," after the Hungarian writer. We entered a large, tastefully decorated room with a fountain at its center. Splashing with water, the fountain threw subdued lights the color of the rainbow about the room. It was sexy and alluring, if one can call a place that. Tables circled the dance floor. It seemed to me the place was filled to capacity with happy, well-dressed, young people in love.

As we crossed the floor, for a split-second I actually felt flattered to be on the arm of such a handsome, attentive man, a man dozens of women would have vied for. If only I misjudged him, or that despite orders from the AVO, his ever present affection was driven by his heart. A strange thought flashed through my mind: am I in love with the wrong man? If I submitted to László, would he actually have the stomach to turn me in? Taking in a deep breath, I reprimanded myself for this weak moment and reminded myself that this was precisely what the AVO counted on. *Be on your toes, Anna*, I thought.

The maitre'd arrived and escorted us to a table for two in a private niche, from which we had an excellent view of the rest of the room. Candlelight flickered across a vase containing a red rose and a yellow one, something that, of course, László had arranged. It seemed he was sparing no expense, and it gave me pause.

The people at the surrounding tables were elegantly dressed, and no one seemed older than thirty-five. I enjoyed watching them and overhearing snatches of conversation as we engaged in idle chit chat. I only wished the circumstances of my being here were different—that I might be sitting beside someone I loved and who loved me in return, not an AVO agent with whom I was playing a cat and mouse game of charades. I wished I could simply be honest with László and challenge the work he was doing. There were so many things I wanted to say.

He brought me back to the present when I heard him ask me whether I liked the work I did. It was a stupid question, and I wanted to tell him so, but instead I said, "No I don't, but there's not much choice for me at this point."

He leaned toward me, his one arm on the table, and his gaze fixed on me. "Of course there is, Anna. There are branches of the government that would send you back to school if you chose to work for them."

I was tempted to say, "Like the AVO?" just to see his reaction, but I reined myself in. "I should look into it, I suppose. Perhaps you can help me with it?"

"Yes, perhaps I can," he said, though his eyes shifted away from me and toward the couples dancing. Following his gaze, I suggested that we join them. As we danced to the lively music, for a time I got caught up in the festive mood and tried to forget who I was with.

Back at the table, he asked about my father and what he had done before the war. It seemed like an innocent question, and so I told him about the vineyard and the orchard, and the horses my father raised for the army. "Horses that have to pull heavy artillery," I explained. "We had a cooperative with two other families near Szolnok by the Tisza River. That's where the horses were raised." Just speaking of it brought images of my youth to mind. "I went there with my father at foaling time. I loved seeing the little foals getting up on their wobbly legs for the first time, and sometimes, I'd run with them."

"Did you learn to harness them?"

"No, we never did. The army trained them. I loved them to run free."

"You are like a filly yourself," he said. "Now I can see where it comes from." He paused, stopping to think for a moment. Then he reached for something in his pocket and pulled out a small gift-wrapped box, which he placed before me. "Perhaps I can harness you with this." He smiled. "Open it."

I untied the ribbon and opened the box slowly. Inside was a delicate gold chain necklace with an unusual amber and gold pendant. The amber head of a cat was encircled in a frame of gold. "It's lovely, Laci, I'm so surprised, I don't know what to say."

"Don't say anything, just give me a kiss," he said. "Here, I'll put it around your neck." I turned so he could fasten it. His hands rubbed against my flesh, and I almost imagined that he was trembling. When he finished, he sat back and admired the effect of his gift. "The amber matches the color of your eyes. You look absolutely stunning. Perfect. Perfect."

Under normal circumstances such a present on such a night after several months of courtship could be expected to lead to something more serious. Of course, I knew what László wanted in return and what I would refuse to give him.

Though he'd been drinking, while I'd been having raspberry soda, after giving me the present, he began to drink more heavily.

After the waiter delivered yet one more drink, he lifted his glass and said, "I claim your promise to have a glass of wine with me."

I smiled. "So be it. A glass of wine to bring in the New Year!"

A few minutes later, the waiter headed toward us. When he was within a couple of feet of our table, László abruptly stood up and, with his back to me, took the tray from the waiter's hands. In that same moment, I had the sudden impulse to reach behind my neck and open the clasp of my new necklace, careful to allow the chain to remain where it was. It was an instinctual movement, strange even in hindsight.

László set down one of the glasses before me and held the other in his hand as if to make a toast. I reached to pick up my glass when I noticed several bubbles rising to the top. The fortune teller's words came hurtling back to me. With a slight shrug, the necklace slid off my shoulders and onto the floor, making a slight pinging sound when it hit. "Oh dear, my necklace," I said, dropping my gaze to the floor. "It fell down."

No sooner had László bent over in search of the necklace than my hand shot out and I switched our two glasses. Of course, it was possible the drink was perfectly safe, but if so, then no harm had been done. László straightened, holding the necklace in his outstretched hand. "Let me put it back on. This time I'll make sure it's closed properly." He fiddled with it a moment. "There, done."

He returned to his chair. Raising his glass, he said, "To our love, Anna."

"That all our wishes might come true," I added, then took a long, slow drink.

I felt him watching me, and only after I'd taken a sip did he drink his. With a smile and his eyes closed to savor the moment, he drank. Fearing the loss of my sensibilities, I tilted my glass and let the remainder of the wine pour down the front of my dress, which, fortunately being black, did not show the stain. By the time László had drained his glass and opened his eyes, my empty wine glass stood on the table.

"The wine, it had a strange taste," I said and lifted the glass of water to my lips, clumsily tipping it so that the water fell on my dress in roughly the same place as the wine had.

László seemed strangely delighted. "Oh, Anna," he said laughing, "don't tell me the wine has gone to your head." He leaned over and wiped my dress with a large white napkin.

Only a few minutes later, he announced that we should get going. There was an urgent note in his voice. "Let's go. I'll get your coat." When he stood up, he seemed slightly unsteady on his feet, and after he'd retrieved my coat and was buttoning it for me, his eyes briefly lost focus. When they returned to normal, there was an animal lust in them I'd never seen before, and it frightened me.

The clinking of glasses and cheering indicated that 1949 had begun.

January 1949

It was cold outside as László and I made our way to the subway station. His grip was strong and he held me tightly as we wound our way down the stairs. At once, I noticed that he was moving toward the platform for trains going in the opposite direction of where I lived. "You are taking us the wrong way, Laci."

"I am not," he said forcefully. "I'm taking you the right way. I am going to teach you how to love," he added in a strange, crude voice. He was either very drunk or under the influence of whatever it was that he'd placed in my glass. His hand encircled my arm in a vise-like grip.

I glanced around, searching for a way out. The platform was crowded with late night revelers, many of them tipsy, loud, and pushy. When the train blasted into the station, everyone swarmed toward the doors. Clutching my hand, László pushed through the throng of people. He fought to get into the car. I tried to pull away from his grasp without success. People were shoving and jostling to enter the train. The mob squeezed from all sides, and for an instant, his grip loosened just enough for me to slip my hand out of his. I took a step back and allowed myself to be swallowed by the crowd.

I heard the car doors sigh as they closed. The train took off, and I was fairly certain László had gone with it. Nevertheless, I bounded off, running up a set of stairs and then down the other side to catch the train home. The train arrived within seconds, and I jumped on it as if the devil himself were chasing me.

Finally in my seat, I caught my breath. Only then did I realize he might find a taxi and come after me. He would know I was headed to my apartment. My hope was that he was in no shape to go anywhere, since he'd had much to drink and even more so if the wine had been combined with a mind-altering drug. I said a prayer to that effect.

Soon enough, the train came to halt in my station. On exiting, I glanced around, still half-expecting to see him, but he wasn't there. I ran up the steps and started for home. Barely a few dozen feet into my flight, I slipped and almost fell on the sidewalk, which had grown icy and treacherous for someone wearing heels. Rather than risk injury, I took my high heels off and ran several blocks on the frigid snow and ice to reach home.

Chattering by the time I entered the apartment building, I wanted nothing more than to get into my bed to warm my frozen feet. My thoughts turned to Stephen, who I imagined might have gone out after he was off duty to celebrate the New Year with Joan or other friends. And yet, what was there to be joyous about?

The light was on when I walked into the apartment. Stephen took one look at my bedraggled appearance and came over to me. "What on earth happened to you?" He took my coat off and threw it on a chair. "Come sit next to me. I'll warm you up." With his arm around my waist, he began to walk me to his bed.

"No, Stephen, I just want to go to my bed and sleep," I said, though part of me wanted to do exactly the opposite. I desperately wanted someone to take care of me.

Probably thinking I was being chaste, he said, "I only want to hold you to take the chill off. Now take off those wet clothes and tell me what happened." He turned the light off, and I removed my stockings and necklace and slid under the covers. Solicitous and kind, Stephen pulled me into his embrace and waited until I'd defrosted enough to talk.

Once I began, the words poured out, and I continued until I'd told him the entire story. "So you think he was trying to drug you?"

"I'm almost certain of it. After he drank the wine, he seemed to lose all common sense and became unusually aggressive. I'm sure he thought the drug would soon take effect and make it easy to get me to his apartment."

Stephen grew quiet and said nothing for some time. I was exhausted, my nerves frayed. A drowsy feeling overcame me. Only half-awake, I felt Stephen's hand floating ever so gently over my body. "It is partly my fault, my poor little mouse. I should have known. These people are beasts." It wasn't long before Stephen fell asleep.

By the time I stole out of his room and went to my own bed, it was almost dawn. Though I thought I'd instantly fall asleep, I didn't. I got up and built a fire in the stove to warm up the chilly room. The events of the last few hours swirled around in my head. Extending my hands for warmth, I realized that the danger that until tonight had remained abstract was now exceedingly real. I'd seen something new in László's eyes, a shade of cruelty I had never noticed. From now on, I sensed he might have to resort to less genteel, less civilized methods to do his job. He would have to; he had no alternative if he wanted to keep his job—and perhaps even his life.

The sound of the buzzer startled me out of my thoughts. It was morning. I went into the kitchen to prepare breakfast, imagining that working would help get my mind onto other things. Stephen asked me to sit down with him and repeat my story. He wanted to get all the facts right, he said. I think he also wanted to be clear that I hadn't exaggerated, that I hadn't in fact had too much to drink. By the time I concluded relaying my experience for the second time, he seemed assured events of the previous night were just as I'd said.

As he finished mopping up the egg on his plate, in a light tone, he said, "I had a strange dream last night. A lovely girl came to me, but when the clock struck, six she disappeared." He arched his brow in a dramatic way, and then pulled something out from behind him. It was one of my shoes. "She left this slipper. Try it on; maybe it fits you."

I got up, but instead of putting my foot into the still soggy shoe, I went to his bedroom. When I returned, I showed him the necklace László had given me. "I suppose this was part of what should have lured me into his bed. Maybe it would even be evidence I had spent the night with him." I grew somber again. "What shall I do?" I asked. "I'm sure he'll be calling to see me again, and I'm afraid to go."

Without even thinking, Stephen told me to call him before he had a chance to call. "You should be sweet and ask him what happened. Tell him you're not even sure how you made it home." He handed me the phone. "Call him right now. Here, with me listening."

I took a moment to compose myself, and then I dialed his number. He picked up after several rings, and though his voice sounded groggy, when he realized it was me, he seemed to grow alert. "It's you," he said.

"Yes, I'm so glad you're home. I was worried about you. I don't understand how we got separated. We were waiting for the train, then somehow you got on and I didn't. I waited for quite some time. At least, I think I did."

"Why would you wait for me?" I could hear suspicion in his voice.

"Well, I thought you'd come back for me," I said. "Then I felt dizzy and groggy, and decided I'd better get home. I woke up a short time ago with a terrible headache. It must have been the wine. See, that's why I don't drink."

He surprised me a little when he told me with what sounded like complete sincerity that he loved me and insisted I see him the following night, Sunday, since it was the day we always spent together. I didn't know what to do but to agree. I looked help-lessly at Stephen.

After we hung up, I turned to him. "I don't want to go with him. If this is how the year begins, what will the rest bring?"

"I don't know. None of us can know exactly, but maybe it's a new beginning."

I couldn't quite believe what he was saying.

"Yes," I said, "a bad beginning."

The following day, on January 2, Lászlo picked me up at four o'clock to go skating on the lake in Park Városliget, near the apartment. We both enjoyed ice skating, and it was an activity that necessitated little eye contact. After what had happened the previous night, I had the sense that looking one another in the eye might be difficult for us both.

Though the air was quite chilly, it was perfect for skating, and after about half an hour had gone by, the exercise loosened us up, and we even enjoyed ourselves—at least as much as was possible under such circumstances. Another hour passed, and he took me to dine at a small restaurant called The Black Gander—Fekete Gúnár—on the nearby Dózsa György Street. The restaurant was a small, relaxed place where they only served soup and dessert. We ordered Gulyás soup and apple strudel. No wine for either of us.

Perhaps to sidestep events of New Year's Eve, he asked whether I knew that the Cardinal had been arrested.

"Of course I know. We prayed for him in church today and also for his accusers."

He seemed surprised. "Why would you pray for them?"

"They need more prayers than the Cardinal does to enter St. Péter's pearly gates," I said, giving him a stern look. Then I turned to the topic I was sure he would rather forget. "I'm sorry about what happened the other night. I am glad you're all right."

He seemed to be groping for a response, his eyes searching mine before he answered. "I don't know how I feel about it. Have you ever felt angry and glad at the same time after you've done something stupid, like I did the other night?"

I briefly wondered if he was about to confess, but then he continued, admitting only that he'd had *one* too many glasses of wine.

"Yes, I know what it's like to do something you regret," I said sympathetically. Then, noticing that his face suddenly looked very tired, I added, "You look ill. Are you not feeling well?"

"I do have a headache," he said. He tried to make light of it. "Don't worry; it's all right. I'm glad you agreed to go out with me."

I suggested that we finish dinner and afterward he should take a taxi home. The cab dropped me off first, and we parted after he'd asked to see me again in a week.

Though I was glad he hadn't questioned me about the events of that night, I did think that I hadn't heard the last of it, which clouded my mind with worry about what he would ask at some point in the future.

When I told Stephen that László hadn't said much about the incident, he said he thought it was a good sign. "Most likely, he cannot remember a thing, and you should relax." Many of Stephen's opinions I agreed with, and often, he turned out to be right. But about this, I was fairly certain Stephen was wrong.

———————⊷•⊶———————

It was hard to believe that in 1949 I would continue seeing László as I had in 1948, but so it seemed. I don't recall seeing much of Stephen in the intervening week, mostly because Minister Chapin kept him busy preparing the American Legation's response to the arrest of Cardinal Mindszenty. And when he was around it seemed that his mind was far away on other matters so I left him alone.

As for news of the Cardinal, the Hungarian press was quiet, as if nothing had happened. In fact, this was when Mindszenty was being interrogated, drugged, and tortured; he was being prepared for his show trial.

January 9, 1949

László invited me to attend an art exhibit of Mária Blasko's paintings. Her name was familiar to me, because of the terrible story Stephen had told me back in June, when Mária had witnessed police harassing a couple near the Buda castle—an incident which had led to the man's death. Though it was with László, I was excited to go.

The event was held in an elegant building just across from the Opera House. By the time we arrived, the place was already packed with people, many of them recognizable from photos in the social pages of the newspapers. László pointed out the artist, a woman who appeared to be in her mid to late forties. She was elegantly dressed in a loose, full-length, light gray dress enhanced by a floor-length silver and blue silk scarf.

Apparently, László knew quite a few people, and as we began to circulate, we got separated, which suited me perfectly. It gave me the freedom to browse the paintings at my own pace, observe the people—including László, and occasionally listen in on snatches of conversation.

I realized that I'd been to another exhibit of hers, but these paintings were new, or at least they hadn't been in the previous show. As I toured the rooms, I found myself enjoying the unique way in which she portrayed her subjects. There was something beautiful and sad about them. She had chosen to illustrate various aspects of the city—a market place, a street corner, a prison, an empty church, children playing in a street, the city in the various seasons and under a variety of weather conditions. The painting that made the greatest impression on me was the royal castle in the spring with a bright red Danube flowing beneath a damaged bridge. It elicited strong emotion in me. As I stood there gazing at it, my mind drifting in assorted directions, a man standing nearby said, "I wonder why the artist painted the Danube red." But I knew why, recalling the story Stephen had told me several months earlier, when she'd witnessed the police chasing a man to his death near the Castle of Buda.

I turned slightly to see who the man was and to whom he was speaking. To my great surprise, it was János Kádár, the Minister of the Interior—the man at the top of the pyramid of secret police and security agents. When I realized who it was, I wanted to shout at him. "Why do you think it's the color of blood? Isn't it obvious? And why can't you just leave me alone?"

Not far from me, a woman I recognized was whispering to another. She was Livia Barankovics, the wife of the head of the Democratic People's Party. It was tempting to move closer to hear what they were saying. Then fortune brought them to me as they wandered my way. "No, István is not here. I can't get him to go anywhere. He only steps out to places he absolutely has to. He worries all the time about being arrested."

I knew she was speaking of her husband.

"And you aren't afraid?" the other woman said.

"Of course I am, but I guess if they want me, they'll find me just as easily in my home as elsewhere."

The other woman laughed lightly. "How right you are. What a depressing thought."

When I glanced around for Lászlo, I found him leaning his head toward Mária Blasko and speaking to her in a friendly confidential manner. It caught me by surprise. She seemed a little too old for him, though she was a stylish woman and perhaps her notoriety appealed to him. I couldn't imagine there was anything else to it.

Later I heard a rumor that she was involved with Father József Jánosi, the Jesuit priest who Stephen had told me was a continual thorn in Barankovics's side. It turned out this was the primary reason for László's interest in Mária Blasko. She represented assurance that Father Jánosi would testify against the Cardinal. If he refused, the government would simply expose the fact that he was having an affair with her, which would ruin him even if it was not really true.

A short while later László and I left for an oriental restaurant that had just opened in the heart of the city not far from the exhibit. I felt the dinner was strained and that he'd looked at me strangely throughout the evening, though why I had no idea. In any case, I was glad when he deposited me back at the apartment. This "courtship" had gone on far too long and had become too stressful. What could I do to bring it to an end?

January 13

With all the turmoil, I often wished I could speak to my parents, but it would only have worried them. This produced a deep sense of loneliness that sometimes held me in its grip for an entire day or two. More than once, the notion that I couldn't go home brought to mind my mother's tearful good-bye at Christmas.

One such day, I was watching the snow float to earth in huge flakes. In a short period of time, it enveloped the streets, the roofs of houses, and the trees. I reached for my coat and went for a walk to the park. There I thought of Dr. Karl Német and how his blindness had locked him inside of himself like a windowless room. I wished very much that I could speak with him and his wife Margo. They had been a source of great comfort.

What would he say if I told him I was in love with Stephen? I gave it some thought and decided he would tell me that we cannot force others to love us. Enjoy your love for him, he might say, and don't expect anything in return. Then you are safe, and you will survive. Don't hold him responsible for your love. He didn't ask you to love him, nor did he force you to, it is your own doing.

I suddenly felt Karl's presence walking beside me in the snow. Yes, Karl, it is my own doing.

"The facts, Anna, the truth, those are the essence of everything. Look for them, not for things that are transient and fleeting."

"My love won't die," I said aloud and heard a quiet laugh.

It startled me and I glanced around, but there wasn't a soul in sight. For a moment, looking behind me, I could have sworn there were two sets of tracks, but of course there weren't. Still, I know that Karl was there with me that day; his philosophical view of life gave me courage and insight as it always had.

When I arrived home, I saw Stephen's blue car parked nearby. Then I heard his voice calling me. He stood there holding a snowball aloft. Before I could make a move the white ball sliced through the air and struck me in the chest, right over my heart.

"I didn't hurt you, did I?" Stephen called out as he strode over to me. I shook my head. "When I saw you standing there, I felt like a school boy wanting to tease a girl I like. Are you warm enough?" he said placing an arm around me. I nodded yes. "Then let's go for a stroll."

I don't know what overcame him, but suddenly he was telling me things I longed to hear. "I'm walking beside you this time, not ahead of you. That's where I always want to walk. Do you believe me, Anna? Do you feel the same way? That you would like to walk with me always? Shoulder to shoulder as you once said?"

"Yes," I said, elated and waiting for a kiss.

Stephen caressed my face instead and suggested we go home. "Your hair is soaked. We need a hot drink. We don't want to catch a cold. And don't ever forget what we talked about. I mean it, and I hope you did too."

When we turned onto our street, he let go of my hand. I knew there were places and situations where we still had to walk alone.

The following morning, an ice storm raged outside. In Hungarian, it's referred to as "lead rain," because it pulls everything down with its weight. The branches were breaking off the trees and the streets were virtually impassable.

Stephen was irritable and moody, because he couldn't find his gloves. He criticized me for not being orderly on a consistent basis.

"You put them on the heater in the library to dry last night," I said and went and retrieved them for him. He took them without a word of thanks and then left. I watched him go, angry and confused. How could he be so mercurial? What happened to all the precious things he'd said the day before? This side of his personality made me uneasy and insecure. Unpredictable, I concluded, exactly like the weather.

January 16, 1949

László and I went out dancing that Sunday. In the middle of a romantic tune, as we glided around the dance floor, he suddenly said, "Anna, you have never told me you love me. Is it because you really don't or something stops you from saying it? You know how I feel about you—tell me how you feel?" He pulled me so close that I could feel his muscular physique.

Answering this question was tricky. I knew I had to give him as truthful an answer as possible without seeming to reject him.

"Laci," I began slowly, "I know so little about you. Where you come from, what you are doing, where you are heading. I only know what I see. That you are handsome and nice to be with. I see you on Sundays, but for the rest of the week you are a stranger to me. I have no idea where you work and what you do."

"If you did know, would you love me?"

"That's an unfair question, Laci, and you know it. All I can say is that I could love you. Whether I would— that depends on knowing more about you." At that moment the clasp of my necklace opened and slipped off of my neck. László picked it up and placed it in his pocket.

Frowning, he said, "I will take it to have it fixed and bring it back to you next Sunday. By the way, I'd like to introduce you to some of my friends. Maybe they can persuade you to quit your job by offering you a better one."

I assumed he meant working for the secret police. On the heels of his declaration of love, was he at last planning to deliver me into the hands of the AVO? I didn't quite know what to say, and so, for lack of anything, better I smiled and said I looked forward to meeting his friends. Anxious thoughts swirled in my mind on our way home.

———◦———

During the week I grew increasingly nervous anticipating my next date with László. Meeting his friends felt laced with danger. Would they abduct me? Would they compromise me, imprison me? But a phone call from László saved me, at least temporarily. He said he wouldn't be able to see me that Sunday. He offered no further explanation, which again made me wonder what was going on.

———◦———

On Thursday, January 20, General Menshikov, one of the Russian envoy sent to oversee the Cardinal's trial, met with AVO officer Colonel Gyula Décsi to review Father Zakár's confession. Among the statements the priest provided voluntarily was the revelation that during one of Minister Chapin and Stephen's visits to Esztergom the Minister had suggested the Legation could be of assistance should the Cardinal decide to flee the country. If so, he should notify Minister Chapin through Stephen, who met regularly with Zakár.

Menshikov concocted a scheme in which one of the AVO agents would pretend to be a secret adherent of the Cardinal and would offer to smuggle out of prison any letter the Cardinal wished to have delivered to the Americans. He believed that this had strong potential because the imprisoned Cardinal was being drugged and, therefore, confused and suggestible. The agent would suggest that he ask the Americans to live up to their promise to rescue him.

Once the letter was written, the plan, Menshikov explained, was to have the AVO agent deliver the note to Minister Chapin at the Legation. Once the Americans developed a plan to rescue the Cardinal, Chapin would most likely have Stephen pass this information on to the agent, the supposed friend of the Cardinal, who would suggest they meet at some clandestine location, not at the Legation, in case he was being followed.

In fact, agents would be hidden at this location. They would photograph them and apprehend them. Though they would release Stephen, they would have photographs of him in the company of the supposed friend of the Cardinal. The agent would confess to the plot at once. This would provide just cause to have Stephen expelled, timed to occur after the press carried reports of the two men's apprehension and the agent's confession.

The agent would then appear as a most damning witness at the trial scheduled for February 3, less than two weeks away. Since the Cardinal would have to confirm that he wrote the letter from prison, everything else to which the agent confessed would appear to be true and done with the knowledge and support of the Americans. What a propaganda coup if all went well.

Sunday, January 23

By the time I came home from church, Stephen was gone. Since my meeting with László had been cancelled, I was free to do as I wished. I made plans to spend time reorganizing my room, something that helped clear my mind, and later spend a few hours with Julia and another friend discussing Julia's wedding.

While I was happy for Julia, her enthusiasm was in such contrast to my own turbulent state of mind that I couldn't get into the spirit of things and left feeling quite depressed and sad. She reminded me to see her father about the job we had discussed. "February 1 at ten o'clock in the morning, sharp," she chirped gaily.

Walking home, I distractedly thought about leaving Stephen's employ and wondered if that would solve some of my problems. I was so locked in my thoughts I hadn't noticed the route I was taking. At once, I realized that I was passing 60 Andrássy Street. It was as if an invisible net dropped over me, enclosing me in its web of fear and terror. I hurried my pace trying to shake the spine-chilling feeling.

I hoped that Stephen had returned from wherever he'd been, but he hadn't. Instead, he'd left me a note saying he was at the Legation office. While disappointed he wasn't home, I took pleasure in knowing he wasn't with Joan, who had recently returned from England after a long vacation.

After lighting a fire in the stove, I sat down at the desk to write a long letter to my parents. The words came pouring out. I related every imaginable thing except my love for Stephen and the situation with László. I told them how much I loved them and that I planned to visit soon.

On the same day, the agent posing as a friend to Cardinal Mindszenty brought him a crumpled sheet of paper and a pen. Managing to fool the Cardinal, and with some prompting, Mindszenty drafted the following letter to Minister Seldin Chapin:

> Mr. Minister,
>
> You must take action by Thursday and I request you to do so, for a death sentence is likely and the trial will be aimed against America. They want to prove that I was paid by America for secret information. Please send a car and an airplane. There is no other way out.
>
> With warmest regards,
> Mindszenty
>
> January 23

The text was sent to Moscow for approval. At the same time Ernő Szücs, also an agent, consulted with Péter Gábor, the head of the AVO, who informed Minister of the Interior János Kádár on the matter. Moscow decided that several more lines should be added.

The final letter included the following two postscripts:

> P.S. Please instruct Koczak immediately to meet the bearer of this letter today to discuss every detail.
>
> Mindszenty

> P.S. Please promise the pilot 4,000 dollars in the interest of the cause. I shall refund it.
>
> Mindszenty

AVO agent Jenő Marko was selected by Ernő Szücs to personally deliver the Cardinal's letter to Minister Chapin. Two days later, on January 25, Marko arrived at the Legation at ten o'clock in the morning and was surprised when he was told that Chapin was out of the country. Counselor Cochran, a recent arrival at the

Legation, had a policy of never receiving Hungarians personally and referred them to one of his subordinates. Marko was told if his message was confidential then he might see Stephen, who agreed to receive him.

In the meeting with Stephen, Marko claimed to be a man who delivered coal to Andrássy Street and carried it to the cells of prisoners for use in the stoves there. He explained that, for this reason, he could speak to those whom he trusted and had managed to tell the Cardinal that he was prepared to smuggle any message the Cardinal wished to anyone on the outside. The Cardinal then asked him to send a message to Minister Chapin. He handed the document to Stephen, who scanned the brief note.

Marko then explained to Stephen how he'd secretly given paper and pencil to the Cardinal to write a note. The Cardinal had completed only the first part when the guards were returning. Mindszenty wanted to write more but had to give the paper back before he could finish. Marko had smuggled the paper back out of the room, and later he'd carried a second sack of coal and returned with it, which was when the Cardinal added the first postscript. He had to return yet a third time to allow the Cardinal to write the second postscript.

Stephen observed Marko closely as he spoke and was certain that the man's account was false and that he very likely was an AVO agent. Stephen knew far too much about operations inside the prison from interviews he'd had with people who'd undergone interrogation and imprisonment there. He surmised that this was a plot of some sort to further establish the Cardinal's treasonous activities with the Americans.

He took a moment to think about how the Legation could turn this plot against the Hungarian puppet regime. He left the agent in his office and went to Cochran, proposing that the text of the letter be sent immediately to Washington and released there as an obvious scheme to entrap the Americans in an alleged plot with Cardinal Mindszenty.

Cochran, an overly cautious diplomat, wanted nothing to do with Stephen's proposal. "You should not have accepted the letter. I'm not going to accept it. Give it back to this man," he ordered.

When Stephen began arguing the merits of accepting it and denouncing it before the trial, Cochran left the room saying, "I don't want to hear another word. I'm sorry I heard this much. Give it back and don't talk to me about it again."

But Marko, astounded when Stephen sought to return the letter, refused, saying that he had endangered himself too much already, and did not dare leave the building with it. So far as he was concerned, he had delivered the Cardinal's letter, and he would report to the Primate that the Americans had received it.

Stephen realized his dilemma. He could not keep the letter because he'd been ordered to return it as if it had never been accepted. And this man was refusing to take it back. There was only one thing to do.

Having already memorized its contents, Stephen tore the letter in half before Marko's wide-eyed stare, then pulled a match from his desk drawer and burned the letter to ashes.

Marko looked on in confusion. He rose and rushed from the room.

Menshikov and Szücs were furious at this turn of events.

Friday, January 28

On this cold afternoon, I walked to Buda, where I would again meet Pista's friend Sándor Tanács who was returning to Nagykörös in a day or two and agreed to take a couple of things back for me. In my arms, I carried a package of coffee for my family and a carefully wrapped baby blanket I'd crocheted for my sister's recently born son.

It was a pleasant distraction to meet up with Sándor. He didn't have much time, but we caught up on one another's news. There was nothing much to report about my family, but he handed me a piece of paper. "Here," he said, "this is from Pista."

It was short and to the point. "Anna, I'm worried about you. Try to get out of this place as soon as possible."

I read the note, then folded it and slipped into my pocket. It disturbed me, but there was little I had to say about it. Shortly thereafter, Sándor and I took leave of one another and wished one another good luck.

As I walked, the note's message reverberated in my mind. It was so like Pista to worry about me. But what about him? He was in even greater danger than I. *Try to get out.* If only we could, Pista. But where would we go?

About mid-way over the Margit Bridge, I stopped for a moment to view the frozen river below. The ice was broken into large slow moving chunks, and for some reason, I thought of the girl in *Uncle Tom's Cabin* who had to flee across a frozen river clutching her baby. As different as our situations were, I felt like that girl, pursued by sinister forces in an ever shifting and uncertain world.

What were my options? Taking the job with Samuel Grunewald? Would that end my value to the AVO and conclude László's courtship? No sooner had these thoughts blazed through my mind than Stephen's face appeared. It was hard to consider a future without him, though of course such thinking was silly, which I'd been telling myself almost since the day I met him. Who knew how much longer he would remain in Budapest. And then what? And worse, what if he married someone else, here in my city, my country. The wedding hovered ghostlike in my thoughts.

Then I noticed something in the water. An elegant white swan gracefully navigated chunks of ice. As I leaned over the rail to get a better look, Pista's note fell out of my pocket and floated down to the river.

A firm hand on my shoulder jerked me away from the railing. "Don't, Miss, don't. It is too cold down there." I turned abruptly. A tinker with a worried frown stood before me.

I smiled at him. "Oh, I wasn't going to jump. I was watching a swan down there. It's so beautiful. Come see," I said pointing.

He looked down. "Miss, what luck you have! To see a swan on a Friday in January is the best thing that can happen. It means you will change your life. The swan will take you onto his back and fly away with you to eternal happiness."

I knew that the old man was doing his best to divert my attention from jumping to my death, and I appreciated his concern more than he could imagine. Perhaps still not trusting me, he asked where the train station was located and suggested I might show him the way.

It wasn't far, and I was happy to have the company. He told me he was going to see his sister—all the family he had left—in Szeged. He went on to explain that he'd been in Austria for two years but had come back.

"Why?" It seemed so odd to return to this mess.

"I couldn't fit in. I couldn't understand their mentality. So I came back, figuring that at my age, it won't matter what goes on here, and I will be satisfied as long as I will be buried in my own country."

We reached the station, and I wished him well on his journey. He took both of my hands in his and said in a very serious tone, "Miss, when the swan comes for you and asks you to go with him, think of no one but yourself. Say yes, hop on its back, and fly away. Don't look back; otherwise, the magic will be broken. God bless you."

Saturday, January 29

The following morning I didn't see Stephen in the apartment, nor had he left a note, which he usually did. I figured he'd been in a hurry and had forgotten. I proceeded to clean the stove, a messy job I liked to do when he wasn't around. All that remained was to remove the ashes when Stephen entered the room.

I apologized for the mess and waited for him say something, but he said nothing. He began to pace the room, and a few times he came to a stop in front of me. He appeared more upset than I'd ever seen.

At once the words burst forth. "I am leaving Budapest tomorrow, Anna," he said.

I had a feeling that he meant a lengthy departure that would end his need to keep me in his employ, but I prayed I was wrong. "You are? Going on vacation?"

"No, Anna," he said, "I have to leave for good."

His words came as a shock. I didn't want to believe I'd heard him correctly, but his expression told me I had. I felt limp and the small ash shovel I held dropped to the floor with a clatter and sent a small cloud of ash into the air.

His voice regained some of its usual composure. "I was called to the Legation early this morning. Apparently, the government has accused me of conspiring with the Cardinal to overthrow the government. I've been declared persona non grata, and I've been ordered to leave the country within forty hours. Your uncle's friend, Foreign Minister Rajk, signed the order."

He paused for a moment as if deciding what to say next, or perhaps organizing his thoughts as was his habit.

"I have to have all my things packed by tomorrow. I plan to leave around eight in the evening. If I'm not gone by midnight, they can arrest me." He started for the door then turned. "I will come back later to help you with my papers. Just attend to the other things now," he said and turned on his heel and left.

I stood up and stared at the door, my thoughts trailing after him. I knew that emotions often left Stephen when a task confronted him. He allowed little to interfere with his job. He was this way before his nighttime journeys to Vienna; he was this way each day when he went to work. He seemed to cordon off his personal life, and I supposed that was the case now. His mind had already jumped ahead to what needed to be accomplished in the little time left to him.

I don't know how long I stood there. Time both stretched before me endlessly and shrank to nothing with the knowledge that I would see Stephen for only a few more hours.

Like an automaton, I collected Stephen's things and packed them into his suitcases and into boxes. By late afternoon, when only his papers were left to be organized, he returned carrying hot coffee and cake. He seemed calmer and surer. For a time, we organized his papers and packed them into a waterproof briefcase. We exchanged few words until everything was done.

"What are you going to do when I'm gone?" he asked suddenly.

Bitterness rose up my throat. What will I do? I wanted to shout. But my voice was flat as I revealed my thoughts of the previous day. "What are my options?" He knew I didn't expect him to answer, and he said nothing.

Sunday, January 30, 1949

László Harsányi was called to a meeting with Ernő Szücs. It was unusual that he was summoned to Szücs's home, instead of AVO headquarters. He supposed the reason might be that it was Sunday. As he climbed the stairs to Szücs's apartment, he recalled his meeting with Anna's uncle nearly a year and a half earlier. So much had happened. He had a moment of nostalgia for that time, which had been far less complicated. And it had not involved Ferenc's niece for whom he'd developed respect, and if he was honest, a great affection.

When he entered the apartment he was surprised to see that little but its occupant had changed in the interval. "Sit down, László. I have a new order concerning Anna Tóth. Since you haven't—" he said, then as if reconsidering what he wanted to say, he added, "We have decided to arrest her tonight."

"Tonight? Why?" László felt a moment of confusion.

"She'll be the one to confront the Cardinal with that damn note Koczak burned. Now that Koczak's been expelled, there won't be anyone at the Legation to make a stink about her arrest. In fact, I doubt they'll even know. Or when they do, they won't much care. She's no one to them, Captain."

"Captain?"

"Yes, Captain. Congratulations! You were promoted on Friday." He pulled something out of his pocket. "Here is your insignia." Szücs handed László the bit of embroidered cloth that represented his promotion.

He took it into his hands and turned it over several times before speaking. "What is the new plan?"

"You will take her on your date to meet your *friends*. While she is with you, we will plant the letter from the Cardinal to the Americans in Koczak's apartment. The agents will show up at your place, and they'll arrest her. They'll go to the apartment with her, search the place and come up with the Cardinal's letter. They will then take her into custody. She will have to confess that the Cardinal's letter was among the papers Koczak had left behind in his rush to leave the country."

"Just one question. If Koczak burned the letter, how can she—?" László didn't finish, but gave Szücs a curious look.

"Yes, well, we have a new one."

"New? I thought the Szulners disappeared?"

Szücs gave him a dismissive frown. "Yes, yes. It's unfortunate. We'll have to do with second best. With Koczak gone, who's to know if the letter is a forgery or not? He's the only American who saw the original."

He paused a moment as if trying to remember where he'd left off. He explained that László should keep her at his friends' until they arrived, and then assured him that they would take care of the rest.

"We're sure she knows plenty about Legation affairs and Koczak's interactions with the Cardinal. We just want her to tell us a few things, sign some papers, and in a few months, if not sooner, she'll be ready to come work for us."

"I don't know," László said. "She's not a very talkative girl. In all the time we've gone out, she's never said a compromising word about Koczak. I've tried."

"I'm sure you have. Leave this to us. We'll get her to testify. Just make sure the two of you are there by nine o'clock." As an afterthought, Szücs added, "Perhaps she'll even work with you." He gave László a conspiratorial grin.

After a moment's hesitation, László saluted his superior and left the apartment. Taking the stairs slowly, he wondered if Anna's dead uncle was watching him now. He'd liked Ferenc Tóth. What would he say? A trace of guilt coursed through him.

———————◆———————

I slept in my own apartment, weighed down by uncertainty and grief. To my amazement, when I woke up on Sunday, I didn't remember that Stephen was leaving the country until I stepped into the hallway where his suitcases stood. I stared at them as the previous day's events came rushing back to me. I grew lightheaded, faint, until I heard Stephen behind me. "Good morning, Anna," he said. "Come, I want to talk to you."

He escorted me to a chair and pulled another close enough to my own that our knees were touching. But I felt none of the usual thrill of his body against mine.

"I thought about you during the course of the night," he began. "The grim fact is that you might very well be arrested the moment I leave because there will be no one here to protect you from them. They will want to know everything about me, and you know far too much. They'll get the information they want, one way or another. I can't let that happen to you. I have a responsibility to you."

The reality of his words sent an icy shiver up my spine. At the same time his concern placated my brittle emotional state. Then I thought I heard him say that I should go with him. "I will take you to Vienna tonight and from there to Salzburg where you will be free."

No sooner had his words sunk in, than the defects of his plan followed. "No, Stephen, there is no need to endanger yourself now. And anyway, I can't leave. Not without seeing my family. I couldn't live with myself."

"I've done this many times. There is nothing different about tonight."

I stared at him blankly.

He took my hands in his. "There's no time to lose. You know what's likely to happen to you. Your family will be happy for you. If not now, with time."

271

Pista's note. He told me to leave. The tinker's fairy tale. "But what happens after I get to Austria? Where will I go? What will I do?"

He responded as if he'd been thinking about the answers to these questions, as if he'd already planned out my life. "Well, you can study languages. It's something you've wanted to do. You can go to Paris to the Sorbonne. You'll regain control over your life, your future."

My mind hopscotched about. "What will you do?" I asked.

"I'll have to return to the United States until they post me elsewhere."

I suppose I had dared wish for more, but Stephen's obvious concern for me and his willingness to take this risk was more than I could or should have hoped for. Before I'd further sorted through things in my mind, I whispered, "When should I be ready?"

"So you are coming?" Stephen said. "Good girl, I like your attitude." He squeezed my hands. "Now listen. We will leave no later than eight o'clock tonight. Until then, I don't want you to leave the house and you cannot speak to anyone—not even to your friends or family. Can you do that?"

As if reading my thoughts, he said, "It will make it worse for them and could endanger them. You must do as I say. Understand?"

I swallowed and nodded. Their images flashed through my mind, and tears threatened. But I had to restrain myself. I knew that. I had to focus on the need to pack. I would no longer have to see László. Then I remembered that I had a date with him at the very time we were supposed to leave. I told Stephen.

"Is he always punctual?"

"Yes, very much so," I said. The specter of his arrival fell over me like a shroud.

"Then we'll leave earlier. Be ready by seven thirty. Now, I have some things to attend to. Hopefully I'll be back early this afternoon."

━━━◆━━━

As Stephen approached the Legation, he glanced all around before exiting the car. He assumed that he was being followed, and after assuring himself that no one was there, he parked and hurried into his office, where he needed to get some personal files out of his desk. He swiped a newspaper off a counter in the reception area and took it with him.

He threw the paper on his desk then rummaged through the drawers collecting the documents and files he needed. After organizing the folders neatly, he placed them into his briefcase. He looked around the room for some small memento to take with him or anything else he might have forgotten. This place had been his office for a year and a half. A wave of emotion came over him. He was sorry to say good-bye to it and to Budapest. He'd been of service to all sorts of people, to Hungarians, the people of his roots, and it was doubtful that any other place would afford the same opportunity.

He was about to pick up the paper and be off when a headline caught his eye—"Underground Leader Hanged." There was a photo of a young man hanging from a tree, and underneath two others were handcuffed and staring off into the distance.

"Good, God." The words escaped his lips. He read the article. It was just a few lines telling that an underground group had been apprehended and their leader a priest, Father Imre, hanged. Two other top members of the group, Sándor Tanács and István Tóth, were arrested and faced potential life sentences.

István Tóth. That must be Anna's brother. He hurried home, worried that I might have seen the report about my brother. When he entered, he looked as though he'd seen some tragedy. "What's the matter?" I asked.

"I just wanted to see how you were holding up. Make sure you haven't changed your mind." He regarded me curiously.

"No, but it's been difficult. I've been thinking about my family and worried that the officials might question them, or even worse."

"I understand. Believe me, I do," he said gazing at me thoughtfully. "Anything to eat?"

I knew he was thinking about so many of the people to whom he'd given passage out of the country. The temptation was great to contact one's family and friends, but the danger to the mission would only increase the more people who knew about it.

After I fixed him a bite, he said he had to attend to some more details.

"But what will I do?" I asked somewhat childishly. "The radio isn't even working. Oh, I know, could you bring me a newspaper before you leave?"

"I'll pick one up on my way back. I won't be gone long." He gave me an intense stare. "Now, remember, no phone calls, and don't even pick up the phone. And for God sakes, don't open the door."

I had few clothes, and all of my twenty-and-a-half years fit into one suitcase. I had packed them in under an hour. When I glanced about my apartment, it no longer felt like home. Nor did Stephen's. There was no sign that he'd ever lived there or, for that matter, that I'd lived there either.

I curled up in the chair where I'd read book after book, often waiting for Stephen. I thought about the ride ahead then tried to put it out of my mind for it only made me nervous. Several times, I stood at the window looking out, then paced back and forth, hoping once again that Stephen would return soon.

Perusing the bookshelf, I half-heartedly pulled a title off the shelf and tried to read, but my mind refused to focus. A newspaper doesn't require much concentration; I only wished I had one. Beside me on the small table sat the telephone. More than once, I reached my hand toward the receiver. Finally, I picked it up. I would chat with Julia. I wouldn't say a word about my departure, but I'd hear her voice one last time and we could catch up on the latest wedding activities.

The key turned in the lock, and I hastily retrieved my hand and pretended to be staring outside. The voice that came from the hallway wasn't Stephen's—Robin Steussy had stopped by. I was pretty sure Stephen had sent him to keep an eye on me, and I was glad he did. Robin was a welcome diversion. Like Stephen, he asked how I was doing.

I mustered a weak smile. "I'm all right."

By the time he left it was already four o'clock. Time ticked by ever so slowly. Countless thoughts entered and left my mind, including all sorts of disastrous events. What if László came early? What if I was discovered in the trunk? I realized I didn't even know if anyone else was coming. Stephen had told me about the woman with the children, and so I selfishly prayed that on this trip there would be no one but me.

When Stephen hadn't arrived back by seven o'clock, I grew terribly worried.

———•———

As László stepped inside the subway train on his way to pick up Anna, he reflected on his meeting with Szücs—in particular, the surprise promotion. It was curious, he thought. Though he'd been reporting on her for the past five months, he'd made little progress toward bringing her into the fold of the AVO. Five months certainly indicated slowness on his part, but he'd hoped to do it with her cooperation and had convinced his superiors that would have a better outcome. If she fell in love with him, he thought he could persuade her to join him in working for the secret police. Then, having lost patience, they'd pressured him, and the result was the botched New Year's Eve incident.

Now, with Koczak's departure, he was assigned to deliver her into their hands. He almost wished that he hadn't been told her capture was imminent, but of course, that was impossible. His thoughts turned to his new status as captain. Why had they promoted him just when their faith in his ability to bring her in had wavered? Had they guessed that he had feelings for her, and they wanted to ensure he didn't defect? He mulled over the situation. More than anything, he wished he didn't have to play a role in her arrest.

———•———

When I tried to imagine my future, I could not. Everything was a blank. The future, the present, the past. Not a single intelligent thought came to mind. I was bursting out of my skin waiting for Stephen. I paced and the clock ticked. It was just shy of 7:30, the sky sinister and the night long and dark. If the phone rang, I decided I would pick it up. Something may have happened— must have happened. Why was I always waiting for Stephen?

Though it was cold in the apartment, perspiration dotted my forehead. I closed my eyes and prayed to the God I'd prayed to for so many years. *Please, God, protect us.* Though, perhaps it's not right, or even useless, to ask for such things, I also prayed that László would not show up promptly, just this once. Or if I was really lucky, perhaps he would cancel. But no, that was unlikely.

———•———

When László exited the subway station, his own misgivings came to the fore.

He walked slowly, thinking about Anna's green eyes, and suddenly a memory rose to the surface, a memory of the day he'd been with her uncle on his way up the staircase and he saw a woman with those same eyes. Only then did he realize Anna was the one who'd passed him. It dawned on him that she had probably recognized him and knew from her uncle that he was an agent. This would explain her cautious behavior towards him, which he'd attributed to old-fashioned modesty. She was an intelligent young woman, more intelligent than he'd realized. She'd known all along that he'd been sent to watch her—to reel her in. *What a fool I've been*, he thought.

———•———

When I heard the key turn in the lock, I almost shouted out with relief. Both Robin and Stephen entered and took the luggage down, with me following behind carrying my own bag. They divided the suitcases between their two cars.

The plymouth, Stephen's car, the vehicle of escape.

By the time Robin pulled away, it was ten minutes before eight. Stephen told me to get into the car, and he'd be back in a minute. He had to check on something.

My voice trembled. "There's not much time," I said, pointing at my watch. "He'll be here any minute."

"I'll be right back," he said crisply.

It was an understatement to say that my nerves were frayed. My entire body shook as I settled into the back seat of the Plymouth, which was parked only one car back from the gate to the apartment. I'd hardly gotten situated when I caught a glimpse of László's tall figure turning the corner. The wind blew his coat open, revealing his long-legged stride.

My body went rigid as I stared at him moving toward me. I knew I had to move away from the passenger window and finally managed to inch my way into the corner furthest from the sidewalk. I sank into the seat and held my suitcase in front of me, propping it on my knees in the hopes that he wouldn't see me.

As László approached the entrance to Anna's building, he came to a halt a short distance from the gate. There, a few cars away from Koczak's Plymouth, he saw a figure astride a motorcycle, appearing to be spying on someone. His sharp instinct, developed by intense AVO training, told him to beware. The street lights cast the man in shadow, obscuring his features. The thought passed through László's mind that in addition to Koczak, the AVO was watching him, to determine whether or not he intended to obey the order Szücs had given him.

László was close enough for me to see his wavy hair, his handsome face, which wore a severe expression so unlike him. He glanced at the Plymouth then his face took on a troubled look. His gaze traveled behind Stephen's car and settled there for a moment, before moving back, looking inside the vehicle, in my direction. I dared not breathe. His gaze lingered.

Where on earth was Stephen? At that precise moment, he emerged from the building and almost knocked into László as he passed him near the gate. I watched László train his eyes on Stephen's back and track his movements until Stephen got to the car. I was terrified. But instead of coming after him, he turned back to the gate to ring the bell. To wait for me.

"We're off," Stephen said, his voice without a trace of anxiety or fear. I could hardly speak.

"What's the matter? Why are you so quiet?" he asked.

"The man you almost bumped into. That was László Harsányi. Didn't you recognize him? He arrived a few seconds before you came down."

"I saw him," he said confidently. Then a worried look crossed Stephen's face. "Did he see you?"

"I don't know."

Stephen zigzagged through the mostly empty streets and alleys of Pest, to ensure he wasn't being followed, though for a time, a motorcycle's roar could be heard behind us. I crouched down into the seat to avoid being seen. Finally, he turned the car onto the avenue that passed the Parliament Building, and we crossed the bridge over the Danube into Buda.

He continued his erratic route. First he drove fast, then slow; he stopped, then sped up to the Budavar Palace at the top of the hill. It was then that I noticed the motorcycle was no longer behind us. Stephen followed a series of narrow winding streets, past the Coronation Church, down to the docks, and back up to the Palace again.

Satisfied at last, he took a few more turns then pulled up to an ugly, unfriendly building. "We have to get out here, just briefly."

Robin's car was already there. He opened the gate, and we all climbed to the second floor where Robin let us into an apartment. With the exception of two chairs, a table, and a friendly, black, Hungarian Puli dog, the place was bare.

Before I could wonder what we were doing there, Stephen announced that I was to wait there, alone, until he and Robin returned. "Don't go near the window and don't open the door for anyone. I will let myself in." With that, he and Robin let themselves out and the lock turned in the door.

I heard the two cars motor up, then drive off, the sound of the engines fading into the distance. I stood in the corner of the room, feeling like an abandoned child. Each minute seemed like forever, and wild questions tossed about in my head. What if Stephen doesn't come back? What if the secret police have managed to follow him and are about to arrest me? Why did he leave me here? Why couldn't I have gone with them?

After thirty or forty minutes, I heard a car door slam and footsteps clatter up the stairs. For an instant, I didn't know whether I was about to be abducted or rescued. Then the key sounded in the door. Stephen called to me in a hushed shout, "Come quickly, and be as quiet as you can."

I could hardly keep up with him as he plummeted down the stairs and wondered why he expected me to be quiet when he was making such a racket. His car was parked on the sidewalk, tight against the entrance to the apartment house. It was almost impossible for me to open the rear door and get inside. Much to my surprise, a man and a woman already sat there, the two occupying most of the space.

He pushed me into the car and hurried to the driver's side, slid behind the wheel and started the motor. As he pulled away from the building I recognized the woman. She was the artist Mária Blasko.

Then Stephen introduced us, and we greeted one another politely. It was obvious that she was as nervous as I was. Father Jánosi too was tense, though less so than the two of us. Until that moment, I'd never met the man, but knew of him as an outspoken priest. Since Stephen did not introduce them to each other, it seemed evident they were familiar.

I was troubled by this turn of events. I didn't know why these two had been added to this trip and wished that Stephen had told me. Moreover, I couldn't imagine sharing a trunk, even one as roomy as the Plymouth's, with two adults. Such close quarters with two strangers took some time to digest.

Stephen's announcement interrupted my thoughts. "The three of you will have about an hour to get acquainted before you'll need to move into the trunk."

In light of my confusion and the sadness I felt at leaving behind my home, I was intent on remaining quiet. Mária Blasko also seemed to avoid talking. Father Jánosi, on the other hand, struck up a conversation as if this were a social gathering like any other.

"Have you ever read the *Youth Paper?*" he asked me. This was another name for the newspaper *Sziv Ujság*.

"Yes," I said, wondering what that had to do with anything.

"Well, it is published by Mária," he said, eyeing her proudly.

"Oh. I knew that."

"Why are you leaving Hungary?" he asked, intent on prolonging the conversation.

"I have my reasons," I said without elaborating.

It shocked me a little when Mária huddled into Father Jánosi's side without embarrassment; clearly they were more than friends. She closed her eyes and her lips began to move, apparently praying in silence.

The warmth of our breath inside the car and the bitter January cold caused the windows to fog up. Stephen turned on the defroster, but the ice clung to the outside of the windshield. Time and again, he had to open the window while driving, allowing the chill of winter inside, and lean out like a contortionist to scrape the windshield.

———•———

At AVO headquarters on Andrássy Street, Gábor Péter was growing concerned. It was 10:30 p.m. and the agents in charge of abducting Anna Tóth had not arrived back. The minute they returned, they were supposed to let him know she was being held in the interrogation room. What was holding them up? He ordered Szücs to call Lászlo who he'd told to stay at the party after Anna's arrest. Szücs had done this to maintain the illusion that Lászlo had nothing to do with the operation, which might come in handy later when trying to gain her cooperation.

Szücs discovered that Lászlo had left an hour earlier with the men who'd come for Anna. Gábor exploded. "Heads will roll unless we find her." He was looking at Szücs, who knew he'd just been given another order.

———•———

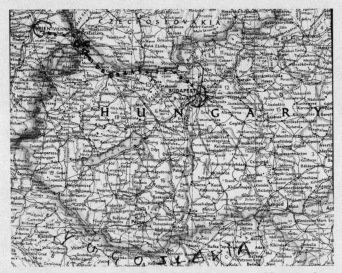

Escape route with the car: Budapest, Hungary to Vienna, Austria.

The rear window was the only one that remained clear. I repeatedly looked back to watch Budapest recede, growing smaller and smaller, and sometimes entirely obscured by the mist that rose from the Danube.

Soul-searching thoughts occupied me. I had read that when people leave behind everyone and everything in their beloved country, they are overtaken by a feeling of indescribable sorrow. I felt little more than dull pain. At the moment that Budapest disappeared altogether, I had a somewhat surreal sensation; I felt as though my soul had been stolen from my body and sat in the front seat watching me. I had no past and an unpredictable future. Only the present moment existed.

Father Jánosi and Mária's hands touched, their fingers intertwined. It was odd to think that they liked each other.

The tires of the car crunched as Stephen maneuvered over the frozen snow, driving through each town and hamlet where we roused dogs who barked in alarm. Otherwise, we were closing in on the border in silence.

After Stephen leaned outside to scrape the window yet again, he announced that soon we would have to get into the trunk. "We don't want to run the risk of being stopped on the road—four people heading toward the border so late at night looks suspicious."

I felt sorry for Stephen. Except for the weather, he could have had a stress-free ride. Instead, he'd decided to undertake one last mission, transporting three fugitives, two of us wanted by the AVO to testify against the Cardinal's coming trial. On the other hand, after doing this time and again, perhaps he'd grown used to the tension. I wondered exactly how many people owed him their freedom. His courage was more than admirable. It was now even clearer to me why so often he'd returned tired and moody from these trips. If not stressful, they had to be exhausting.

The temperature was ten below zero and the wind had picked up, hurling icy snow against the vehicle. Driving was difficult and risky. I wished I could give Stephen a reassuring pat, or that he might direct a comment at me, but neither happened.

———⋯———

In an unfamiliar room inside AVO headquarters, Captain László Harsányi stood before his irate superior. He was frightened by the intensity of Szücs's anger—his red face twisted with rage as he shouted and cursed. László had never experienced this side of him. Only this morning he'd promoted him.

"Tell me once again, Captain Harsányi, what happened? Please be precise this time," he demanded, special emphasis on *Captain*.

He squared his shoulders and spoke as calmly as he could. "Colonel, I was waiting at the gate for Miss Tóth at eight o'clock, the time we had agreed on. Precisely at that moment Koczak was leaving his apartment building, alone. He passed right by me, got into his car, and drove away."

"And you didn't stop him?"

"Was that part of my assignment?"

Szücs shook his head in disgust as though any idiot would have taken that extra step under the circumstances. "Was anyone else in the car?"

"I didn't see anyone, sir." He spoke carefully so that nothing would prove him deceitful. "Then I rang the bell to the apartment, but there was no answer. I tried a few more times, but when no one responded, I hurried up to Anna's room on the top floor. The door wasn't locked, and when I went inside, I saw that her clothing was gone. I stopped by the resident manager's apartment. She said she hadn't seen her for the last two days.

"I then went to the party, knowing the others would be there shortly to arrest her. Obviously, she wasn't there, so we decided to call you, but couldn't reach you."

Colonel Szücs stared beyond László, thinking. "We are in a mess, I tell you," he fumed. "You go to her parents' home first thing tomorrow morning. I've already given an order to search for her here in the city. You are dismissed. I'll call the border police myself."

Relief flooded through László as he left the room. Being harangued by Szücs hadn't been quite as bad as he'd expected. At least he hadn't been tossed into prison. In the subway station on his way home, he reached into his pocket and found Anna's gold necklace there. He fingered it. If she was gone for good, he'd never have a chance to return it to her. He brought the amber cat to his lips. "If you are running away, Anna, run far and fast. I hope they never catch you," he whispered.

———— ·•· ————

Stephen turned off the main road and onto a narrow dirt path that seemed to lead nowhere. After bumping along over the rutted road, the Plymouth rolled to a stop by a tumble-down hut. An old well stood nearby, and two walnut trees extended their frozen branches into the night sky. Against one of them, a tall figure leaned motionless. Then, I saw an auto parked in the shadows.

Stephen got out of the car, and as he shut the door and approached the hut, the frozen figure came to life, moving with the agility of a snake. The three of us looked on, transfixed, until Father Jánosi exclaimed, "My God, Robin Steussy has lost his mind!" We all got out and joined Stephen and Robin. Then two figures emerged from the Chevrolet, which I now recognized as Robin's vehicle.

"Have a last cigarette," Robin said, extending a pack of Pall Malls toward us. Father Jánosi accepted and flicked on his lighter.

As the light illuminated the priest's face, an anguished cry broke forth from the throat of one of the passengers approaching them. "You too, you are here too!" The man who shouted to the priest was István Barankovics, the leader of the Democratic People's Party. His wife walked at his side.

"Yes," Father Jánosi said, the slightest bit shaken. "Mária, too."

It seemed strange to me that these two men, who I knew were political allies, had no idea the other was leaving the country. To escape without telling the other surely had to be a form of betrayal, since the one left behind would bear the burden of testifying against Cardinal Mindszenty. Their disturbed expressions on seeing each other spoke volumes. However, after a few moments their mutual disappointment faded, replaced by more philosophical expressions. I suppose that's what sharing adversity does, especially something so gut-wrenching and terrifying as this.

Stephen told us that we had to get moving. "Remember," he said, "once you are in the trunk, there must be silence. And when we stop at the border, don't breathe."

For a few minutes there was commotion as suitcases were removed from the trunk and packed into the back seats, and the five anxious human beings arranged themselves into the two cars' trunks. Barankovics and his wife in Robin's Chevrolet, and the three of us in the Plymouth. Once we were all settled, if one could call being squeezed into a narrow dark space with two other people "settled," the engine started and we jounced along the dirt path to the main road.

Stephen turned the car west toward the Hungarian border, which we would reach in a little over an hour. Once we crossed into a small spit of land that was Czechoslovakia, we faced one more dangerous checkpoint leading into Austria, though that one wouldn't be nearly as harrowing as the first.

Curled into a fetal position, I occupied the space vacated by the spare tire with my back facing the trunk's lid. Twelve inches of space separated me from Father Jánosi and Mária who huddled together and whispered prayers. At one point, the priest asked if I wanted to join them. I didn't, and said I couldn't put my mind on prayers now.

I shivered from the cold, because to fit into the small space I'd had to remove my coat. The wind fought its way between the cracks of the trunk and blew freezing cold air onto my back. To distract myself, I tried to calculate how many rotations of the wheel for each kilometer, how many blasts of air with each turn, and how many altogether to the border. I tried to imagine being in my mother's womb—warm, safe, and beloved. But this illusion lasted only until another breath of frigid air blew into the icy metal container.

The three of us were startled when the car made a sudden turn, thrusting Father Jánosi and Mária Blasko against one another, wedging her tightly into the corner. I heard Robin's car slipping across the ice behind us and imagined the Chevrolet hurtling into us. After skidding east, then west, the car finally dipped and came to a halt. At most, half an hour had passed. Why were we stopping?

───────◆───────

At the checkpoint, three border guards were playing cards with AVO agent Sergeant Tamás Földi, who, much to the annoyance of the others won each round. Földi was planted at this particular crossing to watch for Stephen, making sure he left Hungary before his midnight deadline. If not, he would be arrested.

The phone jangled and Földi picked it up.

The voice at the other end snapped, "Get Földi on the line!"

"This is Sergeant Földi, sir."

"Colonel Szücs here. Listen carefully. We have reason to believe Koczak is smuggling a girl out of the country. When he arrives, you are to search the car. You, not one of the others. If he objects to opening the trunk, shoot the lock open. We want the girl."

"What if I shoot her by accident?"

There was a pause, then in an irritated tone, he said, "Then you shoot her; we want her in any condition."

"What about Koczak? What should I do with him?"

"Hold him. If the girl is not in the car"—he hesitated—"let him go. Understood?" he barked.

"Yes."

"If he doesn't arrive call me, and if you can't reach me, contact Captain Harsányi at once."

"When is Koczak expected to arrive?"

"How should I know? Any time or not at all." With that Colonel Szücs slammed down the phone.

Földi's brow knitted into a frown. He wanted to leave in fifteen minutes to meet up with his mistress in town. Now he had to wait for that blasted American. He sat back down with the other guards, but instead of resuming the card game, he threw the cards down, and pulled his gun out of the holster. It wasn't often that he used it, and now he'd have the chance. In fact, he'd been ordered to do so. He stroked the barrel and then went about making sure it was in proper working condition. Studying the weapon, he turned it over several times before putting it away.

The crunch of footsteps came to a stop behind the trunk. The three of us held our breath trying to understand what was going on. Then the trunk opened, and Stephen was holding a thermos. He poured dark steaming liquid into three cups, offering one to each of us. We gratefully sipped the cognac laced coffee and braced ourselves for what was to come.

"We're less than an hour from the border," Stephen explained. His voice was firm, but calm. "If I stop anywhere from now on, be quiet no matter what you hear. Absolute quiet, even if it seems that I am being arrested. Can I count on you?"

We nodded in unison, though his words were hardly reassuring. How would we get out if he was arrested? And what would our fates be?

Before he left us, Stephen patted my arm and gave me a smile—an encouraging look, a look that warmed me as much as the coffee, maybe more. Whether he loved me or not, gestures such as his are the ones that keep us humans going. As the wheels clacked on the icy street— round and round—I clung to the feeling he had engendered in me.

The car gave a sudden jerk, and again skittered across the ice. The three of us gasped. With a few correctional maneuvers, the Plymouth righted itself and resumed its forward motion.

Instead of feeling relief, Mária began to cry then sob. Father Jánosi tried to soothe her, but when that failed he scolded her. "Do you want us to get caught? Get a hold of yourself. Nothing happened." Still she cried.

How would this woman behave at the border? I wanted to say something, but couldn't think of anything beyond Father Jánosi's stern warning. My own fears multiplied. I could no longer pretend the trunk was a comforting womb, but instead it took on the shape of a steel coffin.

The cold again seeped inside and into my bones. With each jolt, I focused on Stephen and realized what he meant to me and the extent to which my life and fate depended on him. I believed that if anyone could manage this, he was that man. I tried to gain strength from this thought, but nonetheless wondered if his fear matched mine.

Once, some time ago, Stephen began ruminating about the existence of angelic beings. He claimed they moved from place to place, from thought to thought, with lightening speed. His discourse surprised me, and at first, I thought it strange, even bizarre, that someone so practical might harbor a belief in angels. But I think it gave him the courage and conviction to do what needed to be done, no matter the danger or risk.

Thinking about guardian angels filled me with momentary peace. And a little like the instant before death when you see your life flash before you, I saw myself seventeen months earlier stepping out of the church in Budapest on St. Stephen's Day, removing my shoes and running for cover from the storm. So much had transpired between then and now. Fate? Destiny? Both?

Stephen was reviewing his plan. He'd calculated every move, perfecting it to the tiniest detail. But the question was: would it work? There were always unforeseen variables. What he needed was a bit of luck and angelic intervention.

He checked his watch. What he hadn't told his passengers was that the border crossing had to be timed precisely between 11:50 and midnight. Some time ago, one of the friendly border guards had told him that the AVO had stationed one of their men there to watch for him, but he always left to visit his mistress no later than 11:45 each night, sometimes earlier, so Stephen wanted to arrive after he'd left. On previous trips, it hadn't mattered if he arrived considerably after midnight, but that night was a different matter. His immunity as a diplomat lasted only until the clock struck twelve. He was cutting it close, there was little margin for error.

As the ice again obstructed his view, he rolled down the window and raked the windshield. In his rearview mirror, he saw Robin's car following close behind. A true friend, Stephen thought, one who was willing to risk his own skin to help these people cross. He had told him that he would do the talking, that Robin was to stay in his vehicle until they received the signal to move forward, and his colleague and companion of these numerous trips had agreed.

Shortly before midnight Sergeant Földi noticed the headlights of two vehicles approaching in the distance. He was convinced one of the cars belonged to Koczak. His heart picked up.

To prepare for the American's arrival, he ordered two guards out into the cold. They exchanged a disgusted glance before opening the door wide, and letting a vile, bitter wind sweep inside. "Shut the rotten door," yelled the sergeant.

Stephen slowed the car as he turned into the area beside the border patrol house. He switched on his high beams, to see how many guards were there to greet him. He saw only two. Their rifles hung loosely from their shoulders. He drew up next to them and came to a stop. "Good evening," Stephen said.

"We have to search your car, Mr. Koczak."

In the trunk Mária released a small gasp. Father Jánosi thrust his hand over her mouth. My heart hammered so loudly I was sure it could be heard yards away.

"What time is it?" Stephen asked, though he knew the precise time; they had three, at most four minutes.

"A few minutes before midnight."

"Well, who is going to search it? Let's get on with it."

"The officer inside." He motioned toward the hut. "He's been waiting for you."

"Good, good," Stephen said. "Let me go and give him the keys."

⸻ ⬩ ⸻

Never have I experienced such terror. Hearing Stephen's declaration was like a boot to the chest. I thought Stephen had gone mad. What was he doing? I squeezed my eyes shut, barely breathing, wishing Mária mute.

⸻ ⬩ ⸻

With the two guards at his heels, Stephen stepped inside, focusing all of his considerable energies on getting through the next couple of minutes.

"Good evening. I am Stephen Koczak, American diplomat." He leveled his gaze at the man seated a few feet away.

"Yes, yes, I know. And I am Sergeant Földi, assigned to examine your car." He stretched lazily and opened his mouth to yawn before standing up. The sharp clatter of keys on the table stopped him short. He gazed down to see two sets of car keys.

"I've no time for games," Stephen said forcefully. "I've been expelled by your government and have only three minutes to pass through here, or else."

"Or else what?" Földi stared at him.

"If I'm not out of here by midnight, there will be a huge political scandal, and it will be your fault."

Alert and frowning, Földi hesitated.

"Yes, you will be held responsible." Stephen narrowed his eyes and gave him a half smile. "As a matter of fact, do me a favor and keep me here." He slapped his and Robin's documents on the table. "My people are looking for a reason to have a confrontation with Prime Minister Rakosi and Mr. Stalin. You might even make a little trip to Andrássy Street, so feel free to hold me."

With a sneer, Földi snatched the keys and bumped into Stephen as he hastened past him. The Chevrolet was parked closely behind the Plymouth, its doors open for inspection. He glanced inside Robin's car, saw that it was empty of passengers, then poked his head into Stephen's. He tugged at a couple of the suitcases, but they were obviously too small to contain a human. He moved around to the back of the car and shoved one of the keys into the lock. He wiggled it, but it didn't turn. He withdrew it and tried another key.

"Good God, hurry up. One minute."

Near panic, Földi glanced back and forth between the two cars. He hesitated. Another few seconds passed. Raising the keys, he said, "They don't open the trunk."

"That's your problem," Stephen replied, standing there calmly as if he relished Földi's consternation.

Fumbling, the AVO sergeant tried again.

"Clock's ticking," Stephen said.

"Shut up." He glanced around to see if anyone was watching, then tossed the keys at Stephen.

In an aggressive gesture, Földi motioned Robin's car forward, as if planning to check it again.

"He's with me," Stephen said. "Also an American diplomat."

"Get out of my sight," Földi yelled, "before I change my mind."

———◆———

The motors of the Plymouth and the Chevrolet roared to life. Snug behind one another, they pulled across the border as the last sound of the midnight bells died away.

Despite the cold, Stephen mopped the sweat off his brow. He drove only a short distance, slowed the car and opened the window for air. He gulped in the chill wind, put the flask of cognac to his lips, took a long drink, and resumed cruising speed. "Just a bit longer," he shouted at the captives in the trunk.

At the Czech border, the guard extended his hand for Stephen's passport. Stephen, patting the seat beside him for his documents, kept his gaze fixed on the guard, saying good evening, when he realized the papers weren't there. He turned to make sure he wasn't mistaken. Then he searched the floor, where surely they'd fallen, but they were nowhere to be seen. Such a thing had never happened.

He was at a loss for words as the guard stared at him, waiting. Stephen scanned the entire car. Nothing. His breath grew shallow. Had he forgotten them? Where else could they be? He shoved his hand inside the pocket of his coat. There they were. He withdrew them and passed them to the guard, who merely glanced at them and waved him on. Robin too.

The tongue of Czechoslovakian land that separated Hungary from Austria was only about four miles wide. The trip lasted little more than ten minutes. As the car rolled into Austria, Stephen breathed a deep sigh of relief. The Austrian border guards were slow but polite, and soon we headed toward Vienna.

———————

Never had I experienced such exhilaration. It was over. In unison, the three of us released audible thank yous.

By the time Stephen opened the trunk, I felt frozen in place, my body stiff from the long period of immobilization. Slowly, the three of us climbed out, creaking to life as though our limbs had grown rusty.

While transferring the luggage from the back seat to the trunk, my fingers touched Stephen's and he squeezed my hand. We exchanged a look that I can only describe as deeply heartfelt and a look I think belongs to such dramatic moments as that. I felt as though this seminal event, and everything that had preceded it, bound us for life.

Back in the Plymouth, Father Jánosi waxed on about the frightening moment during the border crossing as if he were addressing a room full of people. I don't recall specifically what he said, except that it was ordinary, nothing spiritual or profound. Here he was like any other refugee. When he finished, Stephen asked me what I had felt.

"I stood before God, and he asked me if I had always been good and merciful."

"And what did you answer?"

"I said I was not—but then neither was He!"

<hr />

It wasn't long until we reached Vienna. Despite the darkness, I was transfixed by the narrow streets and handsome buildings. The spire of a beautiful church reached to the heavens. Only hours ago, we'd been in Budapest, in terrible danger, and now we had reached freedom. It felt like a dream. "So this is Vienna," I finally managed, "the city of Strauss waltzes and castles of the Hapsburgs."

"Yes, here we are," Stephen said.

Shortly before two in the morning on Monday, January 31, we came to a halt on a steep street in front of an impressive, white villa surrounded by a wrought iron fence. It was the only building on the block with its lights on. Stephen rang a bell at the gate. A few seconds later, a young man swung it open to let us in. As we emerged from the two cars, he looked on in amazement to see a procession of seven rather haggard looking men and women marching through the gate and into the building.

This was the Press Club where Stephen usually stayed when coming to town. Inside, several young reporters were sitting in upholstered chairs around two round tables having drinks. Ashtrays overflowing with cigarette butts and paper cups with coffee sat before them. Had it not been for their untidiness, the room would have been lovely as the floor featured Persian carpets and brocade curtains.

Their heads turned to see what the commotion was. Noticing Stephen and Robin, they rose to greet the two. Seeing us, they knew something was up. Eager for information, they launched into a tirade of questions. Despite the enervating journey, Stephen and, to a lesser degree, Robin began to explain what had transpired.

One of the waiters took notice of the five of us huddled by the door and offered us hot coffee. Stephen came over and bade me goodnight. "I'm glad you came," he said.

As we were ushered out of the room, we left behind an animated discussion and the reporters scribbling in their notebooks. Stephen seemed in his element—a diplomat engulfed in conversation about world affairs, depressing though they were.

We were given rooms on the second floor. I was completely spent, and that night, I cried myself to sleep. In the morning, I woke up to the full realization that I'd been robbed of all that was familiar to me and dropped into a life that was alien and frightening. It was one of the worst moments of my life.

Over the course of the next eight days, Stephen was preoccupied and found little time for me. Though sad and moving about in something of a daze, I tried to make the best of things. I spent time exploring the Press Club, a lovely mansion with an elegant stairway leading to the first floor's large reception area where journalists regularly congregated. They smoked cigars and cigarettes, drank coffee and alcohol, gathered the latest news and filed their reports.

I liked to stop at the top of the stairway by a window which had an exquisite view of Vienna, a city partially built on small hills sloping down to the Danube. Often, as I watched the river, I imagined it rolling toward Budapest and dividing my city in two.

Inevitably, my thoughts would turn to my family, my poor parents—how would they feel when they found out I had escaped? I imagined them reading of the news by letter, one that I had written and that Robin had promised to post on his return to

Hungary. I hoped they would understand, and prayed I hadn't put them in more danger than Pista already had, though at that point, I still did not know about Pista's incarceration. In fact I wouldn't find out about Pista and Father Imre's execution until a few more weeks had passed, and then, only by accident.

My mother's tearful good-bye after Christmas haunted me. The memory came unbidden, mostly at night, and then I had to fight back my tears. I tried in vain not to think of them or the past, it was far too painful, but I rarely succeeded and was invariably filled with worry and aching sadness.

On occasion, even László came to mind. What had happened to him as a result of letting me slip out of his hands? Even toward him, I felt a vague regret, but there was no clean way to make such an escape. What was done was done.

Worrisome thoughts of the future also vied for my attention each day. What would I do? Stephen had only told me that I would be going to Salzburg, because Vienna—much of it still in the Russian zone—made it a dangerous place for those without diplomatic immunity. Only small sections of the city were governed by the Americans, British, and French. The entire region between Vienna and Salzburg was under Russian occupation.

Our personal interaction was minimal. I assumed that being part of Stephen's life had come to an end; his duty and obligation to me finished. And no matter what my emotions were for him, I felt I had to remain silent about it. I had to be grateful for all he'd risked and done for me. But it was bittersweet.

On the fourth day, early on Thursday afternoon, there was a knock on the door. I was in the midst of writing a letter to a friend of mine who'd escaped to Tunis two years earlier. The door was unlocked, and I called for the person to come in.

To my shock and surprise Joan Robbins stepped into the room. A few steps behind her was Stephen. On seeing me, she burst into tears, whirled around and threw herself into his arms. Stephen was at a loss as he stood there with Joan wrapped around him crying. I'm sure my own expression didn't help matters. Joan's appearance had once again raised my own feelings of hurt and anger. I wanted to ask him what she was doing in my room but instead waited for an explanation.

"Joan just arrived, and apparently, there's no other room available." He seemed to be signaling that he had no idea what had brought her here and was looking to me for help, but I glared at him. "Of course she can share with me," I said and left the room.

Over the next four days, Joan followed Stephen wherever he went. To his room, to meals, to briefings with the press. She was his shadow day and night. Smiling, holding his hand, sitting as close to him as possible. Even when Stephen spoke with me about the trip to Salzburg, she was there. At night, when he managed to slip away, she would suddenly grow friendly and try to impress me with her ample and elegant wardrobe. Her underlying message was that she was a perfect match for Stephen.

On Tuesday morning, the day I was leaving for Salzburg, I heard that she had been telling everyone she and Stephen were marrying in a month or so. Though it was a blow, I didn't believe it would actually come to pass. I had also come to terms with the fact that while Stephen cared for me, he did not love me. I knew it was an impossible situation, and it made me almost glad to get away from this place.

Stephen arranged and paid for a hotel room for me for one week in Salzburg. He gave me $100 to add to my own $200, which I'd saved while working for him.

Moments before my departure, the door to my room opened, and Joan entered with Stephen. "It's time to go. Are you ready?" He seemed nervous and uncomfortable.

Joan put on her coat and stood at the door. Stephen asked her where she was going, and when she told him that she would accompany him to the airport, he turned red, then, in no uncertain terms, told her she was not coming. "I am taking Anna alone."

Once again Joan burst into childish tears. We stepped past her and out into the hallway. No one bade me good-bye. I left the Press Club as I'd entered—a refugee, alone and vulnerable.

On the road to the airport, Stephen offered some advice in case the Russians forced the airplane down in their zone, which was hardly reassuring. "Just go to a Catholic priest and ask for help." I almost laughed, thinking it was the silliest advice I'd ever heard coming from Stephen Koczak's mouth.

The small military airplane, a two-seater, was ready and waiting for me. The pilot was the same man I'd seen speaking to Stephen at the Press Club. He was roughly Stephen's age and wore a wide grin on his friendly face. When he noticed my suitcase, he shook his head and said something to Stephen.

"He's explaining that there's no room for your suitcase on the airplane."

"What does he want me to do?" Then without waiting for an answer I opened the suitcase and took out my black lace dress, the one I'd worn on New Year's Eve. In front of their astonished eyes I spread the dress out on the snow and dumped the contents of my suitcase onto it. I gathered the corners and tied them into a secure bundle and tossed it into the plane.

I looked at Stephen. "Will I see you again?"

"Of course you will. I'll visit you as soon as I can. In the meantime, you have my address in the States." I nodded. "Stay in touch, all right?"

He leaned forward and kissed me on the forehead. He pushed a small wrapped package at me. "Here, a small gift, but don't open it. Wait until you've arrived in Salzburg."

I wanted to but didn't kiss him. It was all I could do to say, "Thank you for all your kindness."

I had never been on an airplane before. The door didn't latch properly and the entire machine appeared so rickety that I had little faith it would even fly. But it did, and soon Stephen became nothing more than a small notch on the frozen landscape below.

My tears flowed liberally. I was crying not just for Stephen, but for my country and for my family and friends. All these I had lost, possibly forever. What would I do now that I was "free?"

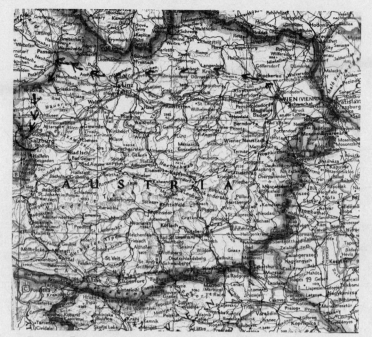

Escape Route with the plane: Vienna to Salzburg, Austria.

Suddenly, I wanted to be back in Hungary, in my mother's kitchen smelling the fresh baked bread, waiting to eat a warm piece of it. *Stop crying; it's no use*, I chided myself.

The plane wobbled through the air, and I hung on for dear life. The view was unimaginably beautiful: snow covered mountains, the small and distant city of Salzburg cradled in its frozen whiteness. A short time after passing over the Inn River we landed at the quaint Salzburg airport.

I descended the plane with the help of the pilot who accompanied me to the gate. There, a gaggle of reporters swarmed around me as though I were a very important person. I wondered what this was all about.

"What is your name? Who are you? How did you get out?" The questions came at me in a polyglot of languages.

I gazed at them, bewildered, wondering what to say. The pilot shrugged when our eyes met. Stephen had asked me not to tell anyone about our escape, which I would not have done in any case. It was then that I realized because I was free I did not have to answer. I walked out of their midst leaving the flabbergasted reporters behind. I heard them switch gears and bombard the pilot with more questions.

Inside the airport I was given a pamphlet written in several languages. On the cover, it provided the address of the Displaced Persons Office. *Displaced person*, I thought. *How perfectly fitting.* I was about to make the trek on the icy road to Salzburg, toward the hometown of Mozart, toward the Office of the Displaced Persons, toward freedom, when I decided I could wait no longer to open the package Stephen had given me. I unwrapped it, my hands shaking. Inside was a single yellow rose and a note.

"Trust me. Love me. Wait for me."

Epilogue

Despite Stephen's note to me, the path to consummating our relationship was not a straight one. Over a stretch of more than five years, I frequently lost confidence in the notion that we should ever become more than just friends, let alone end up together. I think it could have gone either way, but here's what happened, briefly.

After the first week in the hotel, to conserve what little money I had, I moved into a refugee camp at the outskirts of Salzburg—formerly a military barracks. I spent the next six months there, sharing a room with about thirty other single women. Was it bad? Of course, it wasn't home, but we received morning and evening meals, and I learned valuable lessons about human interactions, in particular the give and take required to get along with others under such circumstances.

On the other hand, there was also a sense of despair that permeated our lives. We refugees were more or less stranded, hoping to emigrate somewhere, but where? No country really wanted us, some of us who'd escaped (including me) had no passports, and either one of these things resulted in an interminably slow process.

I spent much time alone, and went into town as much as I could, absorbing the German language, and on occasion, was offered a few days work cleaning and organizing items in small shops.

Stephen visited me unexpectedly after I'd been at the camp for eight weeks. He was returning from the United States and on his way to his new posting in Frankfurt. When he arrived, though he tried not to show his emotions, I could tell that it pained him to see me in that place.

In the course of talking, he realized that I had not yet heard from my parents, which meant I still had no knowledge of what had happened to Pista. Even though I'd been fairly certain something terrible might befall my brother, the news devastated me, especially when I realized that my parents had lost not one but two children within a day of each other.

TEMPORARY TRAVEL DOCUMENT
IN LIEU OF PASSPORT
for Stateless Persons
and Persons of Undetermined Nationality

TITRE DE VOYAGE PROVISOIRE
TENANT LIEU DE PASSEPORT
pour apatrides
et personnes de nationalité indeterminée

VORLÄUFIGER REISEAUSWEIS
AN STELLE EINES PASSES
für Staatenlose
und Personen unbestimmter Staats-
angehörigkeit

№ 0017089

Anna's stateless passport brought to her by Stephen on December 22, 1949.

(Though my parents had received the letter that Robin posted for me, I did not get one in return until the spring of 1951, due to the regime's heavy censorship.)

Stephen left for Frankfurt after two days but not without slipping three hundred dollars into my handbag, which I discovered after his departure. It was money I set aside for the future.

He wrote me a few letters urging me to move to St. Gilgen, a picturesque, quaint, Austrian village on the Wolfgang Sea. It was a destination for many of the financially secure Hungarian refugees, which did not include me. I finally moved there at the end of July, after finding a room in a guesthouse in exchange for doing some work for the owner, such as babysitting. Though the village was beautiful, being tucked into the Alps did not agree with me. I had grown up on the great plains of Hungary, and the proximity of the steep, imposing mountains made me claustrophobic. Homesickness and loneliness were my constant companions.

A month after my move to St. Gilgen, Stephen paid me another visit. We went sightseeing and discussed current events, studiously avoiding a conversation about the future and my situation. Stephen was caring but never said a word about love.

Without any suggestion that our relationship was anything more than platonic, I felt quite abandoned and, on impulse, signed up with a group of friends to immigrate to Australia, a country that provided all documents needed to enter legally. Up to that point, I was a "stateless person" without a passport.

Our departure date was set for December 23. The move to "down under" involved a status that could be likened to indentured servitude, which was to last for five years. At best, I was ambivalent about going. Perhaps subconsciously hoping that Stephen would stop me, I sent him a letter about my decision and once again thanked him for all he had done.

On the day before we were to leave, Stephen arrived unannounced, having braved dangerous, snow-covered, mountain roads. He brought me a stateless person passport issued by the American authorities in Wiesbaden and, in his inimitable fashion, made it clear he would not hear of me going to Australia, as if he was in control of my destiny.

"I thought you wanted to study in Paris? Didn't you tell me that?"

"I do want to go, but how will I find a way to get there?" It wasn't as if I could simply snap my fingers and move to Paris and apply to the Sorbonne.

"I will help you find a way," he said, without elaborating.

Anna's picture in the passport.

And he did. Less than two months later, in February 1950, Stephen not only took me to Paris but also paid for six months of French lessons and two months of room and board. I was able to extend my stay by helping Madame Chasles, my French tutor, with household duties.

In October, I was admitted as a student to the Sorbonne. The next four years, I lived for studying and exploring the beautiful city of light, with the exception of summers, which I spent in Germany, England, and Italy studying those countries' languages. During that time, my parents and I exchanged letters approximately every other month, having figured out how to avoid government censors from destroying our missives. The solution was simple: write nothing important, just stick to things like "How are you; we are fine," and so on. Not a word of politics.

As for Stephen, he and I spent each Christmas and New Year's Eve together, but otherwise, seldom saw each other. I did write him quite often about my studies, my friends, my love for Paris, and whatever else was going on. He usually wrote back a few unromantic lines, though I suppose they were encouraging and caring.

I managed financially by doing some work for a dressmaker named Madame Madrie. With this money, I covered 80 percent of my school fees, which were quite reasonable, and kept a small amount for personal use. Stephen supplied the other 20 percent of the tuition, for which I was very grateful but also reluctant to receive. He saw to it that I had a few lovely outfits, which of course I could not afford. On his holiday visits, Stephen would surprise me with a lovely dress or outfit that he'd paid Madam Madrie to make without my knowledge.

Each time he arrived, I was surprised that he hadn't gotten married, though I was not surprised he hadn't linked himself to Joan, and occasionally, this served to bolster my hope that someday we would be together. He was clearly the man I would always consider my first true love.

Often at night, his visage came to me—his wavy brown hair, high forehead, prominent nose, fashionable mustache and resolute chin. His probing and intelligent eyes searched my thoughts, my heart. But I also had to remind myself that at such remove it is easy to forget a person's negative qualities, and when I simply grew too sad because nothing seemed to be between us, I would conjure up the character traits that most annoyed me—demanding, elusive, overly controlling, and just plain aggravating.

On New Year's Eve in 1953, he invited me for the first time to the Embassy party in Bad Godesberg, Germany, where he had been transferred. It was a lovely affair, and apparently, because of my evening gown and sheer existence, I caused quite a stir. Though Stephen seemed inordinately thrilled by people's enthusiastic acceptance of me, at the end of the visit, he made no declaration of love.

Only five days later on January 5, 1954, I received notice of the sudden death of my mother. The news broke my heart, and I couldn't help but remember her prediction after Christmas 1948 when she had tearfully said she'd never see me again. My mother had known, while I had made light of it. In Paris, I turned my attentions back to my studies for my last semester at the University.

Anna, the day her mother died in 1953. The picture was taken in Stephen's apartment in Badgodesberg, Germany.

In February, six years after we'd met, Stephen paid me another unexpected visit. He took me to a favorite restaurant for a candlelight dinner. He was charming and attentive. My heart danced at the possibility that he might ask me to marry him.

"What are your plans, Anna, after your studies are finished?"

I could see from the expression on his face that there was nothing romantic in his query. It was the pragmatic Stephen wanting to know if I'd thought ahead.

Trying to temper my disappointment, I told him that I had been offered a job in Morocco for at least a year. "All that's left is for me to sign and turn in the papers. Isn't it exciting?" I said bravely.

His eyes searched mine, and he took hold of my hands. "You cannot go, Anna. You owe me something," he said.

I was so taken aback that I thought he meant I needed to reimburse him for his financial support, which of course I would do once I had enough money.

Before I could respond he said, "You have an obligation to me, even if you are in love with someone else. Are you?"

I gaped at him, and before I could stop myself, I heard myself say, "Yes, I am in love—with you. For six long years, in case you hadn't noticed."

He smiled in his irresistible, boyish way. "Anna, I am amazed at you. Wasn't all my concern and interest in you proof that I have also been in love with you for these past six years?"

"But why did you wait so long to tell me?"

"It was important that you find your own way in the world. For a time, you had to walk alone. And you did a splendid job. But now you are at the end of that road, and I am here." He kissed my hands and continued. "We will get married in May in Germany in that little church you love so much."

Obviously, Stephen, my Stephen, had thought through every detail. But this time, it didn't quite turn out as he'd planned.

We didn't get married in May. Without my knowledge, Stephen had submitted his resignation to the Department of State, a prerequisite for requesting permission to marry a non-American citizen. The subsequent investigation took longer than normal because Stephen's superior in Germany informed the Department of State that I was a spy.

Fortunately, in mid-August, Stephen's resignation was not accepted, and he was granted permission to marry me. Three weeks later, we were married in Trenton, New Jersey, Stephen's home town, in the little church he loved so much.

The Little Church, Schwarzenkirchen, We intended
to get married in Rhondorf, Germany.

Stephen and Anna's Wedding - September 4, 1954.

Mr and Mrs. Stephen A. Koczak—ready for life together.

In 1971, I was permitted to reenter Hungary for a visit. Stephen had to wait until 1992 for the same privilege.

On October 15, 1997, after forty-three years of marriage and three daughters and eleven of thirteen grandchildren, Stephen died at home in Washington, D.C. of congestive heart failure a month before turning eighty. He and I had embarked on the writing of this book ten years before his illness took his life. Shortly before his death, he asked me to complete the book, and I promised that I would. In the course of revising and finishing it, I relived many emotions from that time, often finding it painful, and often wishing that he could be here to read the final product.

Washington, DC,
July 2000

On July 20, my birthday, the telephone rang in the middle of the night. A man's deep voice spoke into my ear.

"Hello. Anna." I can't really say whether I recognized the speaker or not, but in the next moment I heard the words: "This is László Harsányi." His voice caught. After a moment's hesitation, he added, "Can I come to see you?"

Mingling in an indescribable way were a sense of shock and the weird notion that I had been expecting his call all these years. My mind alert now, I said, "It's one in the morning, Lászlo. I hope you're not outside, in front of my house."

"No," he said, releasing a small chuckle. "I am in Baltimore at a meeting. I meant to ask if I could see you around two in the afternoon?"

"Yes, that will be fine," I said, as though this conversation were completely normal.

"See you then," he said and hung up.

For a long while, I couldn't return to sleep. After fifty-two years, I would again see Lászlo Harsányi, my nemesis, the man who would have turned me over to the AVO. How could I so blithely let him enter my home after what he'd done? What would it be like? But I also knew that I had many questions I wanted to ask, and finally he would be there to answer them. At least I hoped so.

At 9:15 in the morning, a man from a florist delivered a dozen red roses with a note that only said: "Lászlo."

When the doorbell finally rang, I felt a current of nervousness run through my body. I glanced at myself in the mirror, and though my navy skirt and white jacket were stylish, there was no denying that five decades had passed since I last saw him. What would he think? And would I still recognize him?

I opened the door, and there he stood with his handsome face, now etched with wrinkles, and his dancing black eyes. For some time, we took stock of one another. "Anna, you look so young," he said, his face lighting up.

"Yes," I said nodding, "and so do you." Whether we truly believed this or not didn't matter; it is the sort of thing people say to one another, especially after the lapse of so much time. I also think we were able to see beyond the wrinkles, sagging skin, and graying hair to the youthfulness that once was ours.

He relied on his cane as he followed me inside. I made coffee and served it in the family room which looked out onto the deck and garden. He stared at my family photo gallery, and uttered, "This family could have been mine."

His words surprised me. I had no comment, and an awkward silence ensued. I broke it by asking him why he'd come. "Tell me the truth. I'm sure you didn't travel three thousand miles and cross an ocean to have an idle chat."

His face took on an earnest demeanor. "No, I didn't. I came because I have long wanted to explain some things and to ask you three questions."

I tried to lighten the atmosphere by suggesting that I was like the genie required fulfilling three wishes before being released from the lamp. Though he seemed somewhat ill at ease, he asked his first question with uncharacteristic bluntness. "Were you Stephen's mistress while you were dating me?"

"No, I wasn't. Not in Budapest, nor anywhere else. We married in 1954. I was his wife. Next question."

"Did you ever love me?" When he saw me hesitate he pleaded for me to answer.

"I liked you very much. I might have loved you had you not been working for that detestable regime. You were a fool, László."

He took some time to absorb my words, then he said, "I know. It took me thirty years to come to that same conclusion. I'm sorry." He looked off into the distance as though recalling the past. "How and when did you know that I was working for the AVO?" He wondered if his flash of insight the night I'd escaped had been correct.

"I sensed it the moment you arrived at my door," I said. "The whole thing you made up about my cousin applying for a job and doing a routine background check sounded false. And then later, I remembered seeing you climb the steps to my uncle's apartment as I was leaving. Besides, Stephen checked on you as soon as I told him about you."

"So why did you date me knowing all this?" he asked.

"What choice did I have? I was dating you because I had to; I was afraid not to."

"Yes, you were right. But I hope you believe me when I tell you that I only learned that day that they planned to capture you at my friend's home." He paused, water pooling in his eyes. "I didn't know they planned to… torture you if you didn't cooperate; none of this had been part of their original plan." He looked at me, perhaps trying to gauge my reaction. "It's not much, I know."

"You're right; it's not."

He turned the subject to Stephen. "I was very jealous of him."

"I guess the feeling was mutual. It's long ago; don't be too hard on yourself for that. But now it's my turn to ask questions. When did you discover that I knew your real identity?"

"All the time we were dating, I only once wondered about it, but I was blind with love for you. That's why I asked if you would go away with me if I left Hungary. Had you said yes, perhaps our lives would have ended up quite differently."

I wanted to tell him that I fell in love with Stephen the moment I met him and that fate intended for the two of us to be together, that there was no chance that he, László, and I would have married, but what would have been the point? He was an elderly man, eighty years old; why rob him of his daydreams, if that's what they were.

He went on to explain how he found out for certain that I knew his identity as an agent. "In nineteen fifty-three, your brother was taken from prison to the AVO for interrogation. I sought him out and showed him your photo. At first he denied you were related, but after further questioning, he told me you were in Paris at the University. I offered him a cigarette, but he wouldn't accept it. Instead he turned to me and said, 'So, you're the SOB who was going to betray her?'

"His words stung. 'How do you know about that?' I asked him. 'She told me,' he said. 'We knew from the beginning who you were and that you were sent to spy on her. She hated you, and I hate you! Now you can eat your heart out for the rest of your life.' I never saw him again. He was transferred, but his curse stuck with me. It was my hell to know that you hated me, that you must have despised my touch, my kisses, my words and that you believed them to be lies." László buried his head in his hands and cried.

I felt very sorry for him. "László, listen to me. I never despised you or hated you. You were doing your job, what was required of you, and though it was wrong and I didn't like it, I did know that."

He seemed slightly relieved, and I suggested we have a glass of wine. "Since when do you drink wine?" he asked.

"I always did, just not around you."

László suddenly leaned forward and clutched my hands. He held them tightly, though I noticed that his left hand gripped weakly as if his fingers suffered some sort of paralysis. "I want to tell you how you wore your hair on Sunday evening on January thirtieth. It was not in a bun as you usually wore it. It was loose, flowing down your back with a headband to keep it off of your face."

"How do you know about my hair? Did you see me?" I asked, my heart suddenly pounding as I recalled that night when I'd prayed he hadn't seen me.

"Yes, I did. Just as the car was taking off, you turned around, and I saw you. That's when I realized how much I loved you. I knew I had to let you go, even if with a man I was jealous of, because he was the only one who could save you. I couldn't bear for them to torture you or lose you to Siberia. So I chose to lose you to freedom and the man I thought you loved."

He looked at me beseechingly, hoping that I believed him, and I did. Now it was my turn to tear up. I wanted to say thank you, but my tongue refused to cooperate.

"It's getting late," he said, "maybe I should call my friend to come for me?"

"Would you like to stay here with me tonight?" I asked quietly.

He blushed as he spoke. "Anna, I don't know what to say. Don't you think it's a little late for us? I am too old!"

"Oh, in that case, I'll just put you up in the guest room," I said. We both burst out laughing.

Lászlo kissed my hand and said, "In my wildest dreams, I never imagined I would spend the night with you."

"Nor did I," I answered, "but considering everything, I think we'll survive this excitement in a fashion befitting our age."

Over dinner, in a small Persian restaurant on Wisconsin Avenue, we spoke of our families. He had married a woman who also was an AVO agent; they had a son and a daughter; and now he had a grandson and granddaughter. "I call her Anna," he said, "because she drinks raspberry soda like you used to."

In turn I told him that I'd had a long and satisfying marriage. "It had a mixture of everything that belongs to a marriage—happiness, sadness, anger, excitement. But all in all, we had a wonderful life together."

When we arrived back at my home, he seemed tired, and I offered to read to him from the book I told him I was writing.

He was eager to hear the part about our final New Year's Eve together, and after I read it, he gave me credit for being so clever and said he was glad that I'd switched our glasses. "But you see, you would have made a good spy after all," he said grinning. Another few minutes of conversation, and I saw that he was exhausted. I asked if there was anything he needed from me before he went to sleep.

"Yes. I need a hug from you, and after that, if you would be kind enough to undo my brace. It's fastened between my shoulder blades. I can't reach it by myself."

I gave him a hearty hug, opened up the brace, and bade him good night.

The following morning, I woke up early and went down to make coffee. László was already up, sitting on the deck, smoking. My two cats were keeping him company, accepting his presence as though he were an old friend.

We had our coffee together on the deck, and I asked him some more questions about things that I hadn't been certain of, like my uncle's death. "He was poisoned, wasn't he?"

He seemed astonished that I suspected this. "How did you know?"

"My uncle left me a cryptic note that indicated he only had a few hours left and suspected he was going to be poisoned."

"He was a Titoist, and as you probably know, Stalin purged the government of everyone who'd had anything to do with him. But your uncle was also suspected of collaborating with the underground."

I was interested to hear this. Based on his comment to my father about the grubs buried under the walnut trees, I suppose in a way he was. And the story the Szulners had told me about him in Salzburg and his possible involvement with the prison guards who hid weapons inside the prisons. Perhaps he'd finally seen what these Russian Communists were up to.

Before he left, László told me that he was terminally ill and partially paralyzed. Again, I felt great sadness for him. In June, his doctor had explained that he was beyond improvement and that his months were numbered. "The thought that I might die without talking to you drove me crazy. I could wait no longer." His eyes searched mine. "I hope you can forgive me, Anna."

"Yes, I forgive you."

Before he left, he looked at me with a deep calm. All tension had vanished. He was grateful, he said, that with perhaps only months to live, he'd been able to fulfill one of his life's wishes and couldn't adequately express how glad he was that he'd come—that now he could part from this world in peace. I too was glad that he'd come, very glad. It made a tidy ending for a very messy chapter in my life.

László died in Hungary a few short months later.

Our daughters on their first visit to Hungary in July, 1972. From left to right: Christina (12), Andrea (16), Gabriela (7).

The last time I saw my father in August, 1974.

Josephus Card. Mindszenty
Archiepiscopus Strigoniensis
Primas Hungariae, Bécs, 72. III. 23

Kedves Mr Kocsek,

Thank You note from Cardinal Mindszenty, 1972.

Budapest revisited in June of 1992. The first time Stephen was
permitted to enter Hungary since his expulsion in 1949.

Appendix: What Happened to the People in This Story?

Barankovics, István and Livia: from Austria they went to New York, USA. Occasionally, Stephen visited them. We did not keep close contact.

Blasko, Mária: She lived in Germany for years wanting to come to the USA. It is not known to me if she succeeded.

Boldizsár, Iván: He was under secretary of the Ministry of Information and editor of the Communist Party Journals, one clever survivor of the communist regime. He was also a talented literary man, author of several books. He died on December 21, 1988 in Budapest.

Chapin, Selden: Minister to the American Legation 1947-1948. He was expelled after the trial of Cardinal Mindszenty and left Hungary on February 12, 1949. He was ambassador to the Netherlands 1949-1953, Panama (1954-1955), Iran(1955-1958) and Peru (1960-1960). He died in 1963.

Csertö, Sándor: Father Csertö went from Vienna to Rome to the Vatican. There, after years of study, he joined the Vatican Diplomatic Corp. Stephen visited him whenever he was in Europe.

Jánosi, József: The Jesuit priest moved to Freiburg, Germany. In May of 1965 his body was found next to the railroad tracks near Freiburg. The police did not specify the reason of his death.

Juhász, Vilmos: editor of *Vigilia*, a monthly catholic magazine. After he and his family escaped from Hungary to Austria, they immigrated to New York in the USA.

Julia: my friend married at age twenty-one and had five children. We met in Budapest in 1971, twenty-two years after my escape. That was the first time I was permitted to reenter Hungary for a family visit. She and her husband owned a catering business. She died in Budapest in 1989.

Mindszenty, József Cardinal: imprisoned for life after a show trial in February 1949, he was freed during the Hungarian Revolution (1956) and granted political asylum by the US Embassy in Budapest, where he lived for fifteen years. In 1971, he was allowed to leave the country. He moved to Vienna, where he died four years later in May 6, 1975. He was buried in Mariazell, a pilgrimage place for centuries. In 1991, his remains were repatriated home to Hungary and put to rest in Esztergom in the Basilica.

Péter, Gábor: Head of the AVO. He was a cruel, merciless man. Finally, his fate caught up with him when he became a prisoner himself in 1952. Two years after the Hungarian Revolution, in 1958, he was set free by the János Kádár regime in exchange for testifying against Kádár's tortures. So, hands wash hands. János Kádár became Prime Minister of Hungary after the Revolution.

Rajk, Lászlo: first Minister of Interior, then Foreign Minister, was arrested May 30, 1949 as a "Titoist Spy." He was tortured and promised to be released if he confessed. Despite his full confession, he was sentenced to death and executed on October 15, 1949.

Rakosi, Mátyás: the Deputy Premier rose to become the head of Hungary and the General Secretary of the Hungarian Working People's Party, a position he held until June 1956, when he was removed from office and forced by the Soviet Politburo to move to the Soviet Union. He died in Gorky, USSR in 1971.

Robbins, Joan: She went home to England. She and Stephen had a relationship going on until February 1950 when Stephen ended the relationship.

Slachta, Margit: After the Cardinal's trial, the AVO started to intimidate Margit Slachta. She already had been suspended in the Parliament. In the spring of 1949, she escaped from Hungary and traveled in many countries before coming to the United States. In Buffalo, NY, she established a Mother House of her order. She died there in 1976. In Israel in Yad Washem on September 20, 1985, a tree was planted in her memory and she received "a Distinguished True Human Being" title for saving so many Jews in 1944.

Steussy, Robin: expelled from Hungary as a "spy" on February 10, 1949, a week and a half after Stephen. Though he assumed the position of Vice Consul in 1951 in what is considered modern day Iran, he fell victim to polio and was never able to serve in the Foreign Service again. He studied Russian literature at Harvard, which led to a position at the University of Oregon and Portland State University. He lived in Oregon until his death of age-related causes on February 18, 2009.

Szulner, Lászlo and Hannah: escaped Hungary January 26, 1949. I met the former forgers in Salzburg. Subsequently, because Lászlo escaped Hungary with compromising materials, he was tracked down and was poisoned by the Hungarian AVO in Paris in 1950. Hanna and their son came to the United States and lived in New York.

My Family

Mother: born October 12, 1889 and married at the age of twenty-two. She had nine children, two died in infancy, one died on the Russian front, one was in prison, and one a refugee. She died of influenza on January 5, 1954.

Father: born November 5, 1985 and married at the age of twenty-six. After my mother's death, he lived with my sister's family. My daughters and I visited him in 1972, 1973, and 1974 in Hungary. He died in his sleep after dancing with all the girls at his grandson's Christmas party on December 19, 1974.

Mihaly: Born march 29, 1913, married with two children. He owned a chimney sweep business. He separated from his wife and died on May 25, 1974 due to alcohol poisoning.

Károly: Born February 18, 1915. He was single and a soldier in World War II. He died on the Russian front in 1941—date unspecified.

Margit: Born June 12, 1918, married with three children. She worked in a canning factory and provided a home to our father in his late life. She died on February 6, 2003 from old age.

Gyula: Born September 2, 1920. He was a soldier in World War II. He married and had eight children. He was a farmer producing only vegetables. He separated later in life and died from a motorcycle accident in April of 1984.

Lászlo: Born August 15, 1923. He was a parachuter in World War II. He was widowed two times. He was a landscaper and had two children from his third wife. Two days after the birth of his second child, he died from lung cancer on April 21, 1967.

Pista (István): Born January 2, 1926. He was a volunteer solder in World War II from 1943-44. On January 28 or 29 of 1949 he was put in prison (Vác) for underground activities. He was liberated during the Hungarian Revolution in 1956. He married and had two children. He made small auto parts for the growing auto industry in Hungary. He died of a heart attack on June 10, 1998.